PORTLETS

www.portorials.com

JSR168 Portlet Development

www.portorials.com

ISBN 978-1-59872-904-7

By Cameron McKenzie

A Good Book On JSR168 Portlet Development
by Cameron McKenzie

Second Edition – First Printing
ExamScam Publishing www.portorials.com

Notice of Liability

The information in this book is printed and distributed on an "as is" basis, without any warranty or guarantee of accuracy. IBM WebSphere® and J2EE is a huge technology, so any application of the technology, or following of any suggestions in this book, must be tested and retested before any conclusions are to be made about its validity. While every effort and precaution has been taken in the preparation of this book and materials, the author and publisher shall have no liability to any person, company or entity with respect to any loss, damage, problems or conflicts to be caused directly or indirectly by the instructions contained in this book, or by the hardware and software components described in this book. The content of this book is the opinion of the author. It is the responsibility of the reader to use the technology and test the validity of any opinions or assertions made in this document, and come to their own conclusions.

Trademarks

IBM® and IBM Rational® are registered trademark of International Business Machines in the United States, other countries or both.

WebSphere® is a trademark of IBM as well. IBM also owns DB2®, Informix®, SP® VisualAge®, iSeries®, SP2®, Informix®, MQSeries® Rational® and Sametime®, CICS®, QuickPlace®. These are all trademarks in the United States, other countries or both.

Java® J2EE® J2SE® J2ME® and all Java-based trademarks are trademarks of Sun Microsystems®, Inc

Microsoft®, Windows®, .NET® and the Windows logo are trademarks of Microsoft® Corporation.

Oracle® is a registered trademark of Oracle® Inc.
Palm Pilot® is a registered trademark of palmOne
Netscape® is a registered trademark of Netscape Communications Corporation.
Opera® is a registered trademark of Opera Software AS
Unix is a registered trademark of The Open Group in the US and other countries.
These trademarks and registered trademarks are of the US, other countries or both.

We have attempted throughout this book to distinguish proprietary trademarks from descriptive terms by following the capitalization style used by the manufacturer.

ExamScam is in no way associated with IBM, Microsoft, Oracle or Sun Microsystems. We just really like their products, and we want you to like them too!

ISBN 978-1-59872-904-7

Thanks to all the girls at Tim Hortons.

Table of Contents

Portlet Development: The Basics

Chapter 1
Portlets – The Basics

So, you want to develop portlets, eh? Well, we should probably baseline this whole process with a little bit of a discussion about just exactly what a portlet is.

What is a portlet?

A portlet, in the most vulgar sense, is simply just a content delivery vehicle. That's what a portlet does – it delivers content to a user. Sure, a user can be as simple as a web page, or as voluptuous as a handheld, multimedia device, but that's what a portlet does – it simply delivers content to a user.

Portlets are not web services; web services are web services. Portlets are not web services. Portlets are not EJBs; EJBs are EJBs. Portlets are not EJBs. Portlets are not JavaBeans; JavaBeans are JavaBeans. Portlets are not JavaBeans. Portlets are, quite simply, content delivery vehicles that render themselves within the confines of a portal page.

Partial-Page, Content Generation

Note: the fact that port**lets** are rendered within the confines of a por**tal** page is not a minor point.

When a portlet renders itself, the content it delivers to the user makes up only a portion of the *total* content delivered to the end user. A portlet may make up a large portion of the total content delivered to a user through a handheld device, or it may make up only a quarter of the html page delivered to a client's web browser; but regardless of how much of the *total* content delivered to an end user a given portlet is responsible, the fact remains, that a portlet only generates *part* of the total amount of content delivered to the end user.

The Mighty Portlet Interface

From the standpoint of an application developer, a portlet is any Java class that implements the javax.portlet.Portlet interface.

In many regards, a portlet behaves very much like a servlet from the Servlet and JSP API. Like a servlet, a portlet is a shy little creature that lives peacefully in a war file, leaving everyone alone, and leaves every other portlet to do their own thing. However, get a few drinks into a portlet, and get it *loaded*, and that little portlet is loaded into memory forever, and not unloaded until the portal server shuts down, or the administrator explicitly takes the portlet out of service. Once loaded, the single portlet instance can respond, in a threaded fashion, to an unlimited number of client requests, keeping in mind, of course, the hardware limitations of the portal server on which it runs.

Portlet
init (config : PortletConfig) : void processAction (request : ActionRequest, response : ActionResponse) : void render (request : RenderRequest, response : RenderResponse) : void destroy ( ) : void

Lifecycle Methods of the Portlet Interface

The javax.portlet.Portlet interface defines four lifecycle methods, with the first two lifecycle methods being used to allow a developer to take action when a portlet is first *loaded*, or when a portlet is *unloaded* by the portal server. Similar to the Servlet and JSP API, the method corresponding to a portlet's initialization is very uncreatively named ***init***(PortletConfig config), and the method that maps to the unloading of a portlet is violently named ***destroy***().

The very generic Portlet interface also defines two more, very important, lifecycle methods, namely the ***processAction*** method, which logically is intended to be used during the action processing phase, and the ***render*** method, which as you could imagine, corresponds to the rendering phase, where a portlet generates markup that eventually gets displayed back to the client.

The Abstract Class GenericPortlet

As a JSR-168, portlet developer, you will never create a class that simply implements the Portlet interface. Okay, maybe *never* is a little bit of an exaggeration, but when you code your portlets, you don't directly implement the Portlet interface, but you extend the abstract class GenericPortlet instead, which itself implements the javax.portlet.Portlet interface.

The GenericPortlet class provides default implementations for the four important lifecycle methods defined in the Portlet interface. GenericPortlet is the right class to extend when you want to create your own, customized portlet.

Along with providing a do-nothing constructor, and an implementation of the four lifecycle methods defined by the Portlet interface, the GenericPortlet class defines the pivotally important do<something> methods, namely doView, doEdit, and doHelp. These methods correspond to the three standard rendering modes of a portlet.

The GenericPortlet class also defines and implements a doDispatch() method, which is always called before any of the other do<mode> methods. Clever, eh? A method named *doDispatch* is used to *dispatch* incoming requests to the appropriate do<mode> method.

GenericPortlet

destroy ( ) : void
doDispatch (request : RenderRequest, response : RenderResponse) : void
doEdit (request : RenderRequest, response : RenderResponse) : void
doHelp (request : RenderRequest, response : RenderResponse) : void
doView (request : RenderRequest, response : RenderResponse) : void
getInitParameter (name : String) : String
getInitParameterNames ( ) : Enumeration
getPortletConfig ( ) : PortletConfig
getPortletContext ( ) : PortletContext
getPortletName ( ) : String
getResourceBundle (locale : Locale) : ResourceBundle
getTitle (request : RenderRequest) : String
init ( ) : void
init (config : PortletConfig) : void
processAction (request : ActionRequest, response : ActionResponse) : void
render (request : RenderRequest, response : RenderResponse) : void

Portlets and the Request-Response Cycle

Okay, so far we've discussed what a portlet *is*. In so doing, we have covered the mind numbing details of the *Portlet* interface and the abstract *GenericPortlet* class. That describes what a portlet is, but as developers, we are more concerned with what a portlet *does*, and more to the point, ***how it does it.***

What Portlets Do?

At the most fundamental level, portlets are simply presentation tier components that handle a request-response cycle. When a request comes in from a client, portlets are responsible for inspecting that request, and figuring out exactly what the client is requesting.

Once the portlet has figured out what the crazy client is requesting, the portlet must then figure out how to respond. Before responding to a client, a portlet might use a bunch of EJBs or JavaBeans, web services or JDBC, but eventually, a response must be formulated and sent back to the portal for portal page aggregation, after which, content is finally returned to the client.

The essence of portlet programming is handling the request-response cycle. Conquer the request-response cycle, and the rest of the Portlet API will easily fall under your control.

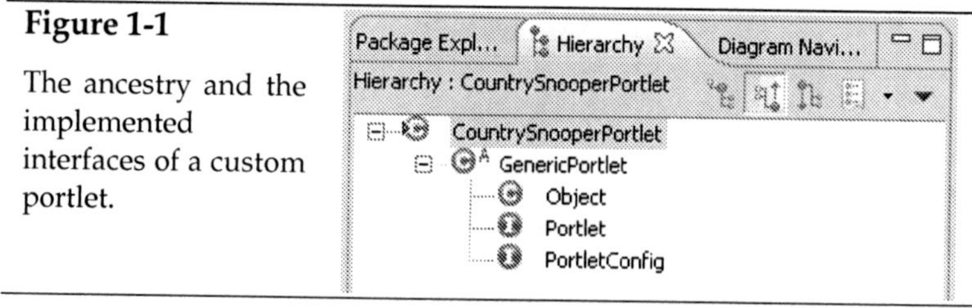

Figure 1-1

The ancestry and the implemented interfaces of a custom portlet.

The Most Basic Portlet

In the most basic sense, a portlet simply handles a web based, request-response cycle. As a Portlet developer, our fundamental responsibility is to simply inspect the incoming request, and subsequently supply an appropriate response back to the user.

The portlet API makes it very easy to develop delicious portlets that can intelligently respond to this web based request-response cycle. To create a portlet that can be viewed on any portal page, we simply create a Java class that extends GenericPortlet, and code a special method called doView.

And what *do* we *do* in the *do*View method? We implement some logic and eventually send some output to the client. The junk we output appears within the confines of a portlet window, on a portal page.

Figure 1-2

Output generated in the doView method is rendered within the confines of a portlet, which appears, aggregated, on a portal page.

```
package com.examscam.portlet;

import java.io.*;
import javax.portlet.*;

public class HelloWorldPortlet extends GenericPortlet {

  public void doView(RenderRequest request, RenderResponse response)
                              throws PortletException, IOException {
    response.setContentType("text/html");
    response.getWriter().print("Hello World");
  }
}
```


The HelloWorldPortlet is an example of a very simple portlet that extends GenericPortlet, and simply outputs data to a client in the doView method.

In this example, when the portlet is displayed on a portal page, the ***doView*** method is invoked, and the ***PortletResponse*** object is used to both set the response type to ***text/html***, and then deliver the ***"Hello World"*** message to the client.

The PortletRequest and PortletResponse

Two supremely important objects are passed to a portlet's doView method:

- *a Portlet**Request** object, as the **Render**Request*
- *a Portlet**Response** object, as the **Render**Response*

Everything a developer wants to ***know about*** the incoming request is stuffed inside the Portlet**Request** object. Anything a developer wants to ***do*** to the client is done through the Portlet**Response** object.

Okay, to say *anything* can be done to the client might be a bit of an exaggeration. The developer can't exactly slap an annoying end user across the face with the PortletResponse object; but a developer *can* send the annoying end user an HTML snippet with some snide comment embedded within it.

Request-Response Programming

Anything a developer wants to know about the incoming request is bundled up inside of the PortletRequest. Anything a developer is *allowed* to do to the client is done through the PortletResponse object. Conquer the request and response objects, and you've conquered portlet programming. Portlet programming is just that simple.

Of course, you don't have to limit your portlets to simple request-response handling. Few developers do. Java programming is all about freedom, and you are free to make your portlets as complex and as crazy as you want.

Fundamentally though, all portlet development can be broken down to inspecting the incoming PortletRequest, implementing some logic, and then using the PortletResponse to deliver an appropriate reply back to the user. How you leverage the various services provided to you through the application server that makes this whole portal thing possible, is up to you. When it comes to portlet development, consider yourself the curator of your own funeral. ☺

Everyone Loves a Good WAR

Portlets don't exist in a peaceful little vacuum, all on their own; quite the contrary, actually, as they exist wrapped up within the confines of a violent war file. As I have said before, in its most banal form, a portlet is simply just a presentation layer component, and in the Java world, the presentation layer is the domain of the *Servlet and JSP API.* Portlets piggyback off the Servlet and JSP API in many ways, and one of the ways they hitch a ride on the Servlet-train is in their packaging. Both Servlet and Portlet applications are packaged and deployed as **W**eb **A**pplication a**R**chives, aka, WAR files.

Like all war files, a portlet war file contains a deployment descriptor named web.xml. The web.xml file pays homage to the Servlet and JSP heritage of the Portlet API, and is an important mechanism for describing how the web container, *which wraps around the portlet container in which a portlet application runs*, should manage a portlet application.

```
<!-- The web.xml file isn't very sexy for a typical portlet
application. The only thing somewhat unusual is the
reference to the portlet custom tag library, portlet TLD-->
<?xml version="1.0" encoding="UTF-8"?>
<!DOCTYPE web-app PUBLIC "-//Sun Microsystems, Inc.//DTD Web Application
2.3//EN" "http://java.sun.com/dtd/web-app_2_3.dtd"  >
<web-app id="WebApp_ID">
  <display-name>ExamScam2</display-name>
  <welcome-file-list>
    <welcome-file>index.html</welcome-file>
    <welcome-file>index.jsp</welcome-file>
  </welcome-file-list>
  <taglib id="PortletTLD">
    <tagliburi>
      http://java.sun.com/portlet
    </taglib-uri>
    <taglib-location>
      /WEB-INF/tld/std-portlet.tld
    </taglib-location>
  </taglib>
</web-app>
```

The Portlet Deployment Descriptor: portlet.xml

Accompanied by the required web.xml file, a portlet application deployment descriptor, named portlet.xml, also resides in the WEB-INF folder of a war file. The WEB-INF folder branches directly off the root of the war. For the HelloWorldPortlet coded in Figure 1-2, the corresponding portlet.xml file would look like this:

```
<?xml version="1.0" encoding="UTF-8"?>
<portlet-app
xmlns="http://java.sun.com/xml/ns/portlet/portlet-app_1_0.xsd"
version="1.0" xmlns:xsi="http://www.w3.org/2001/XMLSchema-instance"
xsi:schemaLocation="http://java.sun.com/xml/ns/portlet/portlet-
app_1_0.xsd http://java.sun.com/xml/ns/portlet/portlet-app_1_0.xsd"
id="examscam2.ExamScam2Portlet.1146144ee0" >

<portlet>
  <portlet-name>HelloWorldPortlet</portlet-name>
  <display-name>HelloWorld portlet</display-name>
  <portlet-class>
    com.examscam.portlet.HelloWorldPortlet
  </portlet-class>
  <supports>
    <mime-type>text/html</mime-type>
    <portlet-mode>view</portlet-mode>
  </supports>
  <portlet-info>
    <title>HelloWorldPortlet</title>
  </portlet-info>
</portlet>
</portlet-app>
```

While both a servlet and a portlet WAR file contain a web.xml file, what sets a portlet application apart from a regular Servlet and JSP war file is the presence of the special deployment descriptor named ***portlet.xml***. For a portlet to truly exist, you must not only code a class that implements the Portlet interface, but your portlet must also be defined in the portlet.xml file.

Conception and the Portlet API

The Java class that extends GenericPortlet, and subsequently implements the Portlet interface, is like the sperm, whereas the definition of the portlet in the portlet.xml file is like the egg. Individually, they are nothing, but when the two of them come together in the ovaries of the portal server, our portlet truly comes to life.

At the very least, the portlet.xml file will define the portlet application, by providing a unique id. A portlet.xml file will then define at least one, and potentially many, portlets. A single ***portlet application*** maps directly to the ***single war file*** that ***contains the portlet.xml file***.

Furthermore, the portlet deployment descriptor will maintain a definition for each portlet contained within the given war file, with the definition including, at a minimum, a reference to the underlying Java class, the markup language and modes the portlet supports, and a title to be displayed above the portlet when it is rendered by the portal server.

The Remaining Elements of a WAR File

So far, we have established that a portlet application is packaged within a war file, and a war file, at the bare minimum, contains compiled Java code, along with a web.xml file, and a portlet.xml file, with those two files being the deployment descriptors for the web module and the portlet application, respectively.

A war file will also contain a special ***manifest*** file, creatively named ***Manifest.mf,*** in a directory named meta-inf, which like the web-inf directory, sprouts out directly off the root of the war file. The manifest file should be used for maintaining the version of your applications. The contents of the manifest file, in a typical portlet application, is usually just a version number: **Manifest-Version: 1.0** If you do not provide a manifest file of your own, the ***java -jar*** utility, or most automated war creation tools, will create one for you.

The Boring Contents of the Manfest.mf File

```
Manifest-Version: 1.0
```

What exactly is a WAR File?

Now I hate to break it to you, but a war file isn't anything special. A war file is simply a compressed file, containing all of your portlet related artifacts, all contained inside of a single zip file, with the extension of the zip file changed to .war. That's all a war file is.

You can actually change the extension of any war file to .zip, and it will open up with any standard zip based utility. Of course, with Java being Java, we can't call a zip file a zip file – everything in the Java world has to have a cute and cuddly name, and nothing exemplifies the ideas of cute and cuddly like a good, wholesome, war.

Packaging Portlet Applications

So, a war file is really just a number of resources, zipped up into a single file, with that zip file maintaining the special folder structure needed for a portlet application.

Along with the required deployment descriptors, a war file will contain compiled Java code, placed in a package aware structure in a subdirectory named **WEB-INF\classes.**

As it has been stated before, a portlet application will also contain two deployment descriptors, named **web.xml** and **portlet.xml**, both of which will be happily placed together in the **WEB-INF** folder directly off the root of the war.

Finally, all war files will contain a rather mundane **Manfiest.mf** file in a directory named **META-INF**, which like the web-inf directory, will be found directly off the root of the war.

Figure 1-3 shows you how the HelloWorldPortlet application, packaged in a file named mywar.war, would look like if you inspected the contents with a WinZip utility.

Figure 1-3 As you can see, a war file can be opened up by any compression utility, such as WinZip, and the contents can be easily discerned. A war file is just a zip file with a .war extension.

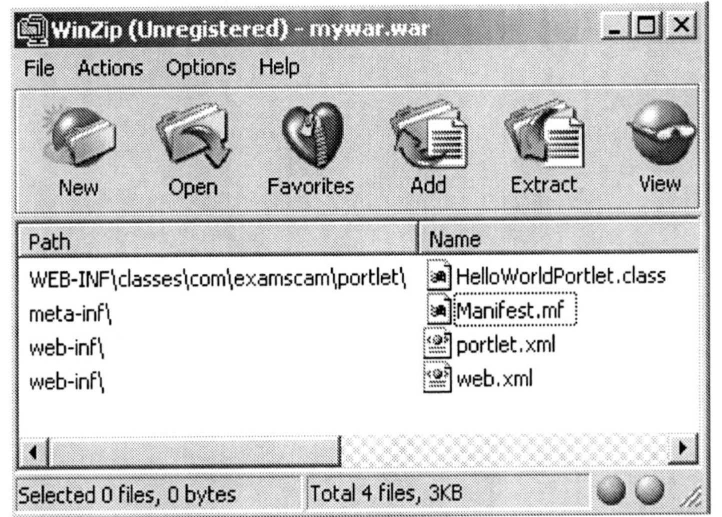

Note the folder locations of the compiled Java class, and the deployment descriptors.

Question 1-1

The four lifecycle methods of a portlet are defined in:
O a) the Portlet interface O b) the GenericPortlet interface O c) the abstract class Portlet O d) the abstract class GenericPortlet

Question 1-2

During a portlet's request-response cycle, which of the following methods will be invoked first?
O a) doView O b) doEdit O c) doHelp O d) doDispatch

Question 1-3

The methods doView, doEdit and doHelp correspond to:
O a) Portlet configs O b) Portlet phases O c) Portlet states O d) Portlet modes

Question 1-4

A typical JSR-168 portlet will:
O a) extend Portlet interface O b) extend GenericPortlet O c) extend AbstractPortlet O d) extend PortletRenderer

Answer 1-1

The four lifecycle methods of a portlet are defined in:

O a) the Portlet interface

O b) the GenericPortlet interface

O c) the abstract class Portlet

O d) the abstract class GenericPortlet

Option a) is correct.

The four lifecycle methods: init, destroy, processAction and render, are all defined in the Portlet interface. The GenericPortlet, however, does extend the Portlet interface and provide default implementations of these four important methods

The GenericPortlet abstract class also defines the various do<mode> methods, but these are hardly lifecycle methods. The Portlet interface is the correct answer to this question.

Answer 1-2

During a portlet's request-response, cycle which of the following methods will be invoked first?

O a) doView

O b) doEdit

O c) doHelp

O d) doDispatch

Option d) is correct.

Before any of the render methods, such as doView or doEdit, are invoked, the doDispatch method is invoked. Since this is the case, it makes sense that when implementing a custom portlet mode, you override the doDispatch method, and check to see if someone is invoking your custom portlet mode; of course, custom portlet modes is a ***very*** advanced topic.

Answer 1-3

The methods doView, doEdit and doHelp correspond to:

- a) Portlet configs
- b) Portlet phases
- c) Portlet states
- d) Portlet modes

Option d) is correct.

We have only briefly mentioned the idea of portlet modes, but it's an idea you better soon get used to. Portlets can have many modes, but they ***must have*** at least ***one***: the ***view*** mode. Other modes, like edit, help, about or print, can be optionally added, depending upon the types of modes your portal server supports.

Answer 1-4

A typical JSR-168 portlet will:

- a) extend Portlet interface
- b) extend GenericPortlet
- c) extend AbstractPortlet
- d) extend PortletRenderer

Option b) is correct.

Extending the Portlet interface is possible, but doing so is so wrong, especially for this question.

When we code a portlet, we extend the GenericPortlet abstract class, which provides default implementations for many important portlet methods. We then pick and choose the methods we wish to override, which always includes the doView method, and perhaps, a few others. I guess it all depends on what you want to ***do***. ☺

Chapter 2 Request-Response Programming

For the most part, portlets are presentation tier components that react to a web-based, request-response cycle.

JSR-168 Portlets are Java based components, and like all Java based components, they can have any number of instance variables defined within them, and they can have any number of business methods as well. However, there is one method that all portlets ***must define*** if they want to be rendered on a portal page, and that ever-important method is the ***doView*** method.

The View Mode and the doView Method

When a portlet is initially displayed on a page, it is said to be in *view mode.* The view mode represents the normal way that a portlet looks when it appears on a portal page.

The doView *method* of a portlet corresponds to the view mode of a portlet. The way that a portlet, in its normal mode, should look on a page, is coded into the doView method. Since it must be possible to view a portlet that is placed on a portal page, every portlet must have a doView method.

```
public void doView
   (RenderRequest request, RenderResponse response)
                 throws PortletException, IOException
```

The doView method of a portlet is fed the RenderRequest and RenderResponse objects, and also throws the intolerable PortletException and IOException.

Along with a concrete implementation of the doView method, to be rendered on a page, a portlet must also define support for the view mode within its deployment descriptors.

```
<supports>
   <mime-type>text/html</mime-type>
   <portlet-mode>view</portlet-mode>
</supports>
```

The PortletRequest Object

A portlet's primary responsibility is to handle a web based request-response cycle. Information about the incoming client request is encapsulated in a PortletRequest object, which is then passed to the pertinent do<mode> method.

The PortletRequest vs. the RenderRequest

The JSR-168 specification defines a PortletRequest data type, but it is actually a subtype of the PortletRequest that is passed into the doView method. This special subtype of the PortletRequest is known as the ***Render*****Request,** which sort of makes sense, as the doView method is invoked when a portlet is required to ***render*** content to be displayed on the client device.

While the doView method of a portlet is passed a RenderRequest, as opposed to the more generic, PortletRequest, the RenderRequest object doesn't actually define any new methods, so the distinction is largely academic. All of the methods available to the RenderRequest, such as ***getLocale()*** and ***isSecure(),*** are actually defined in the PortletRequest interface.

Inspecting the Incoming Request

Any information a developer is allowed to know about the incoming client request is obtained through the request object. Some of the salacious things we can find out about the user through the PortletRequest object include:

- *The preferred language of the user*
- *Any headers served up by a client's browser*
- *What a user typed into a textfield*
- *Which radio button a user selected*
- *The type of browser the client is using*
- *The color of the shirt the user is wearing*

Okay, maybe the PortletRequest can't tell you the color of the shirt your user is wearing, but it can tell you practically anything else. The PortletRequest makes interrogating your client way too easy.

PortletRequest
getAttribute (arg0 : String) : Object
getAttributeNames ( ) : Enumeration
getAuthType ( ) : String
getContextPath ( ) : String
getLocale ( ) : Locale
getLocales ( ) : Enumeration
getParameter (arg0 : String) : String
getParameterMap ( ) : Map
getParameterNames ( ) : Enumeration
getParameterValues (arg0 : String) : String [*]
getPortalContext ( ) : PortalContext
getPortletMode ( ) : PortletMode
getPortletSession ( ) : PortletSession
getPortletSession (arg0 : boolean) : PortletSession
getPreferences ( ) : PortletPreferences
getProperties (arg0 : String) : Enumeration
getProperty (arg0 : String) : String
getPropertyNames ( ) : Enumeration
getRemoteUser ( ) : String
getRequestedSessionId ( ) : String
getResponseContentType ( ) : String
getResponseContentTypes ( ) : Enumeration
getScheme ( ) : String
getServerName ( ) : String
getServerPort ( ) : int
getUserPrincipal ( ) : Principal
getWindowState ( ) : WindowState
isPortletModeAllowed (arg0 : PortletMode) : boolean
isRequestedSessionIdValid ( ) : boolean
isSecure ( ) : boolean
isUserInRole (arg0 : String) : boolean
isWindowStateAllowed (arg0 : WindowState) : boolean
removeAttribute (arg0 : String) : void
setAttribute (arg0 : String, arg1 : Object) : void

RenderRequest

The PortletResponse Object

While the PortletRequest is used to discover information about the incoming request, the Portlet**Response**, or more accurately for methods used during the rendering phase of a portlet, the **Render**Response object, is typically used to send something back, or do something to, the client.

For example, to send HTML back to the client, a PrintWriter can obtained from the RenderResponse object through the call `response.getWriter()`.

Other salacious things we can do to with a PortletResponse object include:

- *Setting the content type for the response*
- *Creating a link back to the current portlet*
- *Obtain a PrintWriter and output content*

PortletResponse vs. the RenderResponse

Only three methods are defined in the PortletResponse interface, namely addProperty, setProperty, and encodeURL. On the other hand, the subtype, the RenderResponse, defines a number of handsome methods, such as createRenderURL, setTitle, setContentType, and of course, getWriter.

A Note About Content Creation within a Portlet

It should be noted that only an html snippet is sent back to the client through a do<mode> method (doView, doEdit, doConfig, doHelp etc).

A portlet should never print out <HTML> or <BODY> tags. The portal *server* takes care of the overall page layout through a theme. The job of a portlet is to simply render a snippet of markup language that will be displayed in a predefined segment of the overall portal page.

Furthermore, any html tags that are opened in a portlet should be closed by that same portlet. Make sure the snippet of markup sent back to the client is well formed, and doesn't leave any dangling html tags, such as a <TABLE> tag that doesn't have a matching </TABLE> tag.

The PortletResponse and RenderResponse

PortletResponse

- addProperty (name : String, value : String) : void
- setProperty (name : String, value : String) : void
- encodeURL (urlToEncode : String) : String

RenderResponse

- getContentType ( ) : String
- createRenderURL ( ) : PortletURL
- createActionURL ( ) : PortletURL
- getNamespace ( ) : String
- setTitle (title : String) : void
- setContentType (contentType : String) : void
- getCharacterEncoding ( ) : String
- getWriter ( ) : PrintWriter
- getLocale ( ) : Locale
- setBufferSize (size : int) : void
- getBufferSize ( ) : int
- flushBuffer ( ) : void
- resetBuffer ( ) : void
- isCommitted ( ) : boolean
- reset ( ) : void
- getPortletOutputStream ( ) : OutputStream

Looking at another Simple Portlet

Here's a simple, yet highly cosmopolitan portlet, that determines a user's preferred language, and prints out an undiscriminating message.

```
package com.examscam.portlet;

import java.io.*;  import javax.portlet.*;

public class CountrySnooperPortlet extends GenericPortlet {

public void
  doView(RenderRequest request, RenderResponse response)
                   throws PortletException, IOException {

  //figure out the user's preferred language
  String language=request.getLocale().getDisplayLanguage();

  //always set the content type before generating output
  response.setContentType("text/html");
  //use the PortletResponse to generate output
  response.getWriter().print("We love people who speak ");
  response.getWriter().print(language);
  response.getWriter().print("!");

  }
}
```

Figure 2-1

Rendering of the above CountrySnooperPortlet

Country Snooper

We love people who speak Spanish!

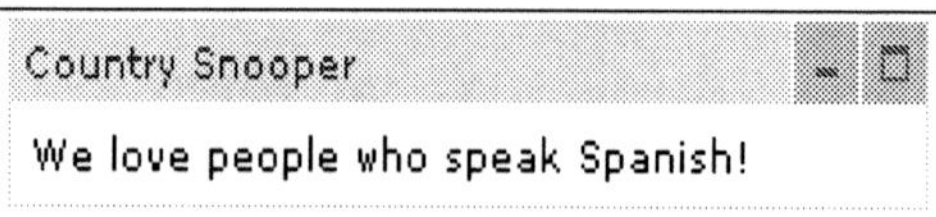

Notice how a method of the Portlet**Request,** through the RenderRequest, is used to find information about the user's country of origin. Also notice how the Portlet**Response**, through the RenderResponse, provides access to a PrintWriter that allows us to send content back to the user.

Generally speaking, anything you want to know about the client is in the request, and anything you want to do to the client is done through the response.

Packaging Portlets Together

If the CountrySnooperPortlet is packaged along with other portlets in the same portlet war file, all of the portlets contained in that war file would be said to be part of the same ***portlet application.*** If the CountrySnooperPortlet was packaged along with the HelloWorldPortlet defined earlier, both would be said to be part of the same ***portlet application***, and we could also say that both portlets share a common ***PortletContext***.

All portlets defined within a portlet application must be declared in the portlet deployment descriptor, portlet.xml. Our CountrySnooperPortlet is no exception.

```
<portlet>
  <description>Snoops on a user's locale</description>
  <description xml:lang="en">
       Snoops on a users locale
  </description>
  <portlet-name>CountrySnooperPortlet</portlet-name>
  <display-name>CountrySnooperPortlet</display-name>
  <display-name xml:lang="en">
    CountrySnooperPortlet
  </display-name>
  <portlet-class>
    com.examscam.portlet.CountrySnooperPortlet
  </portlet-class>
  <supports>
    <mime-type>text/html</mime-type>
    <portlet-mode>view</portlet-mode>
  </supports>
  <portlet-info>
    <title>CountrySnooperPortlet</title>
  </portlet-info>
</portlet>
```

Notice how a few new tags have been added to the portlet definition of the CountrySnooperPortlet. There is a significant amount of meta-data that can be configured in the deployment descriptor, and in this case, we have added a description and a display-name. These are optional tags, but are very useful, both for appropriately internationalizing your portlet, and helping users know the basic use of a portlet when they are deciding to add the given portlet to their portal page.

Full portlet.xml File Containing Two Portlets

```
<?xml version="1.0" encoding="UTF-8"?>
<portlet-app
xmlns="http://java.sun.com/xml/ns/portlet/portlet-app_1_0.xsd"
version="1.0" xmlns:xsi="http://www.w3.org/2001/XMLSchema-instance"
xsi:schemaLocation="http://java.sun.com/xml/ns/portlet/portlet-app_1_0.xsd http://java.sun.com/xml/ns/portlet/portlet-app_1_0.xsd"
id="examscam2.ExamScam2Portlet.1146144ee0">

 <portlet>
  <description>Snoops on a users locale</description>
  <description xml:lang="en">
       Snoops on a users locale
  </description>

  <portlet-name>CountrySnooperPortlet</portlet-name>

  <display-name>CountrySnooperPortlet</display-name>
  <display-name xml:lang="en">
    CountrySnooperPortlet
  </display-name>
  <portlet-class>
    com.examscam.portlet.CountrySnooperPortlet
  </portlet-class>
  <supports>
    <mime-type>text/html</mime-type>
    <portlet-mode>view</portlet-mode>
  </supports>
  <portlet-info>
    <title>CountrySnooperPortlet</title>
  </portlet-info>
</portlet>

<portlet>
  <portlet-name>HelloWorldPortlet</portlet-name>
  <display-name>HelloWorld portlet</display-name>
  <portlet-class>com.examscam.portlet.HelloWorldPortlet</portlet-class>
  <supports>
    <mime-type>text/html</mime-type>
    <portlet-mode>view</portlet-mode>
  </supports>
  <portlet-info><title>HelloWorldPortlet</title></portlet-info>
</portlet>

</portlet-app>
```

Another Portlet Example: Inspecting Headers

Much of the delicious information that comes to the server about the client comes in the form of http headers. Headers, which come in as name-value pairs, represent information that a web browser surreptitiously sends to the server on every client request.

Using the JSR-168 Portlet API, some creative use of the Enumeration class, and a little Haitian Voodoo sprinkled in for good measure, looping through http headers, and seeing what type of data is being sent to the server, is very easy to do. Here's a Portlet that uses the getPropertyNames() method of the RenderRequest object to do just that:

Figure 2-2

The following portlet loops through the various headers sent to the server, and outputs the corresponding name-value pairs within a portlet.

```
package com.examscam.portlet;
import java.io.*;import javax.portlet.*;

public class GettingHeadersPortlet extends GenericPortlet {

  protected void
   doView(RenderRequest request, RenderResponse response)
                    throws PortletException, IOException {

   response.setContentType("text/html");
   PrintWriter out = response.getWriter();
   out.print("<B>These headers were sent:</B><BR/> ");
   java.util.Enumeration enum = request.getPropertyNames();
      while (enum.hasMoreElements()){
        String name = enum.nextElement().toString();
        String value = request.getProperty(name);
        out.print("<BR/>");
        out.print(name + ": " + value);
    }
  }
}
```

Debriefing the GettingHeadersPortlet

Taking the time to try and understand exactly how the GettingHeadersPortlet works will pay off dividends in the future. Code that loops through an enumeration of named objects and then accesses corresponding values, will come up time and time again, not only in this book, but in day to day portlet and servlet based programming.

In figure 2-2, the first line of code in the doView method asks the request object to return all of the various header names in the form of a very flexible collection type called an Enumeration.

```
java.util.Enumeration enum = request.getPropertyNames();
```

Once we have all of the header names in the enumeration, we can move through the collection of names one at a time, using the hasMoreElements( ) method of the Enumeration class.

```
while  (enum.hasMoreElements( )) { //do something }
```

As we loop through the enumeration of header names, we can use the nextElement( ) method of the Enumeration class to grab the current header name.

```
String name = enum.nextElement( );
```

Once we have the name of the header, we can grab the actual value of the header associated with that name.

```
String value = request.getProperty(name);
```

Of course, if we knew the name of a header of interest, we could name it explicitly. For example, 'user-agent' is the name of a header that tells you information about the type of web browser a client is using. We could grab the value associated with the user-agent header by making the following method call:

```
String browser = request.getProperty("user-agent");
```

The above line of code might return the following:

```
(compatible; MSIE 6.0; Windows NT 5.0 )
```

Headers and Other Enumerable Elements

The results of our completed, GettingHeadersPortlet, is a portlet that lists all the header names and corresponding values that are sent to a web server from a web based client.

The header names include accept, referrer, accept-language, user-agent, host, connection and cache-control. Different browsers and device types will send a different set of headers, so the listing will vary from one client to another. Figure 2-3 shows the values associated with these various header names.

Figure 2-3

The rendering of the GettingHeadersPortlet

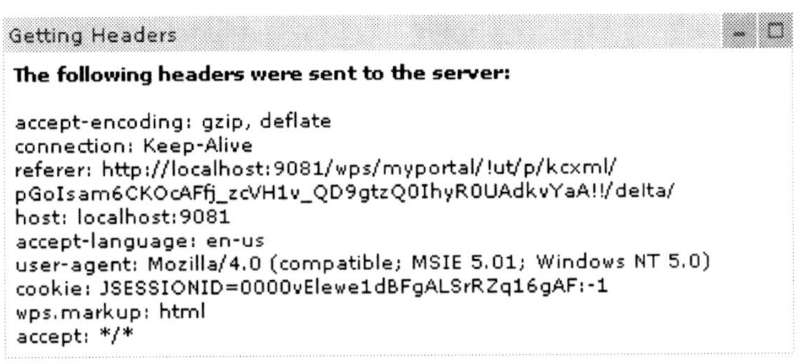

Many objects in both the Servlet and Portlet API return a listing of names as an enumeration, which can be looped through by using code very similar to that that in our GettingHeadersPortlet. Some of those enumerable objects include:

- Initialization Strings stored in the *PortletContext*
- Objects placed in the PortletSession
- Initialization String stored in the PortletConfig

Portlet API Exceptions

When coding the doView method of a Portlet, be aware of two potential exceptions that might be thrown.

The first exception that might occur is the IOException. A portlet has to deliver content to the portal, and subsequently, to the end user, and if any ports or sockets get messed up along the way, an IOException can potentially be thrown. This is also thrown when a portlet takes too long to render, and the portal server decides it will not wait any longer for the portlet to deliver back some yummy markup.

The other exception the doView method of a portlet might throw is the PortletException.

The PortletException is a very general exception, indicating that somehow, the portlet was unable to complete its processing successfully. All of the other exceptions defined in the portlet API use the PortletException as their parent class. These other exceptions include:

- PortletModeException
- PortletSecurityException
- ReadOnlyException
- UnavailableException
- ValidatorException
- WindowStateException

Class Diagram for the PortletException

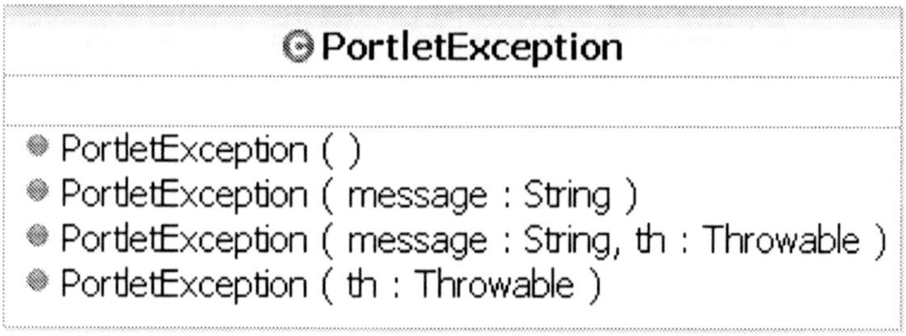

PortletException

PortletException ( )
PortletException (message : String)
PortletException (message : String, th : Throwable)
PortletException (th : Throwable)

Full portlet.xml File For Portlet Application

```
<?xml version="1.0" encoding="UTF-8"?>
<portlet-app
xmlns="http://java.sun.com/xml/ns/portlet/portlet-app_1_0.xsd"
version="1.0" xmlns:xsi="http://www.w3.org/2001/XMLSchema-instance"
xsi:schemaLocation="http://java.sun.com/xml/ns/portlet/portlet-app_1_0.xsd http://java.sun.com/xml/ns/portlet/portlet-app_1_0.xsd"
id="examscam2.ExamScam2Portlet.1146144ee0">

 <portlet>
  <description>GettingHeadersPortlet</description>
  <description xml:lang="en">
    Displays All Http Headers
  </description>
  <portlet-name>GettingHeadersPortlet</portlet-name>
  <display-name>GettingHeadersPortlet</display-name>
  <display-name xml:lang="en">GettingHeadersPortlet</display-name>
  <portlet-class>
    com.examscam.portlet.GettingHeadersPortlet
  </portlet-class>
  <supports>
    <mime-type>text/html</mime-type>
    <portlet-mode>view</portlet-mode>
  </supports>
  <portlet-info>
    <title>GettingHeadersPortlet</title>
  </portlet-info>
 </portlet>

 <portlet>
  <description>Snoops on a users locale</description>
  <description xml:lang="en">Snoops on a users locale</description>
  <portlet-name>CountrySnooperPortlet</portlet-name>
  <display-name>CountrySnooperPortlet</display-name>
  <display-name xml:lang="en">CountrySnooperPortlet</display-name>
  <portlet-class>
    com.examscam.portlet.CountrySnooperPortlet
  </portlet-class>
  <supports>
    <mime-type>text/html</mime-type>
    <portlet-mode>view</portlet-mode>
  </supports>
  <portlet-info><title>CountrySnooperPortlet</title></portlet-info>
</portlet>

<portlet>
  <portlet-name>HelloWorldPortlet</portlet-name>
  <display-name>HelloWorld portlet</display-name>
  <portlet-class>com.examscam.portlet.HelloWorldPortlet</portlet-class>
  <supports>
    <mime-type>text/html</mime-type>
    <portlet-mode>view</portlet-mode>
  </supports>
  <portlet-info><title>HelloWorldPortlet</title></portlet-info>
</portlet>
</portlet-app>
```

Question 2-1

Which of the following files can be found in the web-inf folder of a portlet application?
☐ a) application.xml
☐ b) web.xml
☐ c) manifest.mf
☐ d) portlet.xml

Question 2-2

How many methods are defined in the RenderResponse interface?
O a) 5
O b) 3
O c) 1
O d) 0

Question 2-3

Which of the following exceptions are explicitly thrown in the method signature of the doView method?
☐ a) NullPointerException
☐ b) ServletException
☐ c) IOException
☐ d) PortletException

Question 2-4

Which of the following relationships are true?
O a) a war file can have many web.xml files
O b) a war file can contain many portlet.xml files
O c) a web.xml file can define many portlets
O d) a portlet.xml file can define many portlets

Answer 2-1

Which of the following files can be found in the web-inf folder of a portlet application?
☐ a) application.xml ☐ b) web.xml ☐ c) manifest.mf ☐ d) portlet.xml
Options b) and d) are correct. All portlet war files must contain a web.xml file and a portlet.xml file. The application.xml file is found in the root of an Enterprise Application Archive (EAR), and the manifest file is found in the META-INF folder, not the web-inf folder.

Answer 2-2

How many methods are defined in the RenderResponse interface?
O a) 5 O b) 3 O c) 1 O d) 0
Option d) is correct. Curiously, the RenderResponse defines no new methods, and as such, can be considered a *marker interface*. All of the methods that can be called on the RenderResponse object are defined in the parent type, PortletResponse. Comparatively, the Render***Request*** defines only three of its own methods, inheriting the rest from PortletResponse.

Answer 2-3

Which of the following exceptions are explicitly thrown in the method signature of the doView method?
☐ a) NullPointerException ☐ b) ServletException ☐ c) IOException ☐ d) PortletException
Options c) and d) are correct. All of the do<mode> methods throw both the IOException, and the PortletException. ***Servlets*** throw the ServletException, and while a portlet can indeed throw a NullPointerException, the null pointer is an unchecked exception, and need not be listed in the throws clause.

Answer 2-4

Which of the following relationships are true?
O a) a war file can have many web.xml files O b) a war file can contain many portlet.xml files O c) a web.xml file can define many portlets O d) a portlet.xml file can define many portlets
Only option d) is correct. A war file can have only one web.xml file, and only one portlet.xml file. Portlets are not defined in the web.xml file with JSR-168. However, a portlet.xml file can define ***many*** portlets. It is many portlets working together that makes up a commonly packaged, portlet application.

Chapter 3
Rendering a View with Java Server Pages

In a good model-veiw-controller type of application, a Java centric component should never be polluted with lots of lousy html.

With typical servlet and struts based applications, html is usually generated by a Java Server Page (JSP); in this regard, portlet applications are no different.

However, portlet applications *do* present some unusual complications when deferring to a JSP for markup generation.

How does a JSP link back to a specific portlet on a page? How does a portlet call a JSP? How do we gain access to the portlet specific ***Portlet***Request and ***Portlet***Response object in JSP?

This chapter deals with basic JSP development, and the issues that present themselves when deferring to a JSP for markup generation.

Deferring to a JSP for Markup Generation

While accessing the PrintWriter from the request object, and printing content directly back to the client in the doView method of a portlet is easy to do, it certainly isn't a best practice.

We have been spoiled so far with portlets that are relatively light on html tags. However, for content generation, a portlet should defer to a Java Server Page (JSP). JSPs are web centric artifacts that are written largely in static html, but can be interspersed with Java code to make them more interactive.

Figure 3-1 A Sample Java Server Page (JSP), welcome.jsp

A JSP is mostly markup, with a little bit of Java code (in bold) interspersed. Java Server Pages facilitate the development of complex, dynamic web pages.

```
<%@ page session="false" contentType="text/html" %>
<B>Welcome to this simple JSP<B><BR>
We did some snooping on you.<BR>
This is what we learned about your browser:

<I><BR> <%=request.getHeader("user-agent")%> </I><BR>

And we know what language you speak, it's:

<I> <%=request.getLocale().getDisplayLanguage()%> </I>
```

Invoking the welcome.jsp from a Portlet

While the concept of delegating to a JSP for view generation is relatively simple and straight forward, the code is actually a little bit intimidating. Assuming the code from Figure 3-1 was saved in a file named welcome.jsp, and that welcome.jsp file was saved in the root of the war, invoking the welcome.jsp would require the following lines of code in a portlet:

```
String url = "welcome.jsp";
getPortletContext()
      .getRequestDispatcher(url).include(request,response);
```

PortletRequestDispatcher
include (req : RenderRequest, resp : RenderResponse) : void

Using a JSP for Markup Generation

When a particular portlet is requested, the custom coded Java class that extends GenericPortlet, and is specified in the portlet.xml file, will be invoked by the portal server. The portlet class is then responsible for delegating to a JSP for markup generation. This is done using the ***include*** method of the PortletRequestDispatcher, during the portlet's rendering phase.

The full code for the JSPDisplay portlet that forwards to the welcome.jsp file is as follows:

```
package com.examscam.portlet;
import java.io.*; import javax.portlet.*;

public class JSPDisplay extends GenericPortlet {
  protected void doView
        (RenderRequest request, RenderResponse response)
                throws PortletException, IOException {

    String url = "/welcome.jsp";
    getPortletContext()
      .getRequestDispatcher(url).include(request,response);
  }
}
```

Where is the Portal Finding the JSP?

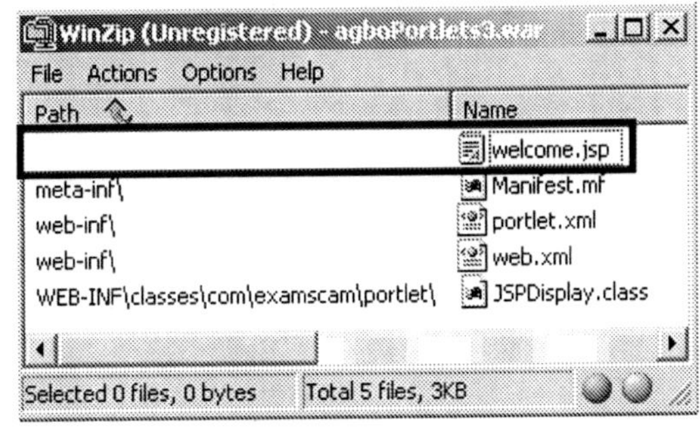

Legacy portal development tools would pull jsp files from a variety of different folders, depending upon the client device and the preferred language of the user making the request. For JSR-168 portlets, the PortletRequestDispatcher quite sensibly searches for jsp files starting from the root of the war.

So, with the JSPDisplay portlet, the welcome.jsp file would be found right there in the root.

JSP Deferment and Multiple Markup Support

For supporting multiple markup languages, it is customary, and automatic with the portlet wizards of many rapid application development tools, that subdirectories exist for each of your markup languages, under a folder named *jsp*. By following this convention, multiple markup languages can be easily integrated by simply creating new JSP files in the appropriately named subfolders, and using these JSPs at the appropriate times.

Figure 3-2

A well formed folder structure helps in the development of multi-device capable portlets.

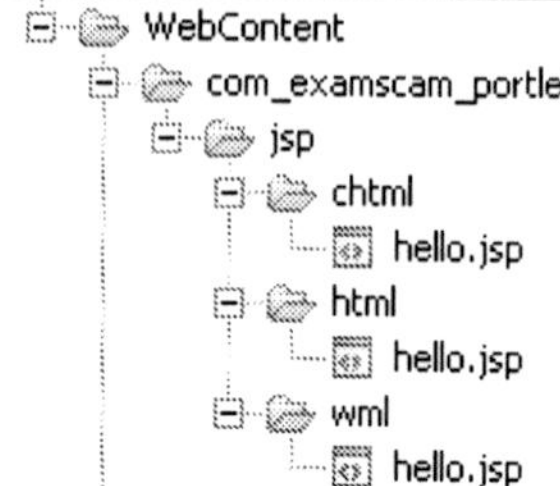

Deployment Descriptor for JSPDisplay Portlet

Assuming the JSPDisplay portlet is packaged in its own war file, the portlet.xml file for the JSPDisplay portlet would be as follows:

```
<?xml version="1.0" encoding="UTF-8"?>
<portlet-app xmlns="http://java.sun.com/xml/ns/portlet/portlet-app_1_0.xsd"
version="1.0" xmlns:xsi="http://www.w3.org/2001/XMLSchema-instance"
xsi:schemaLocation="http://java.sun.com/xml/ns/portlet/portlet-app_1_0.xsd
http://java.sun.com/xml/ns/portlet/portlet-app_1_0.xsd"
id="com.examscam.portlet.JSPDisplay.9afc93cee0" >
 <portlet>
  <description>JSPDisplay</description>
  <portlet-name>JSPDisplay</portlet-name>
  <display-name>JSPDisplay</display-name>
  <portlet-class>
    com.examscam.portlet.JSPDisplay
  </portlet-class>
  <supports>
    <mime-type>text/html</mime-type>
    <portlet-mode>view</portlet-mode>
  </supports>
  <portlet-info><title>JSPDisplay</title></portlet-info>
 </portlet>
</portlet-app>
```

Something Wrong with our welcome.jsp

Portlets build extensively upon the Servlet and JSP API, and the welcome.jsp file in Figure 3-1 was coded as though it were part of a typical Servlet and JSP application. When you're doing ***portlet*** development, not respecting your jsp files as ***portlet artifacts*** is a very bad thing.

A Java Server Page, by virtue of the fact that it runs in a Java web container, has implicit access to eight very important object types defined by the Servlet and JSP API, namely: the ServletRequest, ServletResponse, ServletConfig, ServletContext, HttpSession, JSPWriter, pageContext, and HttpJspPage object.

Now, we're actually not supposed to access these implicit variables within our portlet jsps. Remember, with Portlets, we don't use the ServletRequest and ServletResponse objects, but instead, we use the **Render**Request and **Render**Response objects.

The RenderRequest and RenderResponse objects are not implicitly available to jsp pages that run within a portlet application; however, the portlet API does provide a special custom tag that indeed makes it possible to use them. Any Java Server Page that needs easy and implicit access to classes defined in the portlet API needs only to add a special custom tag, **portlet:defineObjects**, to their JSP page. This makes the RenderRequest, RenderResponse, and even the PortletConfig object, implicitly available with the names renderRequest, renderResponse and portletConfig.

There are several configuration steps required to use the <portlet:defineObjects/> custom tag, namely:

1. a reference to the portlet.tld file must be placed in the web.xml file
2. a taglib directive must be added to the top of the JSP page that uses the portlet.tld custom tags
3. the <portlet:defineObjects/> custom tag must appear in the portlet JSP page

Once you have followed these steps, you can implicitly reference the renderRequest, renderResponse and portletConfig objects within JSP scriptlets, declarations and expressions.

1: taglib Entry in the web.xml file

To access the various custom tags associated with the portlet API, including <portlet:defineObjects/>, a reference to the tag library must be configured in the web.xml file.

```
<?xml version="1.0" encoding="UTF-8"?>
<!DOCTYPE web-app PUBLIC "-//Sun Microsystems, Inc.//DTD Web Application 2.3//EN"
"http://java.sun.com/dtd/web-app_2_3.dtd">
<web-app id="WebApp_ID">
  <display-name>agboPortlets3</display-name>
  <welcome-file-list><welcome-file>index.jsp</welcome-file></welcome-file-list>
   <taglib id="PortletTLD">
     <taglib-uri>http://java.sun.com/portlet</taglib-uri>
   <taglib-location>
     /WEB-INF/tld/std-portlet.tld
   </taglib-location>
  </taglib>
</web-app>
```

2 & 3: Taglib Directive and defineObjects in JSP

After defining the taglib in the web.xml file, you must add a taglib directive, and the <portlet:defineObjects/> tag, to your JSP. After those elements have been added, you have implicit access to the variables named **renderRequest**, **renderResponse** and **portletConfig**.

```
<%@ page session="false" contentType="text/html"  %>

<%@taglib uri="http://java.sun.com/portlet" prefix="portlet"%>

<portlet:defineObjects/>

<B>Welcome to this simple JSP<B><BR>
We did some snooping on you.<BR>
This is what we learned about your browser:<I>
<%=renderRequest.getProperty("user-agent")%>
</I><BR>
And we know what language you speak, it's: <I>
<%=renderRequest.getLocale().getDisplayLanguage()%>
</I>
```

Question 3-1

Which of the following variable names are made available to JSP files with the addition of the <portlet:defineObjects/> tag?
☐ a) portletRequest
☐ b) portletResponse
☐ c) renderRequest
☐ d) renderResponse

Question 3-2

To use the portlet custom tags, the taglib-uri entry must appear in:
O a) the portlet.xml file
O b) the web.xml file
O c) the custom portlet that extends GenericPortlet
O d) JSP pages

Question 3-3

Which of the following methods are defined by the PortletRequestDispatcher?
O a) forward(String url)
O b) include(String url)
O c) forward(RenderRequest req, RenderResponse resp)
O d) include(RenderRequest req, RenderResponse resp)

Question 3-4

Compiled portlet source files are stored in a package aware structure under which folder?

- O a) WEB-INF
- O b) META-INF
- O c) WEB-INF\classes
- O d) META-INF\classes

Question 3-5

In the MVC paradigm, a JSP is typically considered which MVC component?

- O a) View
- O b) Data
- O c) Controller
- O d) Model

Answer 3-1

Which variable names are made available to JSP files with the addition of the <portlet:defineObjects/> tag?

☐ a) portletRequest

☐ b) portletResponse

☐ c) renderRequest

☐ d) renderResponse

Options c) and d) are correct.

When you use the defineObjects tag, you can reference the renderRequest and renderResponse objects within scriptlets and expressions. Furthermore, these objects provide enough getter methods to allow you to navigate to just about any object in the Portlet API. It should also be noted that a third variable, ***portletConfig***, becomes available to a JSP developer when the defineObjects tag is added to a JSP page.

Answer 3-2

To use the portlet API custom tags, the taglib-uri entry must appear in which file?

○ a) portlet.xml

○ b) web.xml

○ c) GenericPortlet

○ d) JSP pages

Option b) is correct.

The taglib-uri must be defined in the web.xml file, otherwise your JSP files will not be able to properly resolve the portlet API custom tags. The JSP pages themselves then need a taglib directive, along with the <portlet:defineObjects/> tag.

For the most part, we steer clear of the web.xml file when we're working in the portlet world. It's important to take note of the few times where we do have to finger the deployment descriptor of the web module.

Answer 3-3

Which of the following methods are defined by the PortletRequestDispatcher?
O a) forward(String url) O b) include(String url) O c) forward(RenderRequest, RenderResponse) O d) include(RenderRequest, RenderResponse)
Option d) is correct. While the Servlet API's RequestDispatcher provides both forward and include methods, only the include method is defined for the **Portlet**RequestDispatcher. The String for the url being forwarded to is provided during the call to getRequestDispatcher(String url).

Answer 3-4

Compile portlet source files are stored in a package aware structure under which folder?
O a) WEB-INF O b) META-INF O c) WEB-INF\classes O d) META-INF\classes
Option c) is correct. All compiled Java code, not to mention property files and resource bundles, must be places in a package aware subfolder of WEB-INF\classes. The only file typically found in the META-INF directory is the manifest file, which should describe the major and minor version number of your portlet application.

Answer 3-5

In the MVC paradigm, a JSP is typically considered to be which MVC component?

O a) View
O b) Data
O c) Controller
O d) Model

Option a) is correct.

A JSP is typically responsible for generating output to the client, which represents the view in an MVC, model-view-controller, architecture.

Chapter 4
Linking Back to the Portal

Forwarding to a JSP to spit out a little 'Hello World' message isn't going to win you any ***Programmer of the Year*** awards. On the other hand, using a JSP to generate an html form that helps process input from the user would be a fastidious application of your programming talents.

Creating Basic HTML Forms for User Input

To grab input from a user, we simply use html forms. For example, if we wanted the user to guess a magic number between one and ten, we might provide an html form that looks something like figure 4-1:

Figure 4-1 Using html Forms to obtain User Input

Web based forms are used to grab input from the user. This form asks a user to enter a number between one and ten and then click *Guess!!*.

NumberGuesserProject portlet

I'm thinking of a number between 1 and 10.

What is it? Guess!!

Using html forms to obtain input from a user is nothing new to a web developer, but using forms in a portlet environment presents a few unique and annoying challenges.

The Number Guesser Portlet

For this chapter, we're going to develop the NumberGuesserPortlet. The idea is that when the portlet is first viewed, it will ask the user to guess a magic number between one and ten:

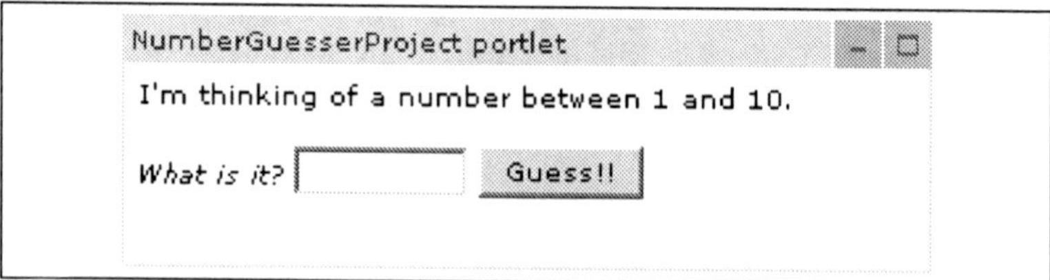
NumberGuesserProject portlet
I'm thinking of a number between 1 and 10.
What is it?
Guess!!

When the user clicks **Guess!!!,** the NumberGuesserPortlet will check to see what the number was that the user typed in, and tell the user whether they guessed the magic number correctly or not. For this example, we will hard code the magic number to be 5.

The Portlet will then generate a response, telling the user if they guessed correctly or not:

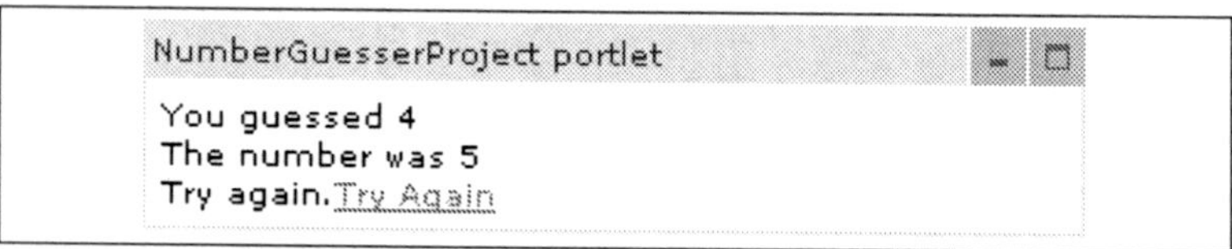
NumberGuesserProject portlet
You guessed 4
The number was 5
Try again. Try Again

The response, telling the user if they guessed correctly, will be generated through print statements in the portlet. The form that takes input from the user will be implemented as a JSP, creatively named numberguesser.jsp

The **Try Again** link will then return the user back to the original screen, prompting the user to guess the magic number. And remember, all of this is being performed on a portlet, that could potentially be sharing screen space with two or twenty other portlets. Furthermore, a portlet can be placed on any number of different pages in the portal. This introduces a level of complexity to your portlet applications that you would never encounter in a typical Servlet and JSP type of application.

Linking Back to a Portlet

Programming portlets presents the web developer with many new challenges, not the least of which is figuring out how to invoke a particular portlet from an html form. A portlet can be placed on a variety of different web pages at runtime. How can we invoke a web-based resource when we don't know the web address of the page on which it will appear?

Another challenge is making sure that the data submitted through our form goes to ***our*** portlet, and ***our*** portlet only. We don't want other portlets on the page using data submitted from our form.

Fortunately, the portlet API addresses these very challenges.

The Challenge of Linking Back to a Portlet

When a user clicks the ***submit*** button on a form, there must be an object sitting on the server that is ready to process the user's request. With typical Servlet/JSP applications, form submissions are forwarded to a servlet, and the name of the servlet is specified as the action of the form; however, we can't do that with a portlet.

For example, if our number guessing application was implemented as a servlet, there would be an HttpServlet, perhaps named NumberGuesserServlet, that would respond to the submission of the form, and subsequently extract the user's input. The Servlet would constitute the ***action*** of the form, and the form tag would look like this:

```
<FORM action = "NumberGuessServlet">
```

But a portlet can't make a direct call back to itself that easily. The best a portlet could do is make a call back to the page the portlet is displayed on, but even that's impossible to configure in an html form, because at development time, we don't know which page, or on how many pages, our portlet will potentially appear.

Submitting HTML Forms to a Portlet

Notice how the action attribute of the html form element in figure 4-2 points to a question mark. Typically, this would point to a Servlet or a CGI script that handles the submission of a form. How can we direct the submission of ***our*** form back to ***our*** portlet?

Figure 4-2

We don't know the name of the page our portlet may appear on at runtime. This makes hard coding a target for the action attribute of the form element impossible. In this case, the action attribute of the form has been left as a question mark (?).

```
<FORM   action = "?"  >
I'm thinking of a number between 1 and 10.<BR><BR>
<I>What is it? </I>
<INPUT type="text" name="number" size="10">
<INPUT type="submit" name="SUBMIT" value="Guess!!">
</FORM>
```

The PortletURL Object

Life would be simple if we could tell a form to directly call the NumberGuesserPortlet, but we can't. When a request is made to the portal server, a single portlet can't be invoked directly. Instead, the user must request a portal page, and the portal server takes care of rendering ***all*** of the portlets that are part of that page.

So, how do we make a new request to the portal to have our portlet, and the portal page with which it is associated, re-invoked? The answer is to have the RenderResponse create a PortletURL object, which essentially represents a link back to the current portal page, along with all of the portlets that appear on that page.

```
response.createRenderURL();  //link back to the portlet
response.createActionURL();  //triggers action phase
```

The PortletURL Object

PortletURL

- setWindowState (windowState : WindowState) : void
- setPortletMode (portletMode : PortletMode) : void
- setParameter (name : String, value : String) : void
- setParameter (name : String, value : String [*]): void
- setParameters (map : Map) : void
- setSecure (flag : boolean) : void

"The `PortletURL` interface represents a URL that reference the portlet itself.

A PortletURL is created through the `RenderResponse`. Parameters, a portlet mode, a window state and a security level can be added to `PortletURL` objects. The PortletURL must be converted to a String in order to embed it into the markup generated by the portlet.

There are two types of PortletURLs:

Action URLs, they are created with `RenderResponse.createActionURL`, and trigger an action request followed by a render request.

Render URLs, they are created with `RenderResponse.createRenderURL`, and trigger a render request."

`Portlet API JavaDoc,`
`http://jcp.org/aboutJava/communityprocess/final/jsr168/`

Creating the RenderURL Link

To create a link back to a portlet from within an html form, we need to dynamically generate that action attribute of our form. This can be done using a JSP expression:

```
<FORM  ACTION = "<%=renderResponse.createRenderURL()%>" >
```

Unfortunately, right out of the box, this line of code will not successfully compile. A little taglib directive, along with a `<portlet:defineObjects/>` custom tag, must be added to the JSP to make everything kosher.

A Refresher on Portlet Custom Tags

While all JSPs understand that the word ***response***, when used inside of an expression or a scriptlet, is a reference to the **HttpServlet**Response object, a standard JSP has no knowledge of what a **portlet**Response object is, even if the reference occurs in a JSP that is part of a portlet application.

To get the Java compiler to understand that when we say ***renderResponse*** in our JSPs, that we are referring to a subtype of the ***Portlet***Response object, we need to add two lines to the top of our Java Server Page:

```
1.<%@taglib uri="http://java.sun.com/portlet" prefix="portlet"%>
2.<portlet:defineObjects/>
```

The first line is the taglib, also known as a tag library directive. This taglib directive indicates that the JSP is going to employ the services of the portlet custom tag library.

The second line, <portlet:defineObjects/>, is an actual portlet custom tag in action. The sole purpose of the <portlet:DefineObjects/> tag is to expose three important portlet API objects:

- *The RenderRequest object: renderRequest*
- *The RenderRepsonse object: portletResponse*
- *The PortletConfig object: portletConfig*

With local access to the renderRequest, renderResponse, and portletConfig objects, you have access all of the other important portlet API components, including the PortletSession, PortletContext, PortletURL and others.

Figure 4-3 demonstrates how to create a PortletURL object, while including the taglib directive, and the `<portlet:defineObjects/>` custom tag.

Figure 4-3 renderResponse.createRenderURL()

To create a link back to the page a portlet appears on, the createRenderURL() method of the RenderResponse must be used. Notice the added custom tag and taglib directive.

```
<%@page contentType="text/html"%>
<%@taglib uri="http://java.sun.com/portlet" prefix="portlet"%>
< portlet:defineObjects />

<FORM action="<%=renderResponse.createRenderURL()%>">

I'm thinking of a number between 1 and 10.<BR><BR>
<I>What is it?</I>
<INPUT name="number" type="text" size="10" />
<INPUT name="submit" value="Guess!!" type="submit" />

</FORM>
```

Grabbing Form Input From Within a Portlet

With an html form that contains a textfield named ‘number’, all we have to do to figure out what a user typed into that textfield is call the getParameter method of the request object, and provide the name of the textfield, in this case ‘number’. The input of the user will be returned as a String.

Again, anything you want to know about the user, which includes what the user typed into a given textfield, is obtained through the PortletRequest object, or more specifically during the rendering phase, the RenderRequest.

With the taglib directive, and the <portlet:defineObjects/> tag, any expression that uses objects defined in the portlet API will compile and run successfully, including references to the action attribute of a form that references the portletResponse and the createRenderURL method.

Coding the NumberGuesserPortlet

The text in figure 4-4 shows the code required to improve our NumberGuesserPortlet to the point where it can extract form data from the user. Notice how this portlet acts largely as a controller, displaying the input form (numberguesser.jsp) if no data has been submitted, and alternatively, if a number has been submitted, the portlet provides interactive feedback to the user, namely information on whether the user correctly guessed the magic number.

Figure 4-4 Code used to grab data from a textfield named *number*.

```
package com.examscam.portlet;
import java.io.*;import javax.portlet.*;

public class NumberGuesserPortlet extends GenericPortlet {

 protected void
    doView(RenderRequest request, RenderResponse response)
                         throws PortletException, IOException
{
/*see if a number is passed to the server as a parameter*/
    String number = request.getParameter("number");

    /*if no number was entered, just show the form*/
    if (number == null) {
      String url = "/numberguesser.jsp";
      getPortletContext()
                    .getRequestDispatcher(url)
                              .include(request, response);
    } else {
 /*if a number was entered, display the correct answer*/
      response.setContentType("text/html");
      PrintWriter out = response.getWriter();
      out.print("You guessed " + number);
      out.print("<BR>The number was 5");
      out.print("<BR>Try again.");

/*create a link back to the portlet using a PortletURL*/
      out.print("<A href=\"");
      out.print(response.createRenderURL());
      out.print("\">Try Again</A>");
    }
  }
}
```

Data Clashes on the Portal Server

With our funky new code, and the clever use of the PortletURL object, our NumberGuesserPortlet works pretty darn good; but there is a hidden little problem buried in the JSP.

Our portlet uses the request.getParameter("*number*") method to figure out what the user typed into the textfield we named '*number*'. But remember, our Portlet isn't necessarily the only portlet on the page.

What if another portlet also uses an html form, with a textfield also named *number*? That other portlet would get access to ***our*** portlet's number, and that isn't good. Furthermore, our portlet might end up reading the number from the other portlet, and respond to a submission with which it had no business interacting. This isn't a good scenario.

Multiple Portlets and Handling Form Data

Remember, our portlets don't exist in a vacuum. The page that contains our NumberGuesserPortlet might also include a StockSellingPortlet that wants to know the *number* of shares a user wants to sell. That same page might also have a SpousalBenefitsPortlet that needs to know the *number* of wives or husbands a user has. If each of those portlets makes a request.getParameter("number") call in their doView method, each one will get the number that was typed into the form of the NumberGuesserPortlet.

When a portal page is rendered, the doView method of every portlet on the page is invoked, not just that one portlet with which you might currently be interacting.

Encoding Form Data with getNamespace( )

To ensure that form data being sent from our portlet to the server doesn't get confused with the form data of another portlet, the RenderResponse object gives us a special method called getNamespace(); this method will return a unique, alpha-numeric character set that uniquely identifies a portlet on a particular page. If we use the getNamespace() call, and attach that identifying String to each data element being sent back to the server, no other portlet on the portal page will mistakenly use our portlet's data.

All form elements should be encoded using the getNamespace() method of the response, and all fields being read in a portlet should assume the field has been namespace encoded.

> Note: For simplicity sake, this book will use examples that exclude the namespace call, which is fine for learning, but is completely unacceptable in development or production. Uniquely identify all of your form data, or JavaScripts, by using the getNamespace call to uniquely encode their names.

***If you encode a field in a JSP, make sure you use the same encoding scheme when retrieving that field on the server, as in the example below:

Encoding an Attribute in the Form:

```
<INPUT name="<%=renderResponse.getNamespace()%>number"/>
```

Un-Encoding the Same Attribute in the Portlet:

```
String num  = request.getParameter(response.getNamespace( ) + "number");
```

Figure 4-5

To ensure form data is only sent back to the intended portlet, the getNamespace method of the RenderResponse object needs to be used.

```
<%@ page contentType="text/html"%>
<%@taglib uri="http://java.sun.com/portlet" prefix="portlet"%>
<portlet:defineObjects />

<FORM action="<%=renderResponse.createRenderURL()%>">

I'm thinking of a number between 1 and 10.<BR><BR>
<I>What is it?</I>

<INPUT name="<%=renderResponse.getNamespace()%>number"/>
<INPUT name="submit" type="submit" value="Guess!!" />

</FORM>
```

```
***Note: a code change must be made in our Portlet in order
to be able to read the namespace encoded field from the
form:
```

```
String number=request.getParameter(response.getNamespace()+"number");
```

Displaying Images in a Portlet

A similar problem to linking back to a portlet, is figuring out how to display an image in a portlet. After all, if we have trouble creating a URL from our JSP to point back to our original portlet, how do we code a JSP to link back to a resource, such as a jpg or gif file, in an images subdirectory of our portlet application?

The solution is to use a special method in the renderRequest called getContextPath(). This returns a path to the root of the portlet application. From there, you can map to resources such as image files in subfolders. So, if you had an image named wiw.jpg in an images folder off the root of the war, the following code would pull the image out:

```
renderRequest.getContextPath() +  "/images/wiw.jpg";
```

To display the image in a portlet, you would combine this code with the standard html IMG tag:

```
<IMG src='<%=renderRequest.getContextPath()+"/images/wiw.jpg" %>'/>
```

Ultimately though, the resource should also be encoded, so the getContextPath() method is nested in a call to encode the URL:

```
<img
src='<%= renderResponse.encodeURL(
                   renderRequest.getContextPath() +
                                  "/images/wiw.jpg") %>'
/>
```

The Updated NumberGuesserPortlet

The NumberGuesserPortlet has been updated to demonstrate the changes that needs to be made in order to read a namespace encoded variable that is accessed as a parameter through the PortletRequest object.

Figure 4-6 Code used to grab user input from a textfield named 'number', taking into account namespace encoded attributes.

```
package com.examscam.portlet;
import java.io.*;import javax.portlet.*;

public class NumberGuesserPortlet extends GenericPortlet {
 protected void
     doView(RenderRequest request, RenderResponse response)
                     throws PortletException, IOException
{
/*see if a number is passed to the server as a parameter/*

    /*String number = request.getParameter("number");*/

    String number =
    request.getParameter(response.getNamespace()+"number");

    /*if no number was entered, just show the form*/
    if (number == null) {
      String url = "/numberguesser.jsp";
      getPortletContext()
                 .getRequestDispatcher(url)
                           .include(request, response);
    } else {

/*if a number was entered, tell the user the correct
answer*/
      response.setContentType("text/html");
      PrintWriter out = response.getWriter();
      out.print("You guessed " + number);
      out.print("<BR>The number was 5");
      out.print("<BR>Try again.");
/*create a link back to the current portlet using a
PortletURL*/
      out.print("<A href=\"");
      out.print(response.createRenderURL());
      out.print("\">Try Again</A>");
    }
  }
}
```

A Quick Look at Some Portlet Custom Tags

Since creating ***render*** and ***action*** URLs, not to mention namespace encoding form variables, are such common tasks in our JSP files, the Portlet API provides a couple of handy-dandy custom tags that make these tasks just a little bit easier.

Comparatively speaking, it is much slicker to use the <portlet:renderURL/> custom tag to spit out a link back to the current portal page, than it is to use the corresponding scriptlet.

With a JSP Expression:

```
<FORM action="<%=renderResponse.createRenderURL()%>">
```

With a Custom Tag:

```
<FORM action="<portlet:renderURL/>">
```

Similarly, using a custom tag to encode a variable name used in a form is much more readable and maintainable than using a JSP expression. Additionally, portlet parameters can be attached to a URL with the param tag:

```
<portlet:renderURL>
  <portlet:param name="book" value="portal"/>
</portlet:renderURL>
```

With a JSP: Expression:

```
<INPUT name="<%=renderResponse.getNamespace()%>number"/>
```

With a Custom Tag:

```
<INPUT name="<portlet:namespace/>number"/>
```

There are five custom tags defined by the portlet tag library descriptor (tld). They include **actionURL**, **renderURL**, **param**, **namespace** and **defineObjects**.

Our Input Form with Portlet Custom Tags

Figure 4-7

Custom tags make Java Server Pages a little easier to write, and a little easier to read.

```
<%@ page contentType="text/html"%>
<%@taglib uri="http://java.sun.com/portlet" prefix="portlet"%>
<portlet:defineObjects />

<FORM action="<portlet:renderURL/>">
I'm thinking of a number between 1 and 10.<BR><BR>
<I>What is it?</I>
<INPUT name="<portlet:namespace/>number"
                            type="text" size="10" />
<INPUT name="submit" value="Guess!!" type="submit" />
</FORM>
```

Figure 4-8 Rendering with Scriptlets vs. Custom Tags

While portlet custom tags are used to develop a JSP, the end user has no knowledge of the behind the scenes implementation.

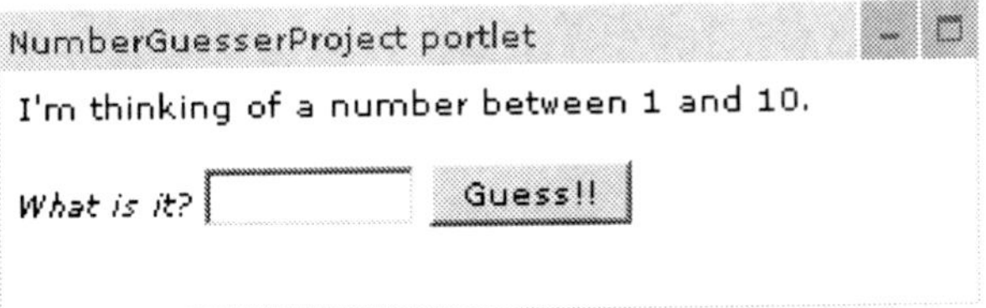
NumberGuesserProject portlet
I'm thinking of a number between 1 and 10.
What is it?
Guess!!

Deployment Descriptors

With the JSPs coded, and the NumberGuesserPortlet doing what it should, the last thing our portlet application needs before being zipped up, is a good portlet.xml file, and web.xml file.

```
<!--portlet.xml file for the NumberGuesserPortlet
application -->
<?xml version="1.0" encoding="UTF-8"?>
<portlet-app xmlns="http://java.sun.com/xml/ns/portlet/portlet-app_1_0.xsd"
version="1.0"xmlns:xsi="http://www.w3.org/2001/XMLSchema-instance"
xsi:schemaLocation="http://java.sun.com/xml/ns/portlet/portlet-app_1_0.xsd
http://java.sun.com/xml/ns/portlet/portlet-app_1_0.xsd"
id="com.examscam.portlet.NumberGuesserPortlet.420453eee0">
<portlet>
  <portlet-name>NumberGuesserPortlet</portlet-name>
  <display-name>NumberGuesserPortlet</display-name>
  <portlet-class>
    com.examscam.portlet.NumberGuesserPortlet
  </portlet-class>
  <supports>
    <mime-type>text/html</mime-type>
    <portlet-mode>view</portlet-mode>
  </supports>
  <portlet-info>
    <title>NumberGuesserProject</title>
  </portlet-info>
</portlet>
</portlet-app>
```

```
<-- web.xml file for the NumberGuesserPortlet Project -->
<?xml version="1.0" encoding="UTF-8"?>
<!DOCTYPE web-app PUBLIC "-//Sun Microsystems, Inc.//DTD Web Application 2.3//EN"
"http://java.sun.com/dtd/web-app_2_3.dtd">
<web-app id="WebApp_ID">
  <display-name>NumberGuesserProject</display-name>
  <welcome-file-list>
    <welcome-file>index.jsp</welcome-file>
  </welcome-file-list>
  <taglib id="PortletTLD">
  <taglib-uri>http://java.sun.com/portlet</taglib-uri>
    <taglib-location>
      /WEB-INF/tld/std-portlet.tld    </taglib-location>
  </taglib>
</web-app>
```

Packaging the WAR

Once the manifest file has been created, which simply states ***Manifest-Version: 1.1***, the NumberGuesserPortlet application can be zipped up as a war file and deployed to the portal server.

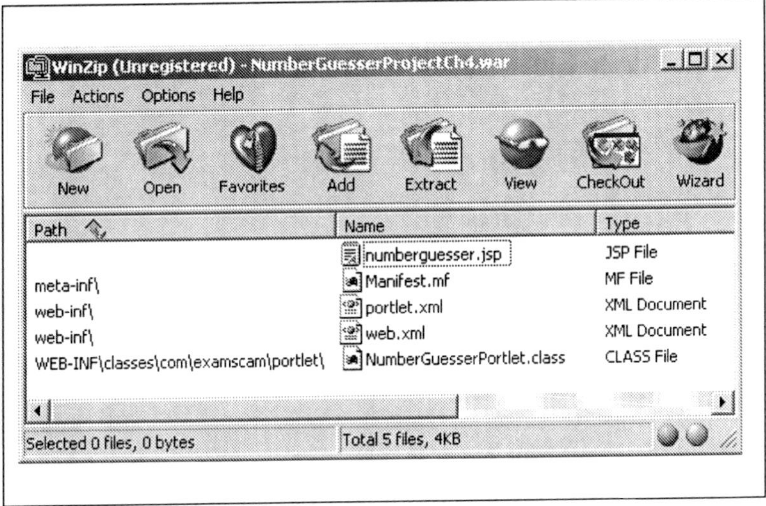

Question 4-1

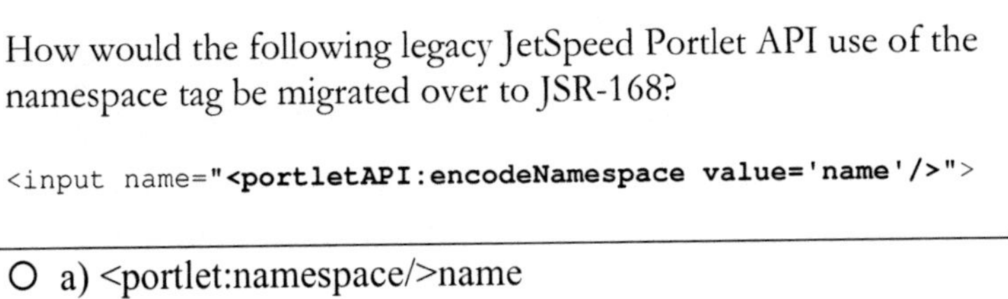

How would the following legacy JetSpeed Portlet API use of the namespace tag be migrated over to JSR-168?

```
<input name="<portletAPI:encodeNamespace value='name'/>">
```

- O a) <portlet:namespace/>name
- O b) <portlet:namespace>name</portlet:namespace>
- O c) <portlet:namespace value='name'/>
- O d) <portlet:namespace name='value'/>

Question 4-2

How would the following code, used to display an image in using the legacy Jetspeed Portlet API, be migrated over to JSR-168?

```
<%=portletResponse.encoeUrl("/img/car.jpg") %>
```

O a)
renderRequest.encodeURL(renderResponse.getContextPath() + "img/car.jpg")

O b)
renderResponse.encodeURL(renderRequest.getContextPath() + "img/car.jpg")

O c)
renderRequest.encodeURL(renderResponse.getContextPath() + "img/car.jpg")

O d)
renderResponse.encodeURL(renderRequest.getContextPath() + "img/car.jpg")

Question 4-3

Which of the following tags are associated with the JSR-168 API?

☐ a) <portlet:defineObjects/>
☐ b) <portlet:actionURL/>
☐ c) <portlet:namespace/>
☐ d) <portlet:parameter/>

Question 4-4

What is the correct usage of the <portlet:param/> tag when placed within a <portlet:actionURL></portlet:actionURL/> tag?

O a)
<portlet:param name="id">007</portlet:param/>
O b)
<portlet:param>007</portlet:param>
O c)
<portlet:param name="id" value="007"/>
O d)
<portlet:param name=id value="007"/>patron</portlet:param/>

Question 4-5

The namespace custom tag uniquely identifies a script or field with:

O a) a particular portlet, as defined in the portlet.xml file
O b) a specific portlet and portlet window on the current portal page
O c) a specific portlet application
O d) a specific portal page

Question 4-6

Which of the following are non-required attributes of the renderURL and actionURL custom tags?

- ☐ a) portletMode
- ☐ b) portletState
- ☐ c) secure
- ☐ d) variable

Question 4-7

The JSR-168 PortletRequestDispatcher allows:

- ☐ a) Forwarding to a JSP
- ☐ b) Forwarding to a Servlet
- ☐ c) Including the output of a JSP
- ☐ d) Including the output of a Servlet

Question 4-8

The JSR-168 PortletRequestDispatcher is directly accessed through which object?

- O a) PortletContext
- O b) PortalContext
- O c) RenderRequest
- O d) RenderResponse

Answer 4-1

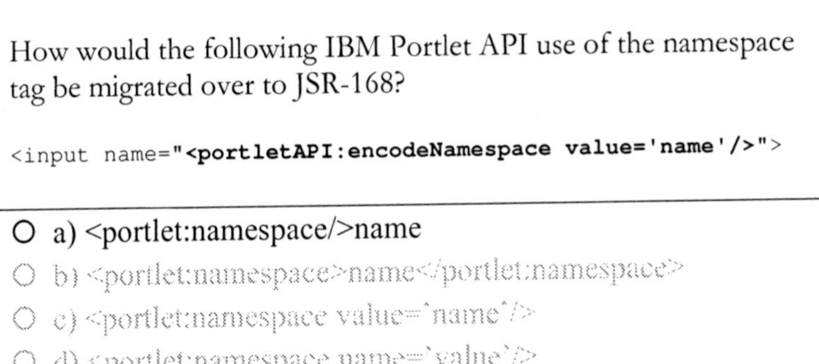

How would the following IBM Portlet API use of the namespace tag be migrated over to JSR-168?

```
<input name="<portletAPI:encodeNamespace value='name'/>">
```

- O a) <portlet:namespace/>name
- O b) <portlet:namespace>name</portlet:namespace>
- O c) <portlet:namespace value='name'/>
- O d) <portlet:namespace name='value'/>

Option a) is correct, although it may be a little non-intuitive. The namespace tag simply prefixes the name of the textfield, so a simple, single tag, sits before the name of the field.

Answer 4-2

How would the following code, used to display an image in using the JetSpeed/IBM Portlet API, be migrated over to JSR-168?
<%=portletResponse.encoeUrl("/img/car.jpg") %>

O a)
renderRequest.encodeURL(renderResponse.getContextPath() + "img/car.jpg")

O b)
renderResponse.encodeURL(renderRequest.getContextPath() + "img/car.jpg")

O c)
renderRequest.encodeURL(renderResponse.getContextPath() + "img/car.jpg")

O d)
renderResponse.encodeURL(renderRequest.getContextPath() + "img/car.jpg")

Option d) is correct. To display an image in a JSR-168 portlet, you first obtain the path from the RenderRequest, and then encode the URL using the renderResponse. Note that the command would work without the *encodeURL*, but would not be as programmatically sound.

Answer 4-3

Which of the following tags are associated with the JSR-168 API?

☐ a) <portlet:defineObjects/>
☐ b) <portlet:actionURL/>
☐ c) <portlet:namespace/>
☐ d) <portlet:parameter/>

Options a) b) and c) are correct.

Along with these three tags, the JSR-168 specification defines a <portlet:param/> tag and <portlet:renderURL/> tag. Choice d) is incorrect, as the proper name is <portlet:param/>, not the full name parameter.

Answer 4-4

What is the correct usage of the <portlet:param/> tag when placed within a <portlet:actionURL></portlet:actionURL/> tag?

○ a) <portlet:param name="id">007</portlet:param/>
○ b) <portlet:param>007</portlet:param>
○ c) <portlet:param name="id" value="007"/>
○ d) <portlet:param name=id value="007"/>patron</portlet:param/>

Option c) is correct.

There can be no content within the body of the <portlet:param/> tag. The information intended to be added as a parameter to the URL must be defined as name and value attributes of the tag, not as body content wrapped by the tag.

Answer 4-5

The namespace custom tag uniquely identifies a script or field with:
○ a) a particular portlet, as defined in the portlet.xml file ○ b) a specific portlet and portlet window on the current portal page ○ c) a specific portlet application ○ d) a specific portal page
Option b) is correct. The namespace feature uniquely identifies a script or field with a particular portlet on a portal page. If the same portlet appears multiple times on a page, each portlet that has its own portlet window, will have its own, unique, namespace identifier.

Answer 4-6

Which of the following are non-required attributes of the renderURL and actionURL custom tags?
☐ a) portletMode ☐ b) portletState ☐ c) secure ☐ d) variable
Options a) and c) are correct. The four attributes of a URL custom tag are portletMode, **window**State, secure and **var**.

Answer 4-7

The JSR-168 PortletRequestDispatcher allows:
☐ a) Forwarding to a JSP ☐ b) Forwarding to a Servlet ☐ c) Including the output of a JSP ☐ d) Including the output of a servlet
Options c) and d) are correct. The JSR-168 PortletRequestDispatcher does not allow any forwarding for content generation. Only *including* content generated by a web based resource is possible for a PortletRequestDispatcher, although using a JSP for content generation is more common than using a servlet. Answers c) and d) are correct.

Answer 4-8

The JSR-168 PortletRequestDispatcher is directly accessed through which object?
O a) PortletContext O b) PortalContext O c) RenderRequest O d) RenderResponse
Option a) is the correct answer. The method getRequestDispatcher is found in the PortletContext.

Chapter 5
The PortletSession

If the user is going to be good enough to provide information to us through html forms and http headers, the least we could do is keep track of that information, if only for the duration of the user's visit to our site.

To provide a stateful experience for portal users, portlet developers rely upon the services of the PortletSession, which, by the way, is remarkably similar to the HttpSession object from the Servlet API.

The PortletSession is easy to use, and helps maintain a stateful experience for the user, overcoming the stateless nature of the HTTP protocol.

This chapter will look at the PortletSession, how the PortletSession works, and will even discuss some of the drawbacks and alternatives to using a PortletSession object.

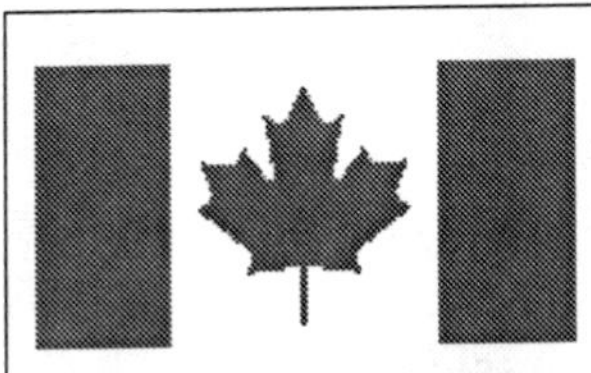

Canada and the http protocol have one thing in common: they are both stateless. Canada has ten provinces and three relatively empty territories, but no states. Of course, they have been eyeing Michigan for a while.

Managing State with the PortletSession Object

When a user visits our site, we often need to keep track of information the user has provided. Information stored in the PortletRequest or PortletResponse objects are purged as soon as a response is sent back to the client, which creates a problem if we want to keep track of information that a user has provided on previous request-response cycles.

To store user specific information for the duration of the user's interaction with the server, the Portlet API provides a special object called the PortletSession. Any useful piece of information, in the form of Java objects, can be stuffed inside a user's session object. That information is then available to our portlet on all subsequent request-response cycles. The PortletSession is effectively tied to the user for which it is created.

The Transient Nature of the PortletSession

One thing to note about the PortletSession is that it is transient – it's the hobo of the Portlet API. If the user leaves our site, doesn't interact with the site for a predetermined amount of time (usually thirty minutes), or even if the user closes their browser, information stored in the PortletSession is lost, or at least, the session containing the information will not longer be tied to the user.

Information stored in the PortletSession is not stored persistently. The job of the PortletSession is to simply create a stateful experience for users while interacting with our site.

Taking Advantage of the PortletSession Object

Figure 5-1 shows a simple portlet that keeps track of the number of times the doView method of a portlet is called. The view count variable is stored in the PortletSession, under the key named *timesvisited*. Every time the doView method of the portlet is called, the view count increases by one. The view count is then displayed back to the user.

Notice how the SimpleSessionPortlet requires some *session-data management.* When the portlet is first viewed, there will be no data stored in the session regarding the view count. On the first iteration, a *timesvisited* key, with an assigned value of 1, is placed into the PortletSession. On subsequent iterations, when the *timesvisited* key is present in the session, the associated value is extracted, incremented, and then stored back in the PortletSession.

Figure 5-1 Taking Advantage of the PortletSession

```
package com.examscam.portlet;
import java.io.*;import javax.portlet.*;

public class SimpleSessionPortlet extends GenericPortlet {

 protected void doView(RenderRequest request, RenderResponse
response)throws PortletException, IOException {

  response.setContentType("text/html");
  PrintWriter out = response.getWriter();
   /*grab the PortletSession out of the PortletRequest*/
  PortletSession session = request.getPortletSession();

  /*pull the visitCount out of the session. On the first
  visit, this will be null*/
  String visitCount =
              (String)session.getAttribute("timesvisited");
  if (visitCount == null) {
    /*if this is the first time viewing the portlet,
    set the timevisited value to 1*/
    session.setAttribute("timesvisited", "" + 1);
    out.print("Welcome to our little portlet!");
    out.print("Click refresh, minimize or maximize!!!");
  }
  else {
    /*if this portlet has been visited before,
    increase the  count*/

    int newCount = Integer.parseInt(visitCount) + 1;
    session.setAttribute("timesvisited", "" + newCount);
    out.print("Number of times visiting this portlet: ");
    out.print(newCount);
  }
 }
}
```

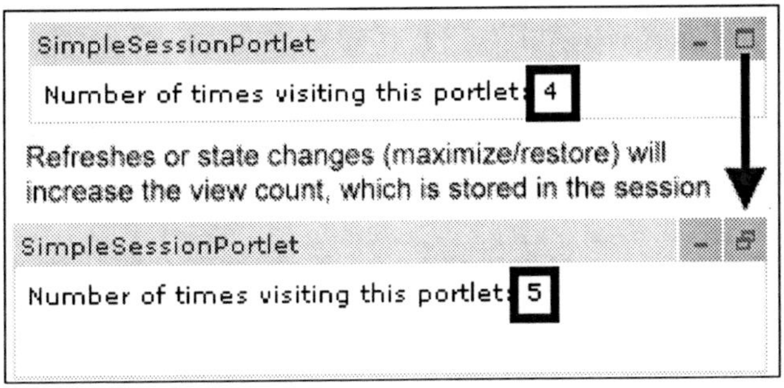

SimpleSessionPortlet

Number of times visiting this portlet: 4

Refreshes or state changes (maximize/restore) will increase the view count, which is stored in the session

SimpleSessionPortlet

Number of times visiting this portlet: 5

PortletSessions and User Portlets

An interesting aspect of the PortletSession is the fact that data stored in the PortletSession, by default, is local and accessible only to the portlet that created it. By default, data stored in the PortletSession by one portlet cannot be shared by any other portlets on the same portal page. If there are four portlets on a portal page, if they all use a PortletSession object, then each one will have a separate, unshared, PortletSession namespace. Even if two instances of the same portlet appear on a portal page, each one will have its own, unshared, PortletSession namespace.

PortletSession and the PORTLET_SCOPE

This default behavior is known as PORTLET_SCOPE, and has been the way the PortletSession object has behaved for years. However, developers have done nothing but moan and groan about the fact that it is incredibly difficult to share information between portlets that exist within the same portlet application (*think **war** file*), so, with the JSR-168 portlet specification, the Java Gods introduced the concept of a shared, APPLICATION_SCOPE, for the PortletSession. When a portlet shoves an object into the PortletSession, and specifies APPLICATION_SCOPE as the visibility of the data, any portlet that is part of that same *portlet application*, can obtain that data by providing the appropriate key when making a call to the PortletSession's getAttribute method.

PortletSession Constants

The JSR-168 API introduces two new constants, or should I say, ***final static*** variables, in the PortletSession class. These two new contains are called APPLICATION_SCOPE and PORTLET_SCOPE, and represent the numbers 0x**01** and 0x**02** respectively.

```
/* constants representing the PortletSession scopes*/

PortletSession.APPLICATION_SCOPE  //0x01
PortletSession.PORTLET_SCOPE  //0x02
```

Newly Overloaded PortletSession Methods

In a typical Servlet and JSP based application, along with legacy JetSpeed and proprietary Portlet APIs, the ***setAttribute*** method is used to save data to the PortletSession. The setAttribute method takes a name/value-object pair as arguments. Data is pulled out of the session with a call to ***getAttribute,*** with the name provided as a parameter; the associated value-object is then returned to the calling program. However, in the JSR-168 Portlet API, the setAttribute and getAttribute methods have been overloaded, with an extra parameter added, that allows for one of the two new portlet scopes to be specified.

```
/* default mechanism for adding to a PortletSession */
session.setAttribute("key", "value");

/* overloaded mechanism for adding to a PortletSession*/
session.setAttribute("key",
                     "value",
                     PortletSession.PORTLET_SCOPE);

/*placing data into the APPLICATION_SCOPE of a PortletSession*/
session.setAttribute("key",
                     "value",
                    PortletSession.APPLICATION_SCOPE);

/* default mechanism for pulling from a PortletSession */
session.getAttribute("key");

/* overloaded mechanism for pulling from a PortletSession*/
session.setAttribute("key", PortletSession.PORTLET_SCOPE);

/*pulling data from the APPLICATION_SCOPE*/
session.setAttribute("key", PortletSession.APPLICATION_SCOPE);
```

PortletSession and the APPLICATION_SCOPE

When data placed into the PortletSession is given APPLICATION_SCOPE, the data is visible to all other portlets that are packaged as part of the same *portlet application.* Portlets are part of the same portlet application

\when they are *defined in a common portlet.xml file, and packaged in a common war file.*

Many developers believe that data stored in the APPLICATION_SCOPE of the PortletSession is available to all of the portlets a users might access on the portal. **This is simply not the case.** While APPLICATION_SCOPE allows a degree of sharing of data, the data is not shared with portlets that are defined in separate war files. All portlets sharing APPLICATION_SCOPE data must be defined in a common portlet.xml file.

C0.lass Diagram of the PortletSession

"The `PortletSession` *interface provides a way to identify a user across more than one request and to store transient information about that user.*

A `PortletSession` *is created per user client per portlet application.*

A portlet can bind an object attribute into a `PortletSession` *by name. The* `PortletSession` *interface defines two scopes for storing objects:*

`APPLICATION_SCOPE`

`PORTLET_SCOPE`

All objects stored in the session using the `APPLICATION_SCOPE` *must be available to all the portlets, servlets and JSPs that belongs to the same portlet application and that handles a request identified as being a part of the same session. Objects stored in the session using the* `PORTLET_SCOPE` *must be available to the portlet during requests for the same portlet window that the objects where stored from.* ***Attributes stored in the*** **`PORTLET_SCOPE`** ***are not protected from other web components of the portlet application. They are just conveniently namespaced.***

The portlet session is based on the `HttpSession`*. Therefore all* `HttpSession` *listeners do apply to the portlet session and attributes set in the portlet session are visible in the* `HttpSession` *and vice versa."*

-Description of the PortletSession from the IBM/Sun Portal API JavaDocs

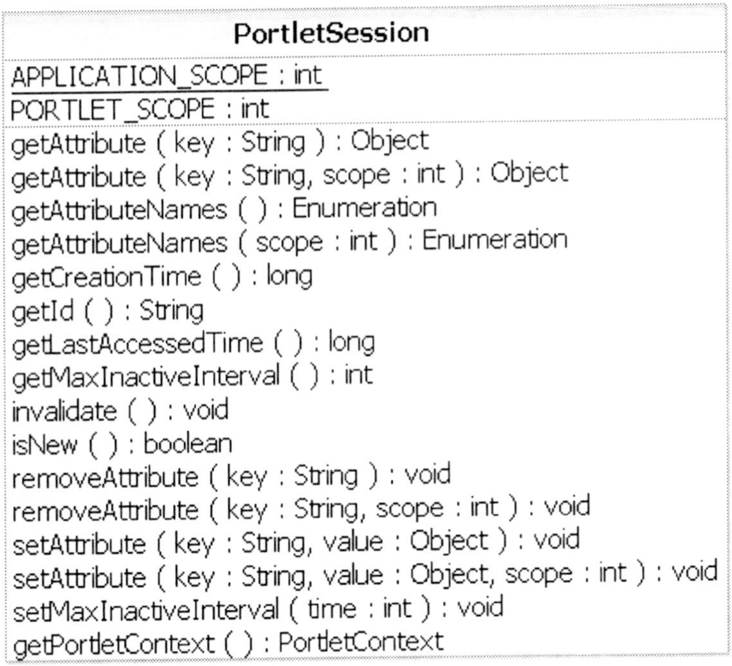

PortletSession
APPLICATION_SCOPE : int
PORTLET_SCOPE : int
getAttribute (key : String) : Object getAttribute (key : String, scope : int) : Object getAttributeNames ( ) : Enumeration getAttributeNames (scope : int) : Enumeration getCreationTime ( ) : long getId ( ) : String getLastAccessedTime ( ) : long getMaxInactiveInterval ( ) : int invalidate ( ) : void isNew ( ) : boolean removeAttribute (key : String) : void removeAttribute (key : String, scope : int) : void setAttribute (key : String, value : Object) : void setAttribute (key : String, value : Object, scope : int) : void setMaxInactiveInterval (time : int) : void getPortletContext ( ) : PortletContext

Reading from the APPLICATION_SCOPE

Our SimpleSessionPortlet defined in Fig. 5-1, places a hitcount into the session using the key *timesvisited.* To allow another portlet to access this hitcount, we could change the scope of the timesvisited key to APPLICATION_SCOPE, and have a second Portlet, which we will name SessionViewerPortlet, pull the key out of the APPLICATION_SCOPE.

```
package com.examscam.portlet;
import java.io.*;import javax.portlet.*;

public class SessionViewerPortlet
                         extends GenericPortlet {
protected void doView
   (RenderRequest request, RenderResponse response)
         throws PortletException, IOException {

  response.setContentType("text/html");
  PrintWriter out = response.getWriter();
  PortletSession session = request.getPortletSession();

  Object count =
  session.getAttribute("timesvisited",
                       PortletSession.APPLICATION_SCOPE);

  if (count != null) {
    out.print("I found the count in the session: ");
    out.print(count.toString());
  } else {
    out.print("Couldn't find the count in the session.");
  }
 }
}
```

While the SessionViewerPortlet looks for the timesvisited key in the APPLICATION_SCOPE, the lookup will be unsuccessful until the SimpleSessionPortlet explicitly places the timesvisited key in the appropriate scope.

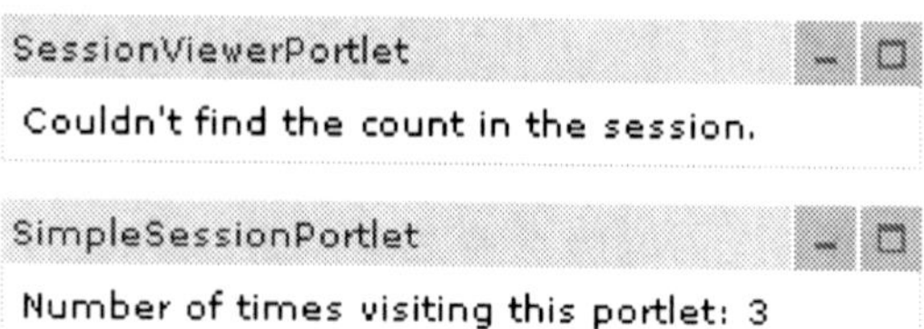

Figure 5-2 Taking Advantage of the PortletSession

```
package com.examscam.portlet;
import java.io.*;import javax.portlet.*;

public class SimpleSessionPortlet extends GenericPortlet {

 protected void doView(RenderRequest request, RenderResponse response)
                          throws PortletException, IOException {
  response.setContentType("text/html");
  PrintWriter out = response.getWriter();
  PortletSession session = request.getPortletSession();

  String visitCount =
    (String)session.getAttribute(
                    "timesvisited",
                     PortletSession.APPLICATION_SCOPE);
  if (visitCount == null) {
    /*if this is the first time viewing the portlet,
    set the timevisited value to 1*/
    session.setAttribute("timesvisited", "" + 1,
                    PortletSession.APPLICATION_SCOPE);
    out.print("Welcome to our little portlet!");
    out.print("Click refresh, minimize or maximize!!!");
  }
  else {

    int newCount = Integer.parseInt(visitCount) + 1;
    session.setAttribute("timesvisited", "" + newCount,
                    PortletSession.APPLICATION_SCOPE);
    out.print("Number of times visiting this portlet: ");
    out.print(newCount);
  }
 }
}
```

Now that the key *timesvisited* is stored in the scope of the application, both the Session ViewerPortlet, and the SimpleSessionPortlet, can share information through the PortletSession. But notice how the two portlets are out of sync, with one showing a count of 2, and the other showing a count of 3? This very issue will lead us into the next chapter on the action processing phase of a portlet.

Portlet.xml File for PortletSession Examples

```
<?xml version="1.0" encoding="UTF-8"?>
<portlet-app
xmlns="http://java.sun.com/xml/ns/portlet/portlet-app_1_0.xsd"
version="1.0" xmlns:xsi="http://www.w3.org/2001/XMLSchema-instance"
xsi:schemaLocation="http://java.sun.com/xml/ns/portlet/portlet-app_1_0.xsd
http://java.sun.com/xml/ns/portlet/portlet-app_1_0.xsd"
id="PortletSessions.8a76e53fe0">

<portlet>
  <portlet-name>SessionViewerPortlet</portlet-name>
  <display-name>SessionViewerPortlet</display-name>
  <portlet-class>
    com.examscam.portlet.SessionViewerPortlet
  </portlet-class>
  <supports>
   <mime-type>text/html</mime-type>
   <portlet-mode>view</portlet-mode>
  </supports>
  <portlet-info>
    <title>SessionViewerPortlet</title>
 </portlet-info>
</portlet>

<portlet>
  <portlet-name>SimpleSessionPortlet</portlet-name>
  <display-name>SimpleSessionPortlet</display-name>
  <portlet-class>
    com.examscam.portlet.SimpleSessionPortlet
  </portlet-class>
  <supports>
    <mime-type>text/html</mime-type>
    <portlet-mode>view</portlet-mode>
  </supports>
  <portlet-info>
    <title>SimpleSessionPortlet</title>
  </portlet-info>
</portlet>

</portlet-app>
```

The NumberGuesser and the PortletSession

Our NumberGuesserPortlet could really use a good dose of the PortletSession object. Currently, our NumberGuesserPortlet thinks up a number, and asks the user to guess it, but it doesn't give the user a chance to keep trying until they guess the magic number correctly.

By incorporating the PortletSession object into the NumberGuesserPortlet, we could store both the magic number and the number of guessing attempts. We could even give the user a hint as to whether they should guess higher or lower. When the user guesses successfully, we can then provide a message that indicates their success, and subsequently displays the number of attempts it took.

Our improved NumberGuesserPortlet appears in Figure 5-3. Be aware that changes will be required in the corresponding JSP in order for the portlet to function properly. The JSP changes are listed in Figure 5-4.

Tips for Manipulating the PortletSession

Information is pulled out of the PortletSession using the **getAttribute(String)** method. Objects are put into the PortletSession using the **setAttribute(String, Object)** method.

The name used to put an object ***into*** the session must **exactly** match the name used to pull the object ***out***. Spellling mistakes, or even a different caSinG of letters will cause the return of a *null* object. Always try to avoid NullPointerExceptions. ☺

The PortletSession also includes a method called **removeAttribute(String).** If you no longer have use for an object you have stored in the PortletSession, that object should be removed from the session.

The misuse of session data is one of the most significant performance bottlenecks a portal server, or *any* J2EE application server for that matter, will encounter. Eliminating unnecessary objects from your PortletSession, and avoiding what is known as *session bloat*, will help you avoid performance problems at runtime.

Figure 5-3 The New and Improved NumberGuesserPortlet

```
package com.examscam.portlet;
import java.io.*;import javax.portlet.*;
public class NumberGuesserPortlet extends GenericPortlet {
protected void doView
 (RenderRequest request, RenderResponse response)
                  throws PortletException, IOException {

PortletContext context = this.getPortletContext();
PortletSession session = request.getPortletSession();

if (session.getAttribute("magicnumber") == null) {
  /* generate a magic number to start the game*/
  int magicNumber = (int) (System.currentTimeMillis() % 9) + 1;

  /* populate the session with pertinent Java objects*/
  session.setAttribute("magicnumber", new Integer(magicNumber));
  session.setAttribute("guesses", "0");
  /* place the message in the session*/
  session.setAttribute("message", "Guess the number!");

} else {
  /* get the magicNumber and number of guesses out of the session*/
  /* NOTE: what will happen if the user didn't type anything in? */
Integer magicNumber
                  = (Integer) session.getAttribute("magicnumber");
  String guesses = (String) session.getAttribute("guesses");
  /* increment the number of guesses*/
  guesses = "" + (Integer.parseInt(guesses) + 1);
  session.setAttribute("guesses", guesses);
  /* what did the user guess? */
  Integer guess = new Integer(request.getParameter("number"));
  /* figure out a message to return to the user*/

  if (guess.intValue() > magicNumber.intValue()) {
    session.setAttribute("message", "Guess lower!");
  } else {
    session.setAttribute("message", "Guess higher!");
  }
  if (guess.intValue() == magicNumber.intValue()) {
    String message = magicNumber + " is correct. Play again!";
    session.setAttribute("message", message);
    /* purge the session of unneeded data*/
    session.removeAttribute("magicnumber");
  }
}
/* forward to the jsp for display  */
String url = "/numberguesser.jsp";
context.getRequestDispatcher(url).include(request, response);
}

}
```

Inspecting the Better NumberGuesserPortlet

The first two lines of our improved portlet simply declares the PortletSession and PortletContext objects for easy access later on in the portlet.

The next step is to see if a *magic number* exists in the session. If there is no magic number in the session, then we assume the user is looking at this portlet for the first time, or they are re-starting the guessing process. In that case, we create a new magic number and stuff that number into the PortletSession. We also set the number of guesses to zero, after all, the number guessing game is just starting.

Once all of our objects have been initialized, and stuffed into the PortletSession, we can forward to a JSP page, but before we do that, we stuff a little message into the PortletSession. The message simply says "Guess the number!!!" This message will be printed out by the JSP.

Figure 5-4 The updated JSP for the improved portlet.

```
✂✂✂
public class NumberGuesserPortlet extends GenericPortlet {
protected void doView
 (RenderRequest request, RenderResponse response)
                  throws PortletException, IOException {

PortletContext context = this.getPortletContext();
PortletSession session = request.getPortletSession();

if (session.getAttribute("magicnumber") == null) {
  /*generate a magic number to start the game*/
  int magicNumber=(int)(System.currentTimeMillis() % 9)+1;

  /*populate the session with pertinent Java objects*/
  session.setAttribute("magicnumber",
                              new Integer(magicNumber));
  session.setAttribute("guesses", "0");
  /*message is set in the session*/
  session.setAttribute("message", "Guess the number!");
}
✂✂✂
}
```

When Form Data is Present

If request.getParameter("number") does not return null, then indeed the user has just submitted a form, trying to guess the magic number. In this case, we grab the ***magic*** number from the session, then we grab the ***number of guesses*** from the session, and finally we grab the ***number guessed*** by the user, using the request.getParameter("number") method.

****Note that we have been lazy so far. If the user clicks submit without typing anything into the textfield, or types in non-numeric data, we are going to have a NumberFormatException.*

If the number is too high, we send them to the numberguesser.jsp file with a message stuffed into the session object instructing them to guess lower.

```
session.setAttribute("message", "Guess lower!");
```

If the number is too low, we send them to the numberguesser.jsp file with a message stuffed into the request object instructing them to guess higher.

```
session.setAttribute("message", "Guess higher!");
```

If the user guesses the magic number correctly, we stuff a friendly message in the session object, indicating that the user has successfully guessed the magic number.

After updating the message, we remove the magic number from the session. After all, it is not needed now that the number has been guessed. If the user wants to play again, we'll just generate a new magic number, and set their number of guesses to zero.

Figure 5-5

```
✂✂✂
if (guess.intValue() == magicNumber.intValue()) {
  String message= magicNumber + " is correct. Play again!";
  session.setAttribute("message", message);
  /* Purge the session of unneeded data */
  session.removeAttribute("magicnumber");
}
✂✂✂
```

Debriefing the NumberGuesser's JSP Pages

A JSP is used to generate the markup needed to display the portlet on a portal page. The JSP used in this example is displayed in Figure 5-6.

Figure 5-6 Generating a View with a JSP

```
<%@ page contentType="text/html"%>
<%@taglib uri="http://java.sun.com/portlet" prefix="portlet"%>
<portlet:defineObjects />
<%=renderRequest.getPortletSession().
                        getAttribute("message")%>
<FORM action="<portlet:renderURL/>">
I'm thinking of a number between 1 and 10. <BR>
<INPUT name="number" size="10" type="text" />
<INPUT value="Guess!!" type="submit" /> </FORM>
Number of guesses:
<%=renderRequest.getPortletSession()
                        .getAttribute("guesses")%>
```

The biggest change for the JSP on this iteration of the NumberGuesserPortlet is the presence of the expression:

<%=renderRequest.getPortletSession().getAttribute("message")%>

just before the input field.

Inside the NumberGuesserPortlet, a message is placed in the session scope, indicating whether a user should guess higher, lower, or if the user is guessing for the first time, simply to guess randomly. This message is then printed out just above the textfield in the numberguesser.jsp page. This script allows a single JSP page to be used dynamically, and render itself slightly differently, depending upon the state of the application.

Our improved form also displays to the user how many guesses they have made at the magic number, based on the ***guesses*** key placed into the PortletSession during the doView method.

```
Number of guesses: <%=renderRequest.getPortletSession()
                              .getAttribute("guesses")%>
```

Question 5-1

What type of data is acceptable for the storage in the PortletSession?

- O a) any class that inherits from java.lang.Object
- O b) any String value
- O c) any serializable Java object
- O d) any serializable String value

Question 5-2

Programmatically, what is the process for storing transient data in the PortletSession?

- O a) call the setAttribute(name, value) method of the PortletSession, followed by the store() method
- O b) call the setAttribute(name, value) method of the PortletSession, followed by the save() method
- O c) call the setAttribute(name, value) method of the PortletSession, followed by the set() method
- O d) call the setAttribute(name, value) method of the PortletSession

Question 5-3

Information stored in the PortletSession with the visibility of APPLICATION_SCOPE:
O a) will be stored persistently O b) will be stored until the portlet application it is associated is stopped O c) will be destroyed when the user's session times out O d) will be stored until the portal server is shut down

Question 5-4

Which of the following is true about the JSR-168 PortletSession?
☐ a) Data stored in the PortletSession is also available to the HttpSession of the Servlet and JSP API ☐ b) Data stored in the HttpSession is also available to Portlets through the PortletSession ☐ c) The PortletSession inherits from the HttpSession of the Servlet and JSP API ☐ d) The PortletSession is based on the HttpSession of the Servlet and JSP API

Question 5-5

A portlet needs to share session data with another portlet defined in the same portlet.xml file. Which PortletSession scope should be used?
O a) PORTLET_SCOPE O b) SESSION_SCOPE O c) APPLICATION_SCOPE O d) This type of session sharing is not possible

Answer 5-1

What type of data is acceptable for the storage in the PortletSession?
O a) any class that inherits from java.lang.Object O b) any String value O c) any serializable Java object O d) any serializable String value
Answer c) is correct. While non-serialized objects can safely be placed in the PortletSession on a non-distributed environment, in order to have portlet applications behave properly in a distributed environment that employs multiple JVMs, you must ensure that any object placed in the PortletSession is serializable.

Answer 5-2

Programmatically, what is the process for storing transient data in the PortletSession?
O a) call the setAttribute(name, value) method of the PortletSession, followed by the store() method O b) call the setAttribute(name, value) method of the PortletSession, followed by the save() method O c) call the setAttribute(name, value) method of the PortletSession, followed by the set() method O d) call the setAttribute(name, value) method of the PortletSession
Answer d) is correct. In order to save data in the PortletSession, you simply call the setAttribute method, providing a name of the object being placed in the session, along with the object itself. Only the PortletPreferences object needs an explicit call to store() in order to ensure that data is saved persistently for the user.

Answer 5-3

Information stored in the PortletSession with the visibility of APPLICATION_SCOPE:

O a) will be stored persistently

O b) will be stored until the portlet application it is associated is stopped

O c) will be destroyed when the user's session times out

O d) will be stored until the portal server is shut down

Answer c) is correct.

PortletSession data, regardless of whether it is APPLICATION_SCOPE or PORTLET_SCOPE, will be only stored transiently.

Answer 5-4

Which of the following is true about the JSR-168 PortletSession?

☐ a) Data stored in the PortletSession is also available to the HttpSession of the Servlet and JSP API

☐ b) Data stored in the HttpSession is also available to Portlets through the PortletSession

☐ c) The PortletSession inherits from the HttpSession of the Servlet and JSP API

☐ d) The PortletSession is based on the HttpSession of the Servlet and JSP API

Answers a) and d) are correct, with d) actually being lifted directly from the PortletSession JavaDoc.

Since the PortletSession is essentially the HttpSession of the user, data stored in the HttpSession becomes available to the user through the PortletSession.

Answer 5-5

A portlet needs to share session data with another portlet defined in the same portlet.xml file. Which PortletSession scope should be used?

O a) PORTLET_SCOPE
O b) SESSION_SCOPE
O c) APPLICATION_SCOPE
O d) This type of session sharing is not possible

Answer c) is correct.

The APPLICATION_SCOPE makes it possible to share session data across portlets that are part of the same portlet application.

Chapter 6 Action Processing

So far, our exposure to handling client requests has limited itself to the rendering phase of portlet processing – all of our examples have placed code in the doView method of our portlets. In our examples, everything from form handling, to view generation, has been done in the doView method. However, this really isn't a good development practice.

Strictly speaking, ***the various do methods of a portlet should only be responsible for generating the markup that needs to be sent back to the client***. Since portlet mode methods, such as doView, doEdit, doConfigure and doHelp, are really only intended for generating the markup that gets sent back to the client, those methods are said to be part of the portlet's *rendering* phase, and as such, these methods are passed a **Render**Request and a **Render**Response object.

Two Phase Portlet Processing

Tasks such as state management, form handling and PortletSession management should not take place during the portlet rendering phase. In fact, certain tasks, such as the manipulation the PortletPreferences object associated with the doEdit mode, or forcing a portlet to display itself in a maximized state, simply ***can't*** be performed during the portlet rendering phase. Such tasks ***must*** be performed before a portlet is asked to render itself, during an important stage known as the *event processing* or *action processing phase.* The event processing phase is associated with a special method called **processAction**.

```
public void processAction
       (ActionRequest request, ActionResponse response)
                   throws PortletException,  IOException {}
```

ActionRequest and ActionResponse

You will notice that the processAction method is passed request and response objects that are different in type to the request and response objects passed to the doView method. The processAction method receives an ***Action***Request and an ***Action***Response object, both of which inherit from PortletRequest and PortletResponse respectively, but provide action phase functionality, as opposed to rendering phase functionality.

ActionRequest
getPortletInputStream ( ) : InputStream
setCharacterEncoding (encoding : String) : void
getReader ( ) : BufferedReader
getCharacterEncoding ( ) : String
getContentType ( ) : String
getContentLength ( ) : int

While it is not a compiler enforced rule, tasks such as state management, session management, and form handling should all be performed in the action processing phase of a portlet. We have cheated a bit in some of our examples, just to keep our portlets as simple as possible, but as a general rule, application processing should occur in the processAction method of a portlet, not the doView method.

ActionResponse
setWindowState (state : WindowState) : void
setPortletMode (mode : PortletMode) : void
sendRedirect (url : String) : void
setRenderParameters (map : Map) : void
setRenderParameter (name : String, value : String) : void
setRenderParameter (name : String, values : String [*]) : void

WindowState and PortletMode Changes

To re-emphasize the point, there are certain things that absolutely **must** be performed in the action processing phase of a portlet, and attempts to do otherwise will fail. For example, only the **Action**Response object has methods such as setPortletMode and setWindowState. If you want a portlet to render itself in a maximized state, this decision must be made before the rendering phase of a portlet takes place. If you want the portlet you are working with to render in the edit mode, or a custom config mode, the setPortletMode method must be invoked during the actionProcessing phase.

Session Management and Action Processing

The PortletSession object can be manipulated during the rendering phase of a portlet, but it is generally not a good idea.

The SimpleSessionPortlet from the previous chapter placed a variable in the APPLICATION_SCOPE of the PortletSession, so that other portlets in the same application could access the variable. However, there is no way to determine the order in which the doView method of various portlets appearing on a portal page will be invoked, and with our SimpleSessionPortlet, the doView method that *manipulated* the PortletSession was invoked *after* other portlets had read the common value placed in the APPLICATION_SCOPE of the PortletSession. As a result, two portlets, on the same portal page, reading the ***same variable*** from the session, actually ended up displaying **different values**. Sometimes, the correct value will appear, but you simply can't be guaranteed which portlet's doView method will be invoked first, and which will be invoked second.

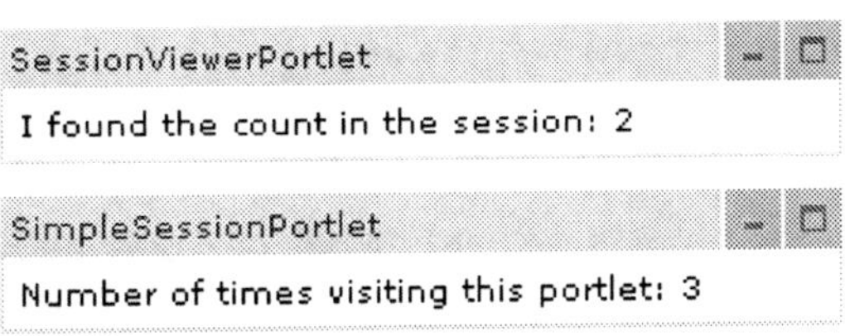

Since the action processing phase always occurs before the rendering phase of any portlet on a portal page, shared variables should always be manipulated in the action processing phase of the portlet.

The ActionResponse vs. the RenderResponse

Both the RenderResponse and ActionResponse inherit from the PortletResponse, but only the ActionResponse has methods that allow for the manipulation of the PortletMode and the WindowState.

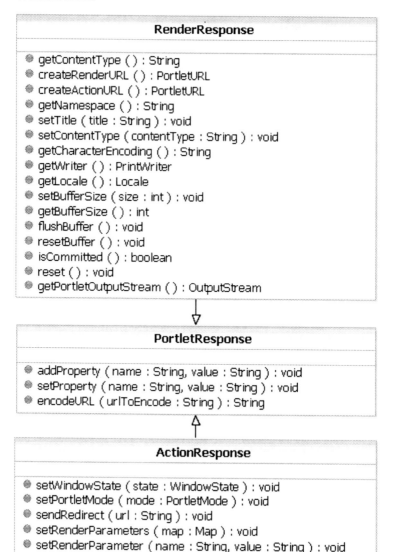

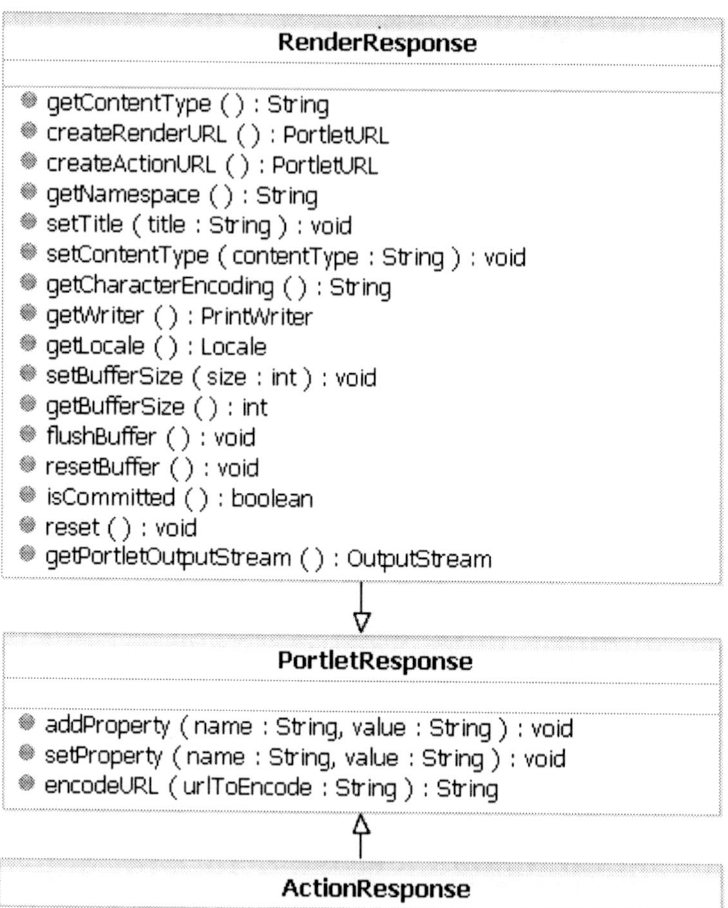

The ActionRequest vs. the RenderRequest

Both the ActionRequest and the RenderRequest inherit from the PortletRequest, although as you can see from the class diagram, the ActionRequest defines infinitely more new methods than the RenderRequest. ☺

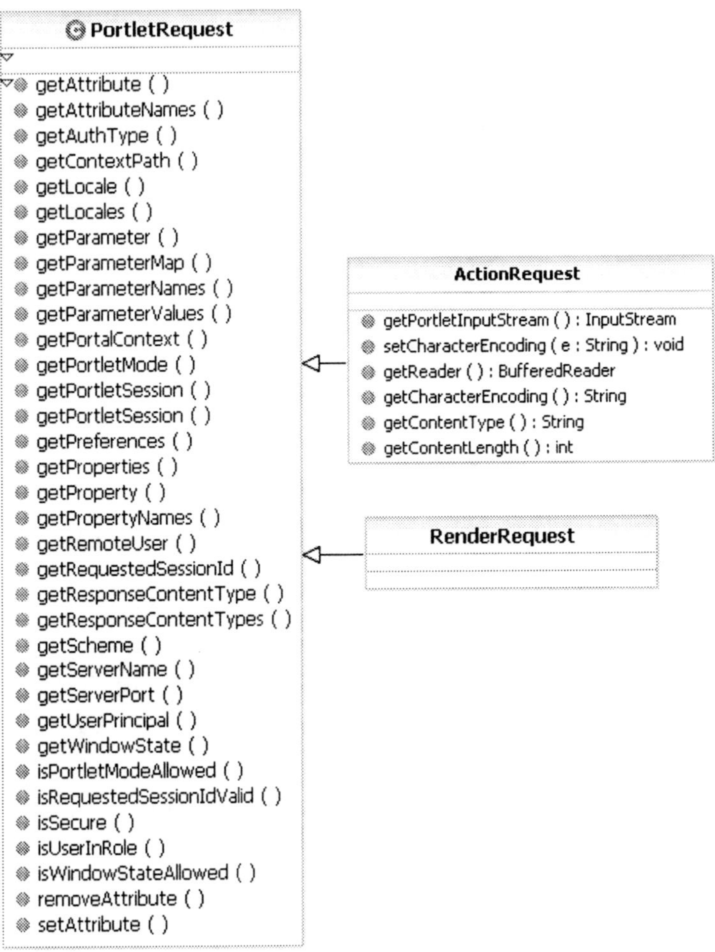

The Event Processing Phase

While the action processing phase always precedes the portlet rendering phase, the portlets we develop do not *automatically* take part in event processing. For a portlet to take part in the event processing phase, a client must invoke the portlet using a special **actionURL**, and the portlet being invoked must implement the **processAction** method.

Let's take a look at a portlet that both implements the processAction method, and triggers itself using an actionURL.

```
public class StateShifter extends GenericPortlet {

/* portlet rendering phase */
public void doView
  (RenderRequest request, RenderResponse response)
                throws PortletException, IOException {}

/* action processing phase  */
public void processAction
   (ActionRequest request, ActionResponse response)
                throws PortletException, IOException {}
}
```

Working with the WindowState Object

WindowState

- NORMAL : WindowState
- MAXIMIZED : WindowState
- MINIMIZED : WindowState

- WindowState (name : String)
- equals (arg0 : Object) : boolean
- hashCode ( ) : int
- toString ( ) : String

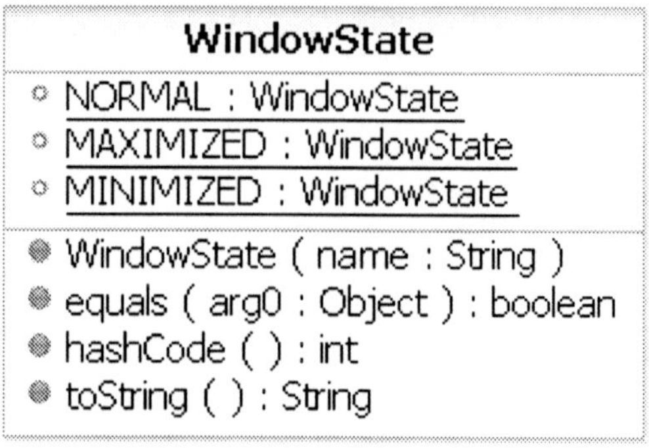

The purpose of this portlet is to move the user from one portlet state to another. The various portlet states are: maximized, minimized and normal. To implement this state shifting portlet, we use the WindowState object to establish the current state of the portlet, and then use the response.setWindowState() method to perform a change.

The Logic of the StateShifter Portlet

If the window is in the normal state, we will switch to the maximized state, and if the window is maximized, we will re-render in the minimized state. The code is relatively straight forward and readable:

```
public void processAction  ✂✂✂
WindowState state = request.getWindowState();
if (state == WindowState.NORMAL) {
  response.setWindowState(WindowState.MAXIMIZED);
}
if (state == WindowState.MAXIMIZED) {
  response.setWindowState(WindowState.MINIMIZED);
}
if (state == WindowState.MINIMIZED) {
  response.setWindowState(WindowState.NORMAL);
} ✂✂✂
```

javax.portlet.WindowState

"The `WindowState` *class represents the possible window states that a portlet window can assume.*

This class defines a standard set of the most basic portlet window states. Additional window states may be defined by calling the constructor of this class.

If a portal/portlet-container does not support a custom window state defined in the portlet application deployment descriptor, the custom window state will be ignored by the portal/portlet container. "

-Description of the WindowState from the IBM/Sun Portal API JavaDocs

Custom Window States

The JSR-168 specification allows portals to define custom window states, such as a pop-up state. If a portlet tries to use a window state that is not supported by the portal server, a ***WindowStateException*** will be thrown.

Figure 6-1 This portlet changes the WindowState when a user clicks on an action link

```
package com.examscam.portlet;

import java.io.*;
import javax.portlet.*;

public class StateShifter extends GenericPortlet {

  public void doView
       (RenderRequest request, RenderResponse response)
                   throws PortletException, IOException {

    response.setContentType("text/html");

    PortletURL url = response.createActionURL();
    url.setParameter("shift", "true");
    PrintWriter out = response.getWriter();
    out.print("<A href=" + url + " >State Shift!!!</A>");
  }

  public void processAction
       (ActionRequest request, ActionResponse response)
             throws PortletException, java.io.IOException {

    if (request.getParameter("shift") != null) {
      WindowState state = request.getWindowState();

      if (state == WindowState.NORMAL) {
        response.setWindowState(WindowState.MAXIMIZED);
      }

      if (state == WindowState.MAXIMIZED) {
        response.setWindowState(WindowState.MINIMIZED);
      }

      if (state == WindowState.MINIMIZED) {
        response.setWindowState(WindowState.NORMAL);
      }
    }
  }
}
```

Moods of the StateShifter

The StateShifter portlet has three different moods, corresponding to the three different WindowState settings.

The StateShifter starts off in a NORMAL state, but when the action link **State Shift** is clicked, the portlet renders itself in the MAXIMIZED state. When **State Shift** is clicked on a maximized StateShifter portlet, the action processing phase sets the WindowState to MINIMIZED.

In the MINIMIZED state, no content is visible, so the restore or maximize button on the portlet must be clicked to change the WindowState to either restore (set WindowState to NORMAL) or maximize the portlet.

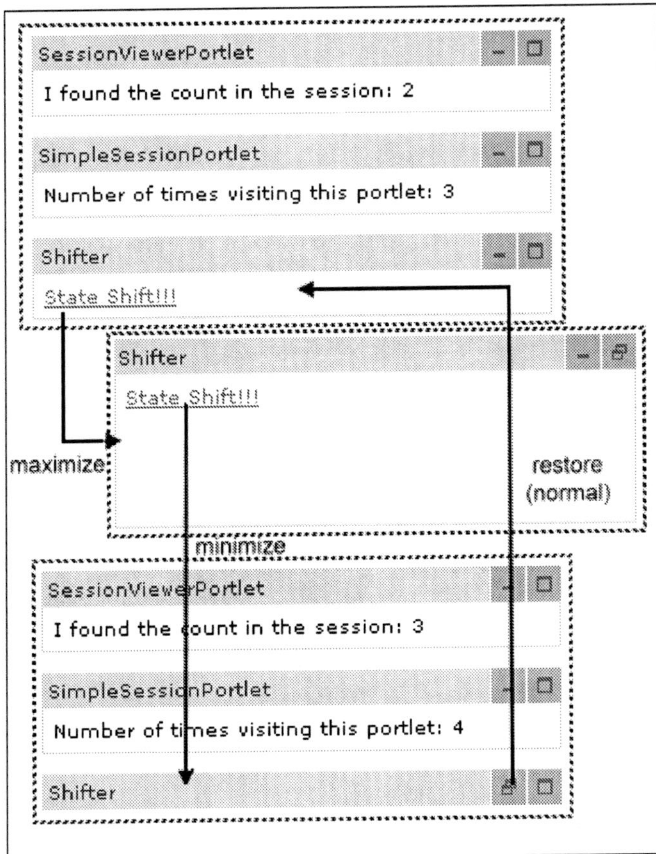

Triggering an Action

Coding the processAction method is the way to ***handle*** an action event, but the processAction method will never be called if a client never actually ***triggers*** an action. To trigger the action processing phase, an action event must be generated. To trigger an action event, a user must click on a link, or submit a form, that has an action explicitly associated with it.

It's easy to create link back to the portal that has an action associated with it, although it is a two or three step process. You start by asking the ActionRequest object to create an **action**URL. Well, there really is not such thing as an ActionURL, but instead, a PortletURL that is ***associated*** with an *action event.*

```
1. PortletURL url = response.createActionURL();
```

Once the PortletURL is obtained, we can optionally add parameters to the PortletURL that help identify the action:

```
2. url.setParameter("shift", "true");
```

Finally, the PortletURL must be used in an html link, or as the action attribute of an html form. In this example, we create an html anchor link that a user can click on:

```
PrintWriter out = response.getWriter();
out.print("<A HREF=" + uri + " > State Shift!!!</A>");
```

If a user clicks on the link generated by the code above, the event processing phase will be triggered on the portal, and an action event associated with the String "**shift**", will be passed to our portlet. ***Encoding*** the attribute probably wouldn't be a bad idea either, but it's been left out for the sake of simplicity.

```
public void doView ✂✂✂ {
   response.setContentType("text/html");
   PortletURL url = response.createActionURL();
   PrintWriter out = response.getWriter();
   out.print("<A href=" + url + " >State Shift!!!</A>");
}
✂✂✂
```

Handling the Right Event Object

When an action event is fired, we want our Portlet to be able to react to the action, figure out exactly what action was triggered, and then execute some type of logic based on the event.

In the doView method, a parameter was appended to our PortletURL named *'shift'*. This parameter, named *shift*, is essentially the name of our action event.

```
public void doView ✂✂✂

   /*create an action URL associated with the value shift*/

  PortletURL url = response.createActionURL();
  url.setParameter("shift", "true");

✂✂✂
```

To make sure our portlet only responds to the *shift* action, and not other actions that might be added to the portlet in the future, we extract the String associated with the event from the ActionRequest object passed into the processAction method.

```
public void processAction ✂✂✂

/*check if the action was associated with shift*/

  if (request.getParameter("shift") != null) {
   ✂✂✂
  }
✂✂✂
```

Deployment Descriptor for the StateShifter

With the processAction and doView method of the StateShifterPortlet coded, the last thing needed to get the portlet running is a definition of the portlet in the portlet.xml file.

```
<!-- portlet.xml for the StateShifter portlet -->

<?xml version="1.0" encoding="UTF-8"?>
<portlet-app
xmlns="http://java.sun.com/xml/ns/portlet/portlet-app_1_0.xsd"
version="1.0" xmlns:xsi="http://www.w3.org/2001/XMLSchema-instance"
xsi:schemaLocation="http://java.sun.com/xml/ns/portlet/portlet-app_1_0.xsd
http://java.sun.com/xml/ns/portlet/portlet-app_1_0.xsd"
id="com.examscam.portlet.StateShifter.9566e4bdf0">
  <portlet>
    <portlet-name>StateShifter</portlet-name>
    <display-name>StateShifter </display-name>
    <display-name xml:lang="en">StateShifter</display-name>
    <portlet-class>
      com.examscam.portlet.StateShifter
    </portlet-class>
    <expiration-cache>0</expiration-cache>
    <supports>
      <mime-type>text/html</mime-type>
      <portlet-mode>view</portlet-mode>
    </supports>
    <supported-locale>en</supported-locale>
    <portlet-info>
      <title>StateShifter </title>
    </portlet-info>
  </portlet>
</portlet-app>
```

Revisiting the NumberGuesser Portlet

Please don't get mad at me for saying so, but our NumberGuesserPortlet violated a number of best practices by handling forms, and processing session state, within the render phase of the portlet. A better design would be to move all of the processing into the action phase of the portlet, and leave rendering tasks to the doView method.

Fig. 6-3 shows the changes required to be made to the NumberGuesserPortlet, while figure 6-2 demonstrates the changes needed in the corresponding JSP to ensure the action processing phase of the portlet is triggered.

Action Processing and Custom Tags

In previous iterations of the NumberGuesserPortlet, we have used the <portlet:renderURL/> custom tag in conjunction with the action attribute of the HTML FORM tag. As you could imagine, the renderURL tag sends a request directly into the render phase of a portlet, completely bypassing the action processing phase. To ensure that the *about to be created* action processing phase of the NumberGuesserPortlet actually gets invoked when a user clicks on the submit button labeled *Guess*, we must replace the old custom tag of <portlet:renderURL/> with the custom tag that triggers the action phase, namely the <portlet:actionURL/> tag.

Figure 6-2 Using the <portlet:actionURL/> Custom Tag

```
<%@ page contentType="text/html"%>
<%@ taglib uri="http://java.sun.com/portlet" prefix="portlet"%>
<portlet:defineObjects />

<%=renderRequest.getPortletSession().getAttribute("message")%>

<FORM action="<portlet:actionURL/>">
I'm thinking of a number between 1 and 10. <BR>
<INPUT name="number" size="10" type="text" />
<!-- The name of the input tag becomes very important -->
<INPUT name="guesssubmit" value="Guess!!" type="submit" />
</FORM>
Number of guesses:
<%=renderRequest.getPortletSession().getAttribute("guesses")%>
```

Refactoring Actions into the NumberGuesser

Much of the content that was in the doView method of the NumberGuesserPortlet has been moved to the processAction method. When session management and form handling tasks have been moved into the processAction method, the doView method, correctly, is left with little more to do than forward to the appropriate JSP page.

Figure 6-3 Responding to Action Events

```
package com.examscam.portlet;
import java.io.*;import javax.portlet.*;
public class NumberGuesserPortlet extends GenericPortlet {

  protected void doView(RenderRequest request, RenderResponse response)
                              throws PortletException, IOException {
  PortletContext context = this.getPortletContext();
  PortletSession session = request.getPortletSession();
  /*This iteration looks for the message, not the magicnumber*/
  if (session.getAttribute("message") == null) {
    /*int magicNumber = (int)(System.currentTimeMillis() % 9) + 1;*/
    /*session.setAttribute("magicnumber", new Integer(magicNumber));*/
    int magicNumber = (int) (System.currentTimeMillis() % 9) + 1;
    session.setAttribute("magicnumber", new Integer(magicNumber));
    session.setAttribute("guesses", "0");
    session.setAttribute("message", "Guess the number!");
  }
  String url = "/numberguesser.jsp";
  context.getRequestDispatcher(url).include(request, response);
 }
 public void processAction(ActionRequest request, ActionResponse response)
                      throws PortletException, java.io.IOException {
  PortletSession session = request.getPortletSession();
  /*make sure name="guesssubmit" is added to the JSP!!!*/
  if (request.getParameter("guesssubmit") != null) {
    if (session.getAttribute("magicnumber") == null) {
      int magicNumber = (int) (System.currentTimeMillis() % 9) + 1;
      session.setAttribute("magicnumber", new Integer(magicNumber));
      session.setAttribute("guesses", "0");
   }
   Integer magicNumber=(Integer)session.getAttribute("magicnumber");
   String guesses = (String) session.getAttribute("guesses");
   guesses = "" + (Integer.parseInt(guesses) + 1);
   session.setAttribute("guesses", guesses);
   session.setAttribute("message", "Guess higher!");
   Integer guess = new Integer(request.getParameter("number"));
   if (guess.intValue() > magicNumber.intValue()) {
    session.setAttribute("message", "Guess lower!");
   }
   if (guess.intValue() == magicNumber.intValue()) {
    String message = magicNumber + " is correct. Play again!";
    session.setAttribute("message", message);
    session.removeAttribute("magicnumber");
   }
  }
 }
}
```

Comparison with and without processAction

Figures 6-4 and 6-5 demonstrate the code used for the NumberGuesserPortlet with figure 6-4 using the ***action processing phase***, and 6-5 ***not*** taking advantage of action processing. When comparing them, you can see that the logic is, for the most part, similar, but the division of tasks, namely state management and view processing, is more elegant when the portlet developer takes advantage of action processing.

Figure 6-4 Responding to Action Events

```
package com.examscam.portlet;

import java.io.*;import javax.portlet.*;

public class NumberGuesserPortlet extends GenericPortlet {
  protected void doView(RenderRequest request, RenderResponse response)
                              throws PortletException, IOException {
  PortletContext context = this.getPortletContext();
  PortletSession session = request.getPortletSession();
  /*This iteration looks for the message in the session*/
  if (session.getAttribute("message") == null) {
    /*int magicNumber = (int)(System.currentTimeMillis() % 9) + 1;*/
    /*session.setAttribute("magicnumber", new Integer(magicNumber));*/
    session.setAttribute("guesses", "0");
    session.setAttribute("message", "Guess the number!");
  }
  String url = "/numberguesser.jsp";
  context.getRequestDispatcher(url).include(request, response);
 }

 public void processAction(ActionRequest request, ActionResponse response)
                        throws PortletException, java.io.IOException {
  PortletSession session = request.getPortletSession();
  if (request.getParameter("guesssubmit") != null) {
    if (session.getAttribute("magicnumber") == null) {
      int magicNumber = (int) (System.currentTimeMillis() % 9) + 1;
      session.setAttribute("magicnumber", new Integer(magicNumber));
      session.setAttribute("guesses", "0");
   }
   Integer magicNumber=(Integer)session.getAttribute("magicnumber");
   String guesses = (String) session.getAttribute("guesses");
   guesses = "" + (Integer.parseInt(guesses) + 1);
   session.setAttribute("guesses", guesses);
   session.setAttribute("message", "Guess higher!");
   Integer guess = new Integer(request.getParameter("number"));
   if (guess.intValue() > magicNumber.intValue()) {
    session.setAttribute("message", "Guess lower!");
   }
   if (guess.intValue() == magicNumber.intValue()) {
    String message = magicNumber + " is correct. Play again!";
    session.setAttribute("message", message);
    session.removeAttribute("magicnumber");
   }
  }
 }
}
```

NumberGuesserPortlet *without* ProcessAction

As you can see, the content of the processAction method was pretty much lifted directly from the else block of the portlet defined in Figure 6-5.

Figure 6-5 Previous Iteration of NumberGuesserPortlet

```
package com.examscam.portlet;
import java.io.*;import javax.portlet.*;
public class NumberGuesserPortlet extends GenericPortlet {
protected void doView
 (RenderRequest request, RenderResponse response)
                 throws PortletException, IOException {

PortletContext context = this.getPortletContext();
PortletSession session = request.getPortletSession();

if (session.getAttribute("magicnumber") == null) {

  int magicNumber = (int) (System.currentTimeMillis() % 9) + 1;

  session.setAttribute("magicnumber", new Integer(magicNumber));
  session.setAttribute("guesses", "0");
  session.setAttribute("message", "Guess the number!");

} else {

 Integer magicNumber
                 = (Integer) session.getAttribute("magicnumber");
  String guesses = (String) session.getAttribute("guesses");

  guesses = "" + (Integer.parseInt(guesses) + 1);
  session.setAttribute("guesses", guesses);

  Integer guess = new Integer(request.getParameter("number"));

  if (guess.intValue() > magicNumber.intValue()) {
    session.setAttribute("message", "Guess lower!");
  } else {
    session.setAttribute("message", "Guess higher!");
  }
  if (guess.intValue() == magicNumber.intValue()) {
    String message = magicNumber + " is correct. Play again!";
    session.setAttribute("message", message);
    session.removeAttribute("magicnumber");
  }
 }

 String url = "/numberguesser.jsp";
 context.getRequestDispatcher(url).include(request, response);
 }
}
```

Question 6-1

If a portlet attempts to transition to a custom portlet state that is not supported by the portal server:

- O a) the portlet will throw a ServletException
- O b) the portlet will throw a WindowStateException
- O c) the portlet will throw a ServletError
- O d) the portlet will throw a WindowStateError

Question 6-2

Which of the following methods are not defined in the ActionResponse class?

- ☐ a) setWindowState(state:WindowState)
- ☐ b) sendRedirect(url: String)
- ☐ c) setTitle(title:String)
- ☐ d) getWriter()

Answer 6-3

The processAction method

- ☐ a) is invoked before every doView method
- ☐ b) is invoked only if a client calls the portlet using an actionURL
- ☐ c) is followed by a the rendering phase of a portlet
- ☐ d) is preceded by the rendering phase of a portlet.

Question 6-4

To participate in the action processing phase, a portlet:

☐ a) must have action processing configured in the portlet.xml file

☐ b) must define a processAction method

☐ c) must define an actionPerformed method

☐ d) must be invoked through an action URL

Question 6-5

Which of the following are not possible during the render processing phase?

☐ a) changing the portlet mode

☐ b) changing the portlet window state

☐ c) accessing the PrintWriter

☐ d) accessing data in the PortletSession

Question 6-6

If a PortletException is thrown during the action processing phase of a portlet, which of the following is true

☐ a) instructions to render the portlet in a Maximized window will be ignored

☐ b) instructions to render the portlet in the edit mode will be ignored

☐ c) other portlets on the page will be forced to stop their rendering process

☐ d) other portlets on the page will continue the rendering process

Answer 6-1

If a portlet attempts to transition to a custom portlet state that is not supported by the portal server:

○ a) the portlet will throw a ServletException

○ b) the portlet will throw a WindowStateException

○ c) the portlet will throw a ServletError

○ d) the portlet will throw a WindowStateError

Option b) is correct.

The WindowStateException just hides in the outskirts quietly, minding its own business, just waiting for a portlet to ask for a WindowState other than MINIMIZED, MAXIMIZED or NORMAL. If it sees an unsupported WindowState being requested, it jumps, and triggers the exception handling features of the portlet.

Answer 6-2

Which of the following methods are not defined in the ActionResponse class?

☐ a) setWindowState(state:WindowState)

☐ b) sendRedirect(url: String)

☐ c) setTitle(title:String)

☐ d) getWriter()

Options c) and d) are correct.

The ActionRequest has the ability to redirect, or set the WindowState. However, accessing the PrintWriter, and changing the portlet title displayed to the user, is purely part of the rendering phase of the portal.

Answer 6-3

The processAction method:

☐ a) is invoked before every doView method

☐ b) is invoked only if a client calls the portlet using an actionURL

☐ c) is followed by a the rendering phase of a portlet

☐ d) is preceded by the rendering phase of a portlet.

Answers b) and c) are correct.

The processAction method is not invoked on every single request-response cycle the portlet takes part in, but instead, only during the request response cycles in which the client has used an actionURL, as opposed to a renderURL. Also, so long as an exception doesn't mess the action processing stage up, the rendering phase follows the action processing phase. The rendering phase will never come before the action processing phase of a portlet.

Answer 6-4

To participate in the action processing phase, a JSR-168 portlet:

☐ a) must have action processing configured in the portlet.xml file

☐ b) must define a processAction method

☐ c) must define an actionPerformed method

☐ d) must be invoked through an action URL

Options b) and d) are correct.

There are no xml configurations that need to be made for a portlet to take part in action processing. All a portlet needs to do is code the processAction method, and subsequently be invoked through an action URL.

The actionPerform method was coded in the legacy portlet API, but not in JSR-168.

Answer 6-5

Which of the following are not possible during the render processing phase?
☐ a) changing the portlet mode ☐ b) changing the portlet window state ☐ c) accessing the PrintWriter ☐ d) accessing data in the PortletSession
Options a) and b) are correct. While the render processing phase actually spits content out to the user, it is really the action processing phase that decides big picture things, like the portlet mode, or the portlet state. Alternatively, the PrintWriter can be accessed during the *rendering* phase. The PortletSession is available in both the action processing, and rendering phase of the portlet.

Answer 6-6

If a PortletException is thrown during the action processing phase of a portlet, which of the following is true
☐ a) instructions to render the portlet in a Maximized window will be ignored ☐ b) instructions to render the portlet in the edit mode will be ignored ☐ c) other portlets on the page will be forced to stop their rendering process ☐ d) other portlets on the page will continue the rendering process
Options a) b) and d) are all correct. If a PortletException is thrown during the action processing phase, all operations performed on the ActionResponse must be ignored, and this includes maximizing the window, or displaying in the edit mode. However, just because one portlet *messes up* in the action phase, doesn't mean the other portlets on the page should suffer. Other portlets will be allowed to render normally, making d) correct as well.

Chapter 7
Portlet Modes

Any preliminary look at the portlet API will elucidate a major similarity between portlets and servlets. Both portlets and servlets handle the request-response cycle, both are Java centric components, and both have access to the J2EE runtime environment when deployed to a J2EE compliant application server. But there are some major differences between portlets and servlets as well.

One of the most significant ways portlets are different from regular servlets is their support for various modes, namely view, edit and help. When it comes to portlet modes, there is no applicable analogy to typical servlet and JSP programming.

This chapter will look at the various modes available to the portlets you create, and how a developer can programmatically take advantage of these modes.

Breaking Away from a *Portlet as a Servlet* Mentality

Handling a request-response cycle is the most fundamental aspect of portlet programming, but inspecting a request and sending out a response is by no means revolutionary. After all, request-response programming is exactly what we do in a Java servlet.

Let's compare a portlet to a servlet: instead of a doView method, a Java servlet has a doPost or a doGet method. Instead of being passed a PortletRequest or a PortletResponse object, a Java servlet is given an HttpServletRequest and HttpServletResponse object. In many ways, handling the request-response cycle of a portlet is very similar to handling the request-response cycle of a servlet. In fact, one of the great things about portlets is the fact that they leverage our existing knowledge of the Servlet and JSP APIs.

But what makes a portlet so incredibly sexy is all of the features and services the Portlet API affords us, *over and above* that of the Servlet API. The most fundamental difference between a Portlet and a Servlet is the various modes in which a Portlet can participate.

A portlet has three standard, and any number of custom, implementable modes, namely:

- *The View Mode*
- *The Edit Mode*
- *The Help Mode*

The most common, and only required mode of a Portlet, is the *view* mode. When a Portlet is displayed on a page, it is typically displaying its view mode. In fact, the specification requires every portlet to have a doView method so that the portlet can render itself on a portal page.

Optionally, a portlet can provide an implementation of any of the other standard modes, with perhaps the most useful mode being edit, and the most helpful, being *help*. ☺

Figure 7-1

The wrench, pencil, and question mark represent the *config*, edit and help modes of a portlet. Note that *config* is a custom mode.

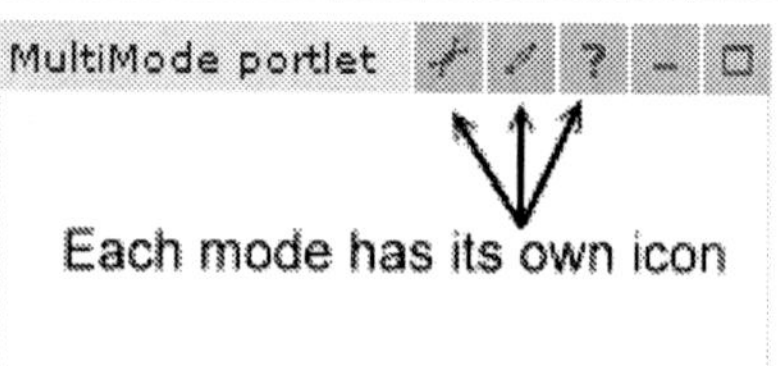

Basic Portlet Mode Implementation

To support all of the standard portlet modes defined in the JSR-168 portlet specification, a portlet must, at the very least, implement a doEdit, doHelp, and doView method.

```
Figure 7-2
-------------------------------------------------

package com.examscam.portlet;
import java.io.*;import javax.portlet.*;
public class MultiModePortlet extends GenericPortlet {

protected void doView(RenderRequest request, RenderResponse response)
                              throws PortletException, IOException {
  response.setContentType("text/html");
  response.getWriter().print("This is the View mode.");
 }

protected void doEdit(RenderRequest request, RenderResponse response)
                              throws PortletException, IOException {
  response.setContentType("text/html");
  response.getWriter().print("This is the Edit mode.");
 }

protected void doHelp(RenderRequest request, RenderResponse response)
                              throws PortletException, IOException {
  response.setContentType("text/html");
  response.getWriter().print("This is the help mode.");
 }
}
```

Along with an implementation of the appropriate do<Mode> method, the deployment descriptor of the portlet must explicitly declare all of the modes the portlet supports.

```
<portlet>
  <portlet-name>MultiModePortlet</portlet-name>
  <display-name>MultiModePortlet</display-name>
  <portlet-class>
    com.examscam.portlet.MultiModePortlet
  </portlet-class>
   <supports>
     <mime-type>text/html</mime-type>
     <portlet-mode>view</portlet-mode>
     <portlet-mode>edit</portlet-mode>
     <portlet-mode>help</portlet-mode>
   </supports>
  <portlet-info><title>MultiModePortlet</title></portlet-info>
</portlet>
```

Portlet Mode Visualization

When the MultiModePortlet from Figure 7-2 is rendered by the portal, the *skin* of the view mode displays edit, help, minimize and maximize icons. Clicking on the question mark generates a pop-up window that displays the contents of the doView method. Clicking on the pencil takes a user into the edit mode of the portlet. The edit mode conveniently contains a *caret* icon that can return a user back to the view mode.

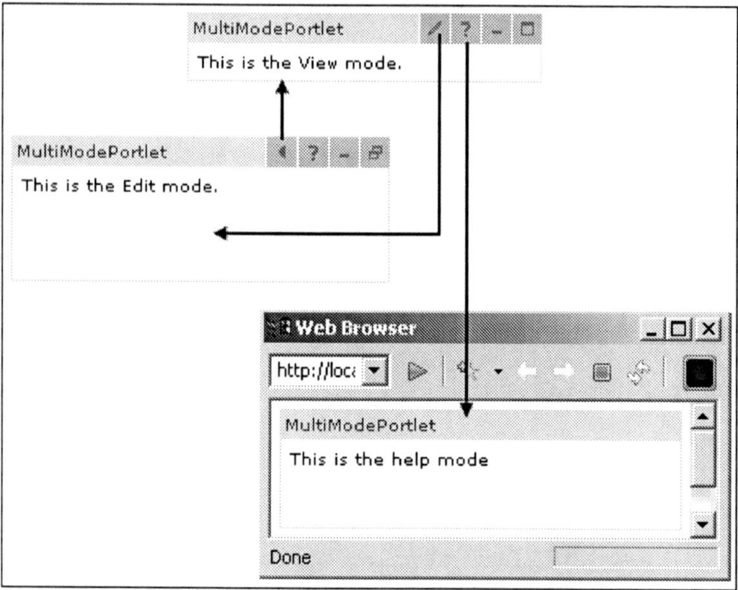

The Help Mode and the doHelp Method

The easiest portlet mode to implement has got to be the help mode. The help mode is designed to simply display to the user information about how to use the portlet. The help mode for the NumberGuesserPortlet will simply inform the user that they need to keep guessing a number until they get it right.

Implementing the help mode simply requires the implementation of a doHelp method in your code *and* an update to the portlet.xml file to inform the portlet container that the help mode is being implemented.

User Customization and the Edit Mode

One of the main benefits of a portlet is the fact that it can be *customized by a user*. If you have gone to any of the mega portals like yahoo.com or excite.com, or have even installed the WebSphere Portal Server and played around with some of the Pinnacore portlets, you have inevitably run into a number of portlets you can customize by providing the portlet any number of personalized parameters.

The ubiquitous weather portlet, the one that tells you the weather for three or four major international cities the first time you see it, but also gives you the ability to customize the portlet by telling it your ZIP code of the city in which you live, is a prime example of a customizable portlet.

The weather portlet provides an *edit mode* that asks the user their zip code or the name of a city of interest. The portlet stores that information permanently, and then the next time the user views the weather portlet, it will additionally display the weather for the specified city or zip code. The edit mode provides the user an opportunity to provide ***personal preferences*** to a portlet. That information is then used in the view mode to deliver customized content to the user.

An **edit mode** provides a user the opportunity to customize a portlet. To handle these user requests for customizations, the portlet API matches the **edit mode** of a portlet, to the **doEdit method** of a developer's portlet code.

Figure 7-3 To implement the help and edit modes, a portlet needs a doHelp and doEdit method.

```
✂✂✂
protected void doHelp(RenderRequest request, RenderResponse response)
                              throws PortletException, IOException {
      response.setContentType("text/html");
      response.getWriter().print("Just guess a number! ");
  }
✂✂✂
protected void doEdit(RenderRequest request, RenderResponse response)
                              throws PortletException, IOException {
  String url = "/numberguesseredit.jsp" ;
  getPortletContext().getRequestDispatcher(url).include(request, response);
}
✂✂✂
```

Edit Mode and PortletPreferences

Any personal preferences provided to a portlet through the edit mode are stored permanently. The next time the user visits that portal page, this personalized information is retrieved for that user.

As you could imagine, storing all of these user preferences persistently, and tying that data to a specific user and a specific portlet on a certain portal page is quite a bit of work. Fortunately, implementing this functionality is not shouldered by the portlet developer. Instead, the portlet API provides a very special component called the PortletPreferences object. While in the action processing phase of the edit mode of a portlet, a developer is allowed to stuff any number of Strings into the PortletPreferences object, using the very straightforward `setValue(name, value)` method.

```
PortletPreferences prefs = request.getPreferences();
if (request.getParameter("guessedit") != null) {
   String newLimit = request.getParameter("newlimit");
   prefs.setValue("upperlimit", newLimit);
   prefs.store();
}
```

Any mode can ***access*** data stored in the PortletPreferences object, but only during the action processing phase of the edit mode can you actually ***change, add or update*** information stored as PortletPreferences.

Store, Store, Store!

When a developer stuffs a String into a portlet's PortletPreferences object (known as PortletData in previous JetSpeed APIs), and subsequently calls the `preferences.store()` method, the data that was stuffed into the preferences object is stored ***persistently***.

A real rookie mistake is forgetting to call the store() method after shoving Strings into the PortletPreferences object. There is no design time type-checking to ensure the store method is called after working with the PortletPreferences object, so you really have to be diligent to ensure that you invoked the store method, and your preferences are subsequently stored permanently.

Initialization of PortletPreferences: portlet.xml

One of the challenges in working with the edit mode is initializing default values for PortletPreferences, or as it was known in the Jetspeed API, PortletData. With JSR-168, each portlet can configure any number of initial values by specifying them in the portlet-preferences section of the deployment descriptor. Furthermore, preferences can be multivalued, and stored as an array of Strings, as opposed to just single value Strings. Finally, PortletPreferences can be set as read-only. This essentially ensures that a given PortletPreference will be common to all users of the portlet.

```
<portlet-preferences>
  <preference>
    <name>upperlimit</name><value>10</value>
    <read-only>false</read-only>
  </preference>
</portlet-preferences>
```

It should also be noted that in order for a portlet to support the edit mode, the portlet.xml file must have the appropriate entry for the portlet. Manipulating PortletPreferences is pretty much a moot endeavor if you haven't specified in the deployment descriptor that the portlet supports the edit mode.

```
<supports>
  <mime-type>text/html</mime-type>
  <portlet-mode>view</portlet-mode>
  <portlet-mode>edit</portlet-mode>
  <portlet-mode>help</portlet-mode>
</supports>
```

PortletPreferences and the NumberGuesser

So, how can we take our simple, NumberGuesserPortlet and complicate it to the n'th degree by adding user customization through PortletPreferences?

Well, by default, the user guesses a number between 1 and 10. But perhaps we want the user to customize their experience by choosing a number between 1 and 100, or 1 and 1000? We could easily make the range customizable through a PortletPreference.

Figure 7-4 Without preferences, our number guessing game always uses 10 as the upper limit.

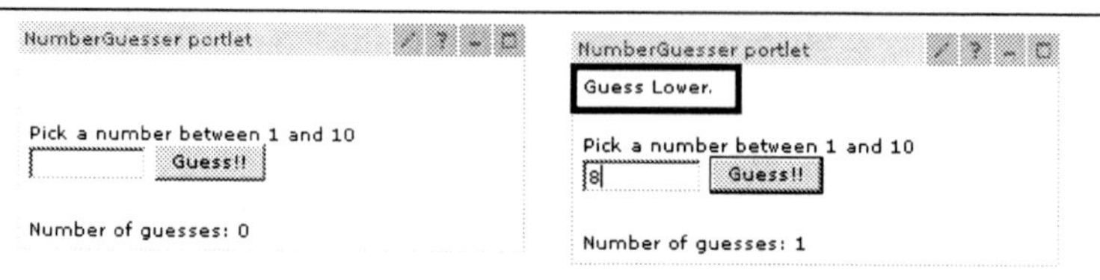

We could store a String value named upperlimit in the PortletPreferences object, and use the portlet.xml file to give this value a default of 10.

```
<portlet-preferences>
  <preference>
    <name>upperlimit</name><value>10</value>
    <read-only>false</read-only>
  </preference>
</portlet-preferences>
```

When the user starts the number guessing game, we could use the ***upperlimit*** value, stored in the PortletPreferences, to generate the magic number.

```
/*obtain the PortlePreferences object from the request*/
PortletPreferences prefs = request.getPreferences();
/*pull the upperlimit String from the preference*/
String upperLimit = prefs.getValue("upperlimit", null);
/*use the upperLimit to generate the new random number to
be guessed*/
long number
    =(System.CurrentTimeMillis()%Integer.parseInt(upperLimit))+1;
/*put the new number in the session*/
session.setAttribute("magicnumber", new Long(number));
```

Figure 7-5 Updating the processAction method.

```
public void processAction
  (ActionRequest request, ActionResponse response)
                  throws PortletException, java.io.IOException {
/* get the preferences and session from the request object */
PortletPreferences prefs = request.getPreferences();
PortletSession session = request.getPortletSession();

/* if we are in the edit mode, get the new range limit */
if (request.getParameter("guessedit") != null) {
  String newLimit = request.getParameter("newlimit");
  prefs.setValue("upperlimit", newLimit);
  prefs.store();
}
/* Obtain application data from the session. */
Long magicNumber = (Long) session.getAttribute("magicnumber");
Long guess = new Long(request.getParameter("number"));
String guesses = (String) session.getAttribute("guesses");
String message = "Guess Higher!!!";

/* If a number was guessed, see if it is correct */
if (request.getParameter("guesssubmit") != null) {

  /* if the magicNumber is null, this is their first guess. */
  if (magicNumber == null) {
    String upperLimit = prefs.getValue("upperlimit", null);

    /* use the range limit from preferences to calc the number */
    long number =
        (System.currentTimeMillis()%Integer.parseInt(upperLimit))   +
1;
    session.setAttribute("magicnumber", new Long(number));
    guesses = "1";
  }else {
    guesses = "" + (Integer.parseInt(guesses) + 1);
  }
  if (guess.intValue() > magicNumber.intValue()) {
    message = "Guess Lower.";
  }
  if (guess.intValue() == magicNumber.intValue()) {
    message = magicNumber + " is correct. # of guesses: " + guesses;
    session.setAttribute("guesses","0");
    session.removeAttribute("magicnumber");
  }
}
/* appropriately set the message and guess number in the session */
session.setAttribute("message", message);
session.setAttribute("guesses", guesses);
}
```

Customization Through the Edit Mode

Figure 7-6

The user sets an custom upper limit through the edit mode.

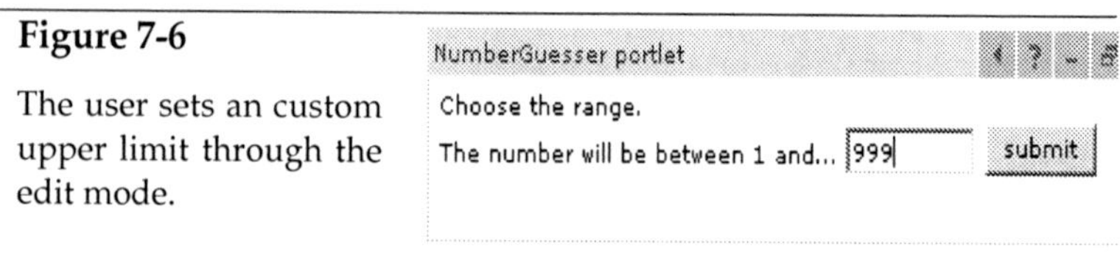

While default values will be provided through the portlet.xml file, the user can change the range by using the edit mode of the portlet. The edit mode could be used to update the preference, allowing the user to set an upper limit that is greater than 10.

```
/*if the user clicked the button named guessedit from the
edit page */
if (request.getParameter("guessedit") != null) {
  String newLimit = request.getParameter("newlimit");
  prefs.setValue("upperlimit", newLimit);
  prefs.store();
}
```

After updating their preference through the edit mode, when the user returns to the view mode, all numbers will be generated based upon the new range, as set in PortletPreferences. An additional code snippet in the jsp allows the new upper range limit to be displayed to the user:

```
<%=renderRequest.getPreferences()
                              .getValue("upperlimit", null) %>
```

Figure 7-7

Notice how the user has set the upper limit to 999, as opposed to the default of 10.

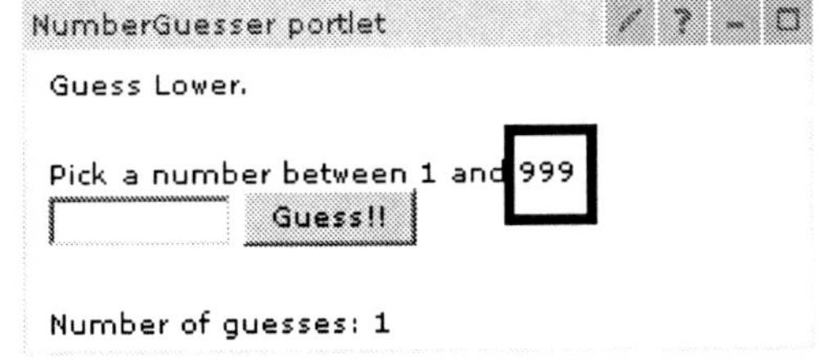

Figure 7-8 Code used for the View JSP in this example. Notice how the message and guesses are coming from the PortletSession.

```
<%@ page contentType="text/html"%>
<%@taglib uri="http://java.sun.com/portlet" prefix="portlet"%>

<portlet:defineObjects />

<%=renderRequest.getPortletSession().getAttribute("message")%>

<FORM action="<portlet:actionURL/>">
Pick a number between 1 and

<%=renderRequest.getPreferences().getValue("upperlimit", null) %>

<INPUT name="number" size="10" type="text" />
<INPUT name="guesssubmit" value="Guess!!" type="submit" />
</FORM>

Number of guesses:
<%=renderRequest.getPortletSession().getAttribute("guesses")%>
```

Fig 7-9 The JSP used for the Edit mode, numberguesseredit.jsp

```
<%@ page contentType="text/html"%>
<%@taglib uri="http://java.sun.com/portlet"
prefix="portlet"%>
<portlet:defineObjects />


<FORM action="<portlet:actionURL/>">
Choose the range.<BR>The number will be between 1 and...

<INPUT name="newlimit" size="10" type="text" />
<INPUT name="guessedit" value="Submit" type="submit" />

</FORM>
```

Figure 7-10 Full portlet.xml file. Notice the support for multiple modes, and the default value given for the upperlimit preference.

```
<portlet>
 <portlet-name>NumberGuesser</portlet-name>
 <display-name>NumberGuesser portlet</display-name>
 <portlet-class>
  com.examscam.portlet.NumberGuesserPortlet
 </portlet-class>
 <supports>
  <mime-type>text/html</mime-type>
  <portlet-mode>view</portlet-mode>
  <portlet-mode>edit</portlet-mode>
  <portlet-mode>help</portlet-mode>
 </supports>
 <portlet-info>
  <title>NumberGuesser portlet</title>
 </portlet-info>
 <portlet-preferences>
  <preference>
    <name>upperlimit</name>
    <value>10</value>
    <read-only>false</read-only>
  </preference>
 </portlet-preferences>
</portlet>
```

Fig. 7-11 The doEdit method simply points to the edit.jsp.

```
protected void doEdit
          (RenderRequest request, RenderResponse response)
                    throws PortletException, IOException {

  String url = "/numberguesseredit.jsp" ;
  this.getPortletContext().getRequestDispatcher(url)
                                 .include(request, response);
}
```

Figure 7-12 NumberGuesser (*Sorry it's so small, but I wanted it all on one page*)

```
package com.examscam.portlet;
import java.io.*;import javax.portlet.*;
public class NumberGuesserPortlet extends GenericPortlet {
 protected void doView(RenderRequest request, RenderResponse response)
                          throws PortletException, IOException {
  PortletContext context = this.getPortletContext();
  PortletSession session = request.getPortletSession();
  if (session.getAttribute("message") == null) {
    session.setAttribute("guesses", "0");
    session.setAttribute("message", "Guess the number!");
  }
  String url = "/numberguesser.jsp";
  context.getRequestDispatcher(url).include(request, response);
 }
  protected void doHelp(RenderRequest request, RenderResponse response)throws
                               PortletException, IOException {
  response.setContentType("text/html");
  response.getWriter().print("You should be able to figure this out!!!");
 }
 protected void doEdit(RenderRequest request, RenderResponse response)
                          throws PortletException, IOException {
  String url = "/numberguesseredit.jsp";
  getPortletContext().getRequestDispatcher(url).include(request,response);
 }
 public void processAction(ActionRequest request, ActionResponse response)
                  throws PortletException, java.io.IOException {
  PortletSession session = request.getPortletSession();
  /* obtain the PortlePreferences object from the request */
  PortletPreferences prefs = request.getPreferences();
  if (request.getParameter("guessedit") != null) {
    String newLimit = request.getParameter("newlimit");
    prefs.setValue("upperlimit", newLimit);
    prefs.store();
  }
  if (request.getParameter("guesssubmit") != null) {
    if (session.getAttribute("magicnumber") == null) {
    /* pull the upperlimit String from the preference */
    String upperLimit = prefs.getValue("upperlimit", "3");
    /* use the upperLimit to generate the new random number to be  guessed */
    int magicNumber = (int)((System.currentTimeMillis() %
                          Integer.parseInt(upperLimit)) + 1);
    /* put the new number in the session */
    session.setAttribute("magicnumber", new Integer(magicNumber));
    session.setAttribute("guesses", "0");
   }
   Integer magicNumber = (Integer)session.getAttribute("magicnumber");
   String guesses = (String) session.getAttribute("guesses");
   guesses = "" + (Integer.parseInt(guesses) + 1);
   session.setAttribute("guesses", guesses);
   session.setAttribute("message", "Guess higher!");
   Integer guess = new Integer(request.getParameter("number"));
   if (guess.intValue() > magicNumber.intValue()) {
     session.setAttribute("message", "Guess lower!");
   }
   if (guess.intValue() == magicNumber.intValue()) {
     String message = magicNumber + " is correct. Play again!";
     session.setAttribute("message", message);
     session.removeAttribute("magicnumber");
   }
  }
 }
}
```

Figure 7-13 The JSP used for the View mode, numberguesser.jsp

```
<%@ page contentType="text/html"%>
<%@ taglib uri="http://java.sun.com/portlet" prefix="portlet"%>

<portlet:defineObjects />

<%=renderRequest.getPortletSession().getAttribute("message")%>

<FORM action="<portlet:actionURL/>">

I'm thinking of a number between 1 and

<%=renderRequest.getPreferences()
                           .getValue("upperlimit", null) %>

<INPUT name="number" size="10" type="text" />
<INPUT name="guesssubmit" value="Guess!!" type="submit" />
</FORM>
Number of guesses:

<%=renderRequest.getPortletSession().getAttribute("guesses")%>
```

Fig 7-14 The JSP used for the Edit mode, numberguesseredit.jsp

```
<%@ page contentType="text/html"%>
<%@taglib uri="http://java.sun.com/portlet" prefix="portlet"%>
<portlet:defineObjects />

<FORM action="<portlet:actionURL/>">

Choose the range.<BR>
The number will be between 1 and...
<INPUT name="newlimit" size="10"type="text" />
<INPUT name="guessedit" value="Submit" type="submit" />
</FORM>

Upper Limit:

<%=renderRequest.getPreferences().getValue("upperlimit", null)%>
```

PortletPreferences and the PreferencesValidator

Part of the JSR-168 API is a convenient interface called the **PreferencesValidator**. PortletPreferences provide the end user the ability to customize their user experience, but as with any type of input taken from a user, there is the possibility that data provided to the server won't be valid for a particular scenario. To provide some level of control over how users configure a particular preference, a PreferencesValidator can be coded, and subsequently configured in the portlet.xml file.

The PreferencesValidator has only one method that needs to be overridden: the validate(PortletPreferences prefs) method. The job of the developer is to code a custom class that implements this interface, and then configure the portlet.xml file, thus making the portal server aware of the validator. The contract between the portlet.xml file and the portal server ensures that before any data is saved into PortletPreferences, the validate method of the PreferencesValidator will be invoked. If validation fails, the validate method must throw the special ***ValidatorException***, which is part of the JSR-168 Portlet API.

To ensure that only numeric data is stored as an upper limit of the number guessing game, a class that implements the PreferencesValidator was coded, and configured in the portlet.xml file.

PreferencesValidator and ValidatorException

PreferencesValidator
validate (preferences : PortletPreferences) : void

ValidatorException
ValidatorException (s : String, c : Collection)
ValidatorException (s : String, t : Throwable, c : Collection)
ValidatorException (t : Throwable, c : Collection)
getFailedKeys ( ) : Enumeration

NumberGuesserValidator

As you can see, the NumberGuesserValidator is relatively straight forward. The preference of interest, the ***upperlimit***, is pulled from the preferences object passed into the validate method, and if the ***upperlimit*** field does not pass muster, then a ***ValidatorException*** is thrown.

```
package com.examscam.portlet;  import javax.portlet.*;
public class NumberGuesserValidator implements
                                        PreferencesValidator {
  public void validate(PortletPreferences preferences)
                                   throws ValidatorException {
    try {
     String upperLimit = preferences.getValue("upperlimit", null);
     if (upperLimit != null) {
       Integer.parseInt(upperLimit);
    }
    } catch (NumberFormatException nfe) {
      throw new ValidatorException("upperlimit", nfe, null);
    }
  }
}
```

Catching PortletPreference Exceptions

If you code a PreferencesValidator, it makes sense that you would then catch the corresponding ValidatorException in your portlet code; *specifically*, when you add new data to your PortletPreferences. Notice that there are actually three exceptions being handled in the following code snippet:

```
✂✂✂
if (request.getParameter("guessedit") != null) {
  String newLimit = request.getParameter("newlimit");
  try {
    prefs.setValue("upperlimit", newLimit);
    prefs.store();
  } catch (ValidatorException e) {e.printStackTrace();
  } catch (ReadOnlyException e) {e.printStackTrace();
  } catch (IOException e) {e.printStackTrace();
  }
}
✂✂✂
```

PortletPreference Related Exceptions

PortletPreferences are typically stored in a centralized database, where the portal server can easily retrieve user customizations. Because the act of storing data to a database, or even just sending data across a network, can be problematic, the store method of the PortletPreferences object can potentially throw the java.io.**IOException**.

More curiously though, the store method can throw the javax.portlet.**ReadOnlyException**. In the portlet.xml file, PortletPreferences can be configured, and default values can be assigned to them. These default values will be used unless a user goes to the edit mode and further customizes their preferences. However, in the portlet.xml file, a preference can be marked as read-only. If a preference is marked as read-only in the portlet.xml file, and an attempt is made to edit that preference at runtime, a ReadOnlyException is thrown.

Finally, we should mention again that the store method of the PortletPreferences object can potentially throw the ValidatorException. If a PreferencesValidator is configured in the portlet.xml file, and that validator throws an exception when a particular field is placed into the PortletPreferences, a ValidatorException will be triggered.

Class Diagram of the ReadOnlyException

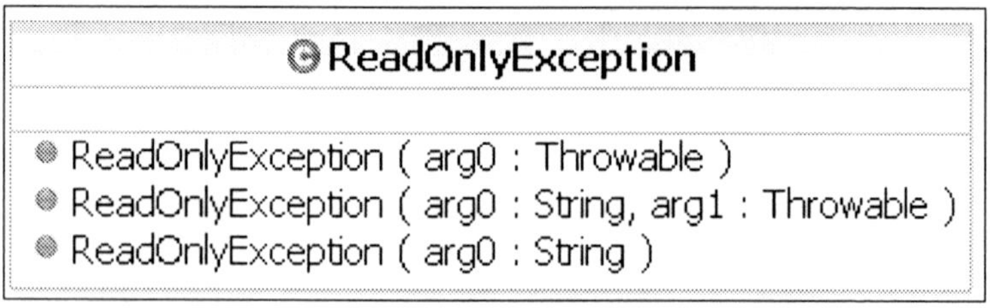

ReadOnlyException
ReadOnlyException (arg0 : Throwable) ReadOnlyException (arg0 : String, arg1 : Throwable) ReadOnlyException (arg0 : String)

PreferencesValidator and the portlet.xml File

```
<?xml version="1.0" encoding="UTF-8"?>
<portlet-app
xmlns="http://java.sun.com/xml/ns/portlet/portlet-app_1_0.xsd"
version="1.0" xmlns:xsi="http://www.w3.org/2001/XMLSchema-instance"
xsi:schemaLocation="http://java.sun.com/xml/ns/portlet/portlet-app_1_0.xsd http://java.sun.com/xml/ns/portlet/portlet-
app_1_0.xsd"
id="com.examscam.portlet.NumberGuesserPortlet.420453eee0">
  <portlet>
    <portlet-name>NumberGuesser</portlet-name>
    <display-name>NumberGuesser portlet</display-name>
    <portlet-class>
      com.examscam.portlet.NumberGuesserPortlet
      </portlet-class>
    <supports>
      <mime-type>text/html</mime-type>
      <portlet-mode>view</portlet-mode>
      <portlet-mode>edit</portlet-mode>
      <portlet-mode>help</portlet-mode>
    </supports>
    <supported-locale>en</supported-locale>
    <portlet-info>
      <title>NumberGuesser portlet</title>
    </portlet-info>
    <portlet-preferences>
      <preference>
        <name>upperlimit</name>
        <value>10</value>

<!--Setting read-only to true will trigger a ReadOnlyException if
the preference is updated at runtime.-->
        <read-only>false</read-only>
      </preference>

<!-- If validation fails, a preferences-validator will throw a
ValidatorException.-->
      <preferences-validator>
        com.examscam.portlet.NumberGuesserValidator
      </preferences-validator>
    </portlet-preferences>
  </portlet>
</portlet-app>
```

Question 7-1

The decision as to which of the various do methods to invoke, such as doEdit or doHelp, occurs in which method?

- O a) init
- O b) destroy
- O c) actionProcess
- O d) doDispatch

Question 7-2

PortletPreferences are not being saved. What are two possibilities as to why this might be happening

- ☐ a) the store() method is not being invoked
- ☐ b) the save() method is not being invoked
- ☐ c) the PortletPreferences are being configured in the doView method
- ☐ d) the PortletPreferences are being manipulated in the processAction method

Answer 7-3

What are the standard, JSR-168, portlet modes?

- ☐ a) edit
- ☐ b) view
- ☐ c) help
- ☐ d) config

Question 7-4

To ensure a PortletPreference has a default value, even if the user hasn't customized their portlet, the best plan of action is to:

- ☐ a) code a default value in the web.xml file
- ☐ b) code a default value in the portlet.xml file
- ☐ c) provide a default value as the second parameter of the PortletPreferences getValue() method
- ☐ d) accept a null value as a valid PortletPreference

Question 7-5

Which of the following checked exceptions could be thrown by a call to the PortletPreferences' store method?

- ☐ a) ReadOnlyException
- ☐ b) PortletException
- ☐ c) ValidatorException
- ☐ d) IOException

Question 7-6

Minimize, Maximize and Normal are all valid:

- O a) window states
- O b) window modes
- O c) Portlet states
- O d) Portlet modes

Question 7-7

Where is a PortletPreference defined as being read only.
O a) programmatically through the PortletPreferences object
O b) by adding a read-only parameter to the portlet.xml file
O c) by adding a read-only parameter to the web.xml file
O d) PortletPreferences are always editable

Answer 7-1

The decision as to which of the various do methods to invoke, such as doEdit or doHelp, occurs in which method?

O a) init
O b) destroy
O c) actionProcess
O d) doDispatch

Option d) is correct.

The init method is called when a portlet is first loaded, and destroy is called when the portlet is unloaded, but neither of those lifecycle methods have anything to do with the render phase of a portlet.

It is the ***doDispatch*** method that is responsible for figuring out which of the do<mode> methods should be invoked for portlet rendering.

Answer 7-2

PortletPreferences are not being saved. What are two possibilities as to why this might be happening

☐ a) the store() method is not being invoked
☐ b) the save() method is not being invoked
☐ c) the PortletPreferences are being configured in the doView method
☐ d) the PortletPreferences are being manipulated in the processAction method

Options a) and c) are correct.

There are two common reasons why PortletPreferences don't get saved. First of all, developers forget to call the store method, and secondly, developers try to manipulate PortletPreferences in the wrong mode. You should only be editing portlet preferences in the appropriately named, ***edit*** mode.

Answer 7-3

What are the standard, JSR-168, portlet modes?

☐ a) edit
☐ b) view
☐ c) help
☐ d) config

Options a) b) and c) are correct.

All JSR-168 compliant portal servers must support view, edit and help modes. However, portal servers are free to support any number of custom modes. For example, the WebSphere Portal Server has built in features for supporting a configure mode.

Answer 7-4

To ensure a PortletPreference has a default value, even if the user hasn't customized their portlet, the best plan of action is to:

☐ a) code a default value in the web.xml file
☐ b) code a default value in the portlet.xml file
☐ c) provide a default value as the second parameter of the PortletPreferences getValue() method
☐ d) accept a null value as a valid PortletPreference

Options b) and c) are correct.

Making sure there's a default value for a user-configurable property is always a challenge. With PortletPreferences, we can code a default value in two ways: first, we can put a preference value in the portlet.xml file; secondly, the getValue() method takes two parameters, the first being the name of the property you wish to extract, and the second parameter being a default value, just in case the property you are looking for doesn't exist.

Answer 7-5

Which of the following checked exceptions could be thrown by a call to the PortletPreferences' store method?

- ☐ a) ReadOnlyException
- ☐ b) PortletException
- ☐ c) ValidatorException
- ☐ d) IOException

Options a) c) and d) are correct.

PortletPreferences are stored persistently, typically in a centralized database, and that database write can throw an IOException. Furthermore, PortletPreferences can be associated with a PreferencesValidator, which throws a ValidatorException if a preference doesn't pass a validation test. Finally, PortletPreferences can be configured as being read-only, and if someone tries to overwrite a read-only preference, a ReadOnlyException is thrown.

Answer 7-6

Minimize, Maximize and Normal are all valid:

- O a) window states
- O b) window modes
- O c) Portlet states
- O d) Portlet modes

Answer a) is correct. Minimize, maximize and normal are the three standard window states. Sometimes the terms *state* and *modes* are easily confused. View and edit are modes, minimize and maximize are states.

Answer 7-7

Where is a PortletPreference defined as being read only.
O a) programmatically through the PortletPreferences object O b) by adding a read-only parameter to the portlet.xml file O c) by adding a read-only parameter to the web.xml file O d) PortletPreferences are always editable
Answer b) is correct. There is no programmatic way to set a PortletPreference to be read-on; this can only be done by setting the preference through the portlet.xml file, and subsequently adding a tag indicating that the preference is read only.

Chapter 8
Custom Portlet Modes

The JSR-168 portlet specification requires all portal servers to provide support for the three standard portlet modes: view, edit and help. However, portal providers are allowed to provide support for any number of extra portlet modes they think would be helpful.

For example, it is envisioned that many portlets would benefit from a print mode, that would make it possible to print out the content of a portlet with the simple click of a button. IBM always provided support for a configure mode with their legacy portlet API, so it's no surprise that the WebSphere Portal Server comes with *built in* support for a configure mode.

Portal Support for Custom Modes

First of all, I want to make it clear that you can follow all of the programming steps required to create a portlet that has a custom mode, but if the portal server to which you are deploying doesn't support that custom mode, that custom mode just *ain't* going to work. If you want your portlets to render a custom portlet mode, that custom portlet mode must be enabled on the portal server to which you are deploying.

Now, the WebSphere Portal Server supports the configure mode, so I will demonstrate how to write a portlet that supports the configure mode. The assumption here is that we will be deploying to the WebSphere Portal Server.

Implementing Custom Portlet Modes

The first step in coding a custom portlet mode is overriding the inherited doDispatch method of the GenericPortlet. The doDispatch method is always invoked before the doView or doEdit modes, so, if we override this method, and inspect to see if our custom portlet mode is being invoked, we can capture the request, and send it to our own custom *do* method, which in this case, will be doCustomConfig().

And what *do* we *do* in our *do*CustomConfig() method? Well, anything we want. This method will be responsible for rendering the config mode of the portlet. This method can do anything you want it to do, but in all likelihood, the method will just forward to a JSP file.

Figure 8-1 WebSphere Portal Server 6.x has inherent support for the custom config mode. Even if custom modes are coded properly, if a portal server is not configured to support that custom mode, the custom mode simply will not be available to the end user.

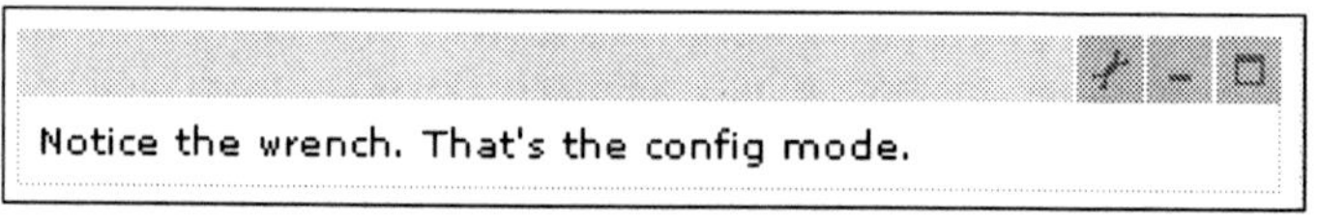
Notice the wrench. That's the config mode.

The Custom do<mode> Method

When the custom configure mode is being requested, we call to our custom do<mode> method, named doCustomConfig(). In our example, the config mode simply prints a message about its own self-actualization to the console. However, this method will never be called, unless we **override** the **doDispatch** method.

```
protected void doCustomConfig(
    RenderRequest request, RenderResponse response)
          throws PortletException, IOException {

 response.setContentType("text/html");
 response.getWriter().print("I have a custom config mode!!!");

}
```

Overriding the doDispatch Method

When overriding the doDispacth method, we first check to see if the portlet is minimized. The mode being requested really doesn't matter if the portlet is minimized, so if it is, we just skip the whole render phase processing.

If the portlet isn't minimized, then we check to see if the portlet mode being requested is the config portlet mode. If it is, then we call our doCustomConfig method. If our custom portlet mode is not being invoked, we simply call super.doDispatch(), which essentially allows the portlet to run as though our custom, overridden, doDispatch method, was never called.

```
protected void doDispatch(
    RenderRequest request, RenderResponse response)
                    throws PortletException, IOException{

  /* don't do anything if the window is minimized */
  if (!WindowState.MINIMIZED.equals(request.getWindowState())) {

    /* find out which portlet mode is being requested */
    PortletMode requestedMode = request.getPortletMode();
    PortletMode customPortletMode = new PortletMode("config");

    /* if our custom mode is requested, call our custom do method */
    if (requestedMode.equals(customPortletMode)) {

      /* this is the call to our custom do <mode> method */
      doCustomConfigure(request, response);
      return;
    }
    /*if our custom portlet wasn't called, allow the regular portlet
    mode processing happen*/
    super.doDispatch(request, response);
  }
}
```

Editing the Portlet Deployment Descriptor

Along with the overridden doDispatch method, and the custom do<mode> method, the deployment descriptor of the portlet application must be updated to indicate that a new portlet mode is being supported.

```
<?xml version="1.0" encoding="UTF-8"?>
<portlet-app
xmlns="http://java.sun.com/xml/ns/portlet/portlet-app_1_0.xsd"
version="1.0"
xmlns:xsi="http://www.w3.org/2001/XMLSchema-instance"
xsi:schemaLocation=http://java.sun.com/xml/ns/portlet/portlet-
app_1_0.xsd http://java.sun.com/xml/ns/portlet/portlet-app_1_0.xsd

id="com.examscam.portlet.CustomModePortlet.051cf00ef0" >

 <portlet>
   <portlet-name>CustomModePortlet</portlet-name>
   <display-name>CustomModePortlet</display-name>
   <display-name xml:lang="en">
      CustomModePortlet
   </display-name>
   <portlet-class>
     com.examscam.portlet.CustomModePortlet
   </portlet-class>
   <expiration-cache>0</expiration-cache>
   <supports>
     <mime-type>text/html</mime-type>
     <portlet-mode>view</portlet-mode>

<!-- This entry indicates the portlet supports the config mode -->
     <portlet-mode>config</portlet-mode>
   </supports>
   <supported-locale>en</supported-locale>
   <portlet-info>
     <title>CustomModePortlet</title>
   </portlet-info>
 </portlet>

<!-- This entry indicates the portlet application supports config-->
 <custom-portlet-mode>
   <portlet-mode>config</portlet-mode>
 </custom-portlet-mode>
</portlet-app>
```

The Full CustomModePortlet

```
package com.examscam.portlet;
import java.io.*;import javax.portlet.*;

public class CustomModePortlet extends GenericPortlet {

protected void doView
   (RenderRequest request, RenderResponse response)
      throws PortletException, IOException {
 response.setContentType("text/html");
 response.getWriter().println("Custom Portlet View Mode");
}

protected void doCustomConfigure
   (RenderRequest request, RenderResponse response)
      throws PortletException, IOException {
  response.setContentType("text/html");
  response.getWriter().println("Custom Config Mode!!!");
}

protected void doDispatch
    (RenderRequest request, RenderResponse response)
                         throws PortletException, IOException{

  /* don't do anything if the window is minimized */
  if (!WindowState.MINIMIZED.equals(request.getWindowState())) {

    /* find out which portlet mode is being requested */
    PortletMode requestedMode = request.getPortletMode();
    PortletMode customPortletMode = new PortletMode("config");

    /* if our custom mode is requested, call our custom do method */
    if (requestedMode.equals(customPortletMode)) {

      /* this is the call to our custom do <mode> method */
      doCustomConfigure(request, response);
      return;
    }
    /*if our custom portlet wasn't called, allow the regular portlet
    mode processing happen*/
    super.doDispatch(request, response);
  }
 }
}
```

Question 8-1

Special icons associated with a particular custom portlet mode are defined:

- O a) in the web.xml file
- O b) in the portlet.xml file
- O c) in the render phase of the portlet
- O d) in a portal skin

Question 8-2

Which method must be overridden to allow the portal server to forward a request to a custom portlet mode?

- O a) doDispatch()
- O b) doMode()
- O c) doView
- O d) getRequestDispatcher()

Answer 8-1

Special icons associated with a particular custom portlet mode are defined:

O a) in the web.xml file
O b) in the portlet.xml file
O c) in the render phase of the portlet
O d) in a portal skin

Option d) is correct.

The cute little icons, such as the pencil for the edit mode, or the wrench for the custom config mode, are part of a portal skin, and are defined outside of the actual portlet application.

The fact that icons for custom portlet modes are defined at the portal server level, and not the portlet level, is part of the reason why portlets cannot simply define custom portlet modes on their own.

Question 8-2

Which method must be overridden to allow the portal server to forward a request to a custom portlet mode?

O a) doDispatch()
O b) doMode()
O c) doView
O d) getRequestDispatcher()

Option a) is correct.

The doDispatch method is responsible for invoking the appropriate do<mode> method, so if you want your custom portlet mode recognized by your portlet, you need to override the logic in this very important method.

Chapter 9
Config Objects

We've covered just about every object in the Portlet API, with the exception of two of the most important ones. It's hard to believe we've made it this far without touching upon them.

The JSR-168 API defines two configuration objects, namely the Port**let**Context and the PortletConfig. In this chapter, I'm also going to throw the Por**tal**Context into the mix as well, as it is *phonetically* pretty close to Port**let**Context. ☺ It's pretty easy to get the two of them confused.

The PortalContext

PortalContext

- getProperty (arg0 : String) : String
- getPropertyNames ( ) : Enumeration
- getSupportedPortletModes ( ) : Enumeration
- getSupportedWindowStates ( ) : Enumeration
- getPortalInfo ( ) : String

The Por**tal**Context is a relatively straight forward object containing five important methods. These methods basically represent a handle from the portlet we code, back to the Portal Server. From the PortalContext, we can discover the supported ***modes*** of the portal (just in case we want to code a custom portlet mode), along with the supported window ***states***. This is good information to know when creating a portlet that may be deployed to a variety of different portal servers.

The PortletConfig Interface

The PortletConfig object is really just a handle back to the information about a portlet that is configured in the portlet.xml file. Methods like getPortletName(), getResourceBundle() and getInitParameters() are all methods that essentially read information that is written about a portlet in the portlet.xml deployment descriptor.

Since all of these parameters come from a text file that cannot be edited at runtime, all of these parameters are read-only. If you want to change the data obtained by PortletConfig, you need to edit the portlet.xml file and bounce your portlet application.

The PortletConfig becomes most interesting when you use it for initialization parameters. The method getInitParameter() can pull data from the portlet.xml deployment descriptor based upon the name, in a name-value pair. The data is always returned as a String; after all, you can't exactly code *objects* into the portlet.xml file.

The neat thing about the PortletConfig is that it is common to the Portlet, regardless of the user interacting with the portlet. Unlike the PortletSession object, where data is unique to the user, and not persisted, or the PortletRequest, where data is unique to a user, but purged after every request-response cycle, data obtained from the PortletConfig is always the same, regardless of the user invoking the Portlet. The only way to change the data pulled from the PortletConfig object is to physically edit the portlet.xml file, which isn't possible while an application is running.

PortletConfig
getPortletName ( ) : String
getPortletContext ( ) : PortletContext
getResourceBundle (locale : Locale) : ResourceBundle
getInitParameter (name : String) : String
getInitParameterNames ( ) : Enumeration

The PortletContext and the ServletContext

Similar to the PortletConfig interface, the Portlet**Context** has a method called getInitParameter(), which can spit out read-only String values that are configured in a deployment descriptor. ***Which deployment descriptor,*** you ask? Well, that's a very good question.

The PortletContext is really just a wrapper placed around the glorious ServletContext from the Servlet and JSP API. The true nature of the PortletContext is revealed when you discover that the init-parameters the PortletContext reads, are actually pulled from the same place the ServletContext init-parameters are pulled: the **web.xml** file. Yes, init-parameters for the Portlet**Context** are actually configured in the deployment descriptor of the *web* module.

So, what exactly is the PortletContext? Well, essentially, the PortletContext represents the shared space in which all of the portlets associated with a common war file reside. So, if information is stored in the PortletContext of a portlet application, any portlet that is deployed as part of that portlet application can access that information.

The PortletContext and the Portlet Application

So, any portlet deployed as part of a common war file can share and access information made available through the PortletContext. Now, this doesn't mean every portlet running on a *portal server* has access to the same portlet context. Every portlet application, which essentially means all of the portlets that are defined in a common portlet.xml file, has a common PortletContext. However, a portlet defined in one portlet.xml file will never be able to access the PortletContext of a portlet defined in a different portlet application.

For example, one resource that all Portlets and JSPs in a portlet application need access to is the PortletRequestDispatcher, which has been used many times to allow a portlet to delegate to a JSP for markup generation. The PortletRequestDispatcher is a service that must be available to all portlets running in a portlet application, so it only makes sense that it be made available through the PortletContext.

Another helpful service made available through the PortletContext is the logging service. Two overloaded log() methods are available to portlets through the PortletContext. Messages written through this logging service are written to a special log file, as defined by the portlet container vendor.

The PortletContext also provides utility methods, such as getMajorVersion() and getMinorVersion(), for figuring out what version of the Portlet API your application is using; but by far, the most powerful methods of the PortletContext are the ones that provide access to the read-only initialization parameters, and the editable runtime attributes that can be added and deleted from the PortletContext.

Class Diagram for he PortletContext Interface

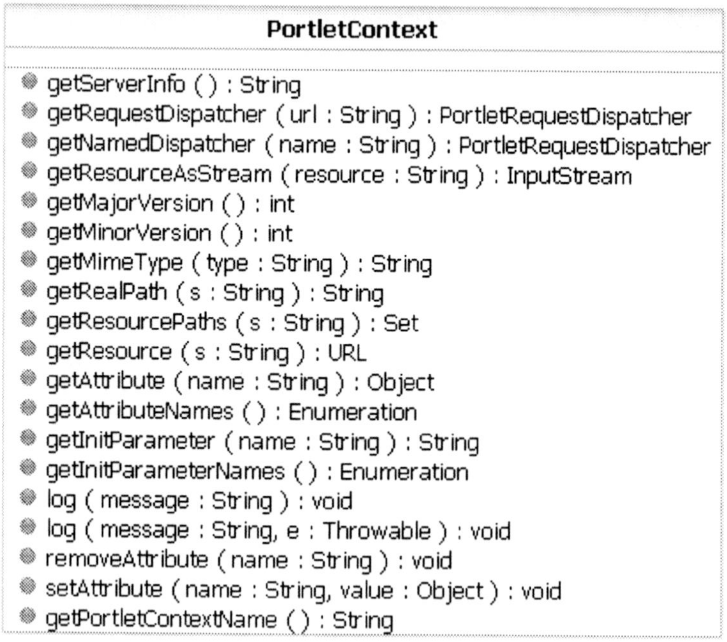

PortletContext
getServerInfo ( ) : String
getRequestDispatcher (url : String) : PortletRequestDispatcher
getNamedDispatcher (name : String) : PortletRequestDispatcher
getResourceAsStream (resource : String) : InputStream
getMajorVersion ( ) : int
getMinorVersion ( ) : int
getMimeType (type : String) : String
getRealPath (s : String) : String
getResourcePaths (s : String) : Set
getResource (s : String) : URL
getAttribute (name : String) : Object
getAttributeNames ( ) : Enumeration
getInitParameter (name : String) : String
getInitParameterNames ( ) : Enumeration
log (message : String) : void
log (message : String, e : Throwable) : void
removeAttribute (name : String) : void
setAttribute (name : String, value : Object) : void
getPortletContextName ( ) : String

Templatized Portlets

Many textbooks and references that talk about ServletConfig and ServletContext objects, which essentially correspond to the PortletConfig and PortletContext objects, gloss over the power of these objects, and simply give lip-service to the act of reading parameter values from deployment descriptors. Well, I'm not going to do that. I'm going to show you a very simple example of a templatized portlet, that can have a profound effect on a developer's ability to generate a multitude of useful and configurable portlets.

Take a look at the following GenericTaxPortlet. How many portlets do you see there? One? Well, you're wrong – *there are hundreds.*

```
package com.examscam.portlet;

import java.io.*;import javax.portlet.*;

public class GenericTaxPortlet extends GenericPortlet {

protected void doView(RenderRequest request, RenderResponse response)
                        throws PortletException, IOException {

  response.setContentType("text/html");
  PrintWriter out = response.getWriter();
  PortletContext context = this.getPortletContext();
  PortletConfig config = this.getPortletConfig();

  String fedRate = context.getInitParameter("fedrate");
  String regionName = context.getInitParameter("regionname");

  String regionalRate = config.getInitParameter("regionalrate");


  out.print("<BR>The federal tax rate is: " + fedRate);
  out.print("<BR>The " + regionName + " tax rate is: ");
  out.print(regionalRate);

 }
}
```

Deployment Descriptors and InitParameters

The GenericTaxPortlet reads in three values from the deployment descriptors, namely ***fedrate*** and ***regionname*** from the web.xml file, and ***regionalrate*** from the portlet.xml file.

But imagine if we wanted to create a bunch of portlets, based on the GenericTaxPortlet, that displayed the federal and state tax obligations for each of the fifty U.S. states? Well, we could create an entry in the portlet.xml file for each state, and configure each state with a different tax rate. We could have one entry for the FloridaTaxPortlet, another for the TexasTaxPortlet, and a third for the NevadaTaxPortlet. We could configure each as a separate portlet in the portlet.xml file, point to the same GenericTaxPortlet as the implementing class, and provide a unique value for each state's tax rate.

Okay, these three states are bad examples, because none of them actually have a state tax, but you get the point!

```
✂✂✂
<portlet>
  <description>OhioTaxPortlet</description><portlet-name>OhioTaxPortlet</portlet-name>
   <display-name>OhioTaxPortlet</display-name>
   <portlet-class>
       com.examscam.portlet.GenericTaxPortlet
   </portlet-class>
   <init-param>
     <name>regionalrate</name><value>4</value>
   </init-param>
  <supports><mime-type>text/html</mime-type><portlet-mode>view</portlet-mode></supports>
  <supported-locale>en</supported-locale>
  <portlet-info><title>Ohio</title></portlet-info>
</portlet>
<!-- You can make as many portlets as you like!!!-->
<portlet>
  <description>FloridaTaxPortlet</description><portlet-name>FloridaTaxPortlet</portlet-name>
   <display-name>FloridaTaxPortlet</display-name>
  <portlet-class>
       com.examscam.portlet.GenericTaxPortlet
  </portlet-class>
   <init-param>
     <name>regionalrate</name><value>5</value>
   </init-param>
  <supports><mime-type>text/html</mime-type><portlet-mode>view</portlet-mode></supports>
  <supported-locale>en</supported-locale>
  <portlet-info><title>FloridaTaxPortlet</title></portlet-info>
</portlet>
<portlet>✂✂<name>regionalrate</name><value>5</value></portlet>✂✂
```

Web Deployment Descriptor (web.xml)

```
<?xml version="1.0" encoding="UTF-8"?>
<!DOCTYPE web-app PUBLIC "-//Sun Microsystems, Inc.//DTD Web Application 2.3//EN" "http://java.sun.com/dtd/web-app_2_3.dtd">
<web-app id="WebApp_ID">
  <display-name>US TaxProject</display-name>
   <context-param>
     <param-name>fedrate</param-name>
     <param-value>35</param-value>
     <description>Federal Tax Rate</description>
   </context-param>
   <context-param>
     <param-name>regionname</param-name>
     <param-value>state</param-value>
     <description>Region Name</description>
   </context-param>
  <welcome-file-list>
    <welcome-file>index.jsp</welcome-file>
  </welcome-file-list>
</web-app>
```

Portlet Deployment Descriptor (portlet.xml)

```
<?xml version="1.0" encoding="UTF-8"?>
<portlet-app xmlns="http://java.sun.com/xml/ns/portlet/portlet-app_1_0.xsd" version="1.0" xmlns:xsi="http://www.w3.org/2001/XMLSchema-instance"
xsi:schemaLocation="http://java.sun.com/xml/ns/portlet/portlet-app_1_0.xsd http://java.sun.com/xml/ns/portlet/portlet-app_1_0.xsd" id="com.examscam.portlet.GenericTaxPortlet.fb9b06d0f0">
 <portlet>
   <description>GenericTaxPortlet</description>
   <portlet-name>GenericTaxPortlet</portlet-name>
   <display-name>GenericTaxPortlet</display-name>
   <portlet-class>
      com.examscam.portlet.GenericTaxPortlet
   </portlet-class>
    <init-param>
      <name>regionalrate</name>
      <value>5</value>
    </init-param>
   <supports>
     <mime-type>text/html</mime-type>
     <portlet-mode>view</portlet-mode>
   </supports>
   <supported-locale>en</supported-locale>
   <portlet-info><title>GenericTaxPortlet</title></portlet-info>
  </portlet>
</portlet-app>
```

Repackaging the WAR

So, by creating multiple entries in the portlet.xml file, we can create a multitude of portlets based upon the GenericTaxPortlet. But all of these portlets are really focused on the United States. What about other countries?

Well, we could configure all of the American states in one portlet.xml file, and export that entire portlet application as a single war file, perhaps called USTaxesPortletApp.war. We could then create a second portlet application for Canada, called the CanadianTaxesPortletApp.war. And if people outside of North American started buying my books, we could create portlet applications for those countries too!

For the CanadianTaxesPortletApp, our portlet.xml file would have entries for each of the Canadian provinces, and the web.xml file, where PortletContext parameters are configured, would look like this:

```
<?xml version="1.0" encoding="UTF-8"?>
<!DOCTYPE web-app PUBLIC "-//Sun Microsystems, Inc.//DTD Web Application 2.3//EN" "http://java.sun.com/dtd/web-app_2_3.dtd">
<web-app id="WebApp_ID">
  <display-name>Canadian TaxProject</display-name>
  <context-param>
    <param-name>fedrate</param-name>
    <param-value>45</param-value>
    <description>Federal Tax Rate</description>
  </context-param>
  <context-param>
    <param-name>regionname</param-name>
    <param-value>provincial</param-value>
    <description>Region Name</description>
  </context-param>
  <welcome-file-list>
    <welcome-file>index.jsp</welcome-file>
  </welcome-file-list>
</web-app>
```

PortletContext Attributes

Both the PortletContext and PortletConfig objects can read information from deployment descriptors, but only the PortletContext provides a scope for storing readable and writable properties.

The PortletRequest provides a scope for storing user centric information that is purges as soon as the current request-response cycle is completed. The PortletSession provides a transient data storage mechanism that can store user-centric data for as long as the user is visiting our website. The PortletPreferences object provides permanent storage for user preferences. But each of these mechanisms work on a per-user basis. How can information be shared across all users, and all portlets, that are part of the same portlet application (aka, packaged in the same war file) ?

Well, the PortletContext provides a getAttribute() and setAttribute() method that allows objects to be stored, and shared across all users and all portlets in a portlet application. The PortletContext, and its close cousin, the ServletContext, are two incredibly powerful scope storage mechanisms, and unfortunately, two of the most under-utilized. I love the PortletContext, and believe that it should be used more often in applications.

There is one drawback to the PortletContext though. The PortletContext is not always synchronized across JVMs in a cluster. As a result, objects placed in the PortletContext should be largely read from, and rarely written to.

On my websites, I provide a variety of online mock exams for certification preparation. In my Java apps, I always store the set of questions in the PortletContext or ServletContext. The questions are loaded into the context as soon as the application starts up, and are not really ever changed at runtime. Of course, almost every JSP, Servlet, Portlet, Filter, or other web artifact must access the exam object, so having it in the context is very convenient.

Use the PortalContext when it makes sense. Your users will love you for it!

Question 9-1

PortletConfig initialization parameters are:
☐ a) defined in the web.xml file
☐ b) defined in the portlet.xml file
☐ c) read only and cannot be changed at runtime
☐ d) read/write, but may get out of sync across multiple JVMs

Question 9-2

The PortletConfig object is
O a) shared amongst all portlet instances
O b) unique to a particular portlet instance
O c) unique to a particular user
O d) is unique to a particular session

Question 9-3

Which of the following statements are true:
☐ a) the PortletContext is accessed through the *this* of a portlet
☐ b) the PortletConfig is accessed through the *this* of a portlet
☐ c) the PortletContext is accessible through the PortletConfig
☐ d) the PortletConfig is accessible through the PortletContext

Question 9-4

The PortalContext:
☐ a) can provide a list of window states supported by the portal
☐ b) can provide a list of portlet modes supported by the portal
☐ c) provides access to the RequestDispatcher
☐ d) provides access to the portal logging mechanism

Answer 9-1

PortletConfig initialization parameters are:
☐ a) defined in the web.xml file ☐ b) defined in the portlet.xml file ☐ c) read only and cannot be changed at runtime ☐ d) read/write, but may get out of sync across multiple JVMs
Answers b) and c) are correct. In the old IBM API, PortletConfig was defined in the web.xml file, but with JSR-168, initialization parameters are all maintained in the portlet.xml file. Also, initialization parameters for a portlet are read only. PortletConfig does not have a problem being managed across JVMs. Synchronization across JVMs is only a problem with the PortletContext.

Answer 9-2

The PortletConfig object is
O a) shared amongst all portlet instances O b) unique to a particular portlet instance O c) unique to a particular user O d) is unique to a particular session
Answer b) is correct. PortletConfig provides initialization parameters to a particular portlet instance. That data is then available to any user, session or any method call made at any time to that particular portlet.

Answer 9-3

Which of the following statements are true:
☐ a) the PortletContext is accessed through the *this* of a portlet
☐ b) the PortletConfig is accessed through the *this* of a portlet
☐ c) the PortletContext is accessible through the PortletConfig
☐ d) the PortletConfig is accessible through the PortletContext
Answers a), b) and d) are the correct answers. There is a getPortletContext() method in the PortletConfig object, but the PortletContext method has not facilities for accessing the PortletConfig object.

Answer 9-4

The PortalContext:
☐ a) can provide a list of window states supported by the portal
☐ b) can provide a list of portlet modes supported by the portal
☐ c) provides access to the RequestDispatcher
☐ d) provides access to the portal logging mechanism
Options a) and b) are correct. The PortalContext has five methods, including getPortalInfo, getPropertyNames, getProperty, getSupportedPortletModes and getSupportedWindowStates. The object used to access the PortletRequestDispatcher and the portal logging mechanism is the similarly named PortletContext object.

Chapter 10
i18n of Portlets

Multi-language support is an important aspect of any application we create, and portlet applications are no exception.

There really is no magic in providing international (i18n) language support to portlet applications. The standard mechanism is to simply code a single portlet, and then, depending upon the language of the user viewing the portlet, text strings are pulled from a properties file that corresponds to the language of the user.

Figuring out the language to display to a user is a fairly straight forward, although multi-step, endeavor. When a user registers with a portal, they usually are asked to specify a preferred language. The portal typically uses this information to figure out which property file, aka resource bundle, from which to pull the language appropriate text string.

If a user hasn't logged on, or has never specified a preferred language, the http headers a web browser sends to the server usually includes a preferred language or locale heading.

Furthermore, if a preferred language or http header doesn't enlighten us as to the preferred language of the user, then a portlet itself usually has a default language, which will be used as the language to display to the user.

Finally, if a portlet doesn't specify a preferred language, then there is always a portal wide setting, configured on the portal server, that specifies a preferred language to use if no other language settings are detected.

So, the portal does a lot of work to figure out from which properties file to pull language appropriate text strings. Still, it is up to the portlet provider to actually *provide* the various, language appropriate, properties files. If you haven't provided a Zulu properties file, then users who speak Zulu won't be given language appropriate text translations, no matter how hard the portal worked to figure out that the user in question indeed speaks Zulu.

Implementing i18n

Internationalization (i18n), is implemented through a combined use of language appropriate properties files, JSTL custom tags, and deployment descriptor configurations to help point a portlet to the appropriate resource bundle (property file).

Starting with the portlet.xml deployment descriptor, there should be a listing of all of the languages your portlet supports, along with a pointer to the name of the corresponding resource bundle. It is important to list all of the supported modes of a portlet, as some portal servers will not display a portlet to a user for page selection if their preferred language is not supported. Within the portlet.xml file, there should also be an internationalized display name defined for each of the supported languages.

```
<?xml version="1.0" encoding="UTF-8"?>
<portlet-app xmlns="http://java.sun.com/xml/ns/portlet/portlet-app_1_0.xsd" version="1.0" xmlns:xsi="http://www.w3.org/2001/XMLSchema-instance"
xsi:schemaLocation="http://java.sun.com/xml/ns/portlet/portlet-app_1_0.xsd http://java.sun.com/xml/ns/portlet/portlet-app_1_0.xsd" id="com.examscam.portlet.Multi18nPortlet.[illegible]">
<portlet>
  <portlet-name>IntenationalPortlet</portlet-name>
  <display-name>IntenationalPortlet</display-name>
  <display-name xml:lang="en">The i18n Portlet</display-name>
  <display-name xml:lang="fr">Le i18n Portlet</display-name>
  <display-name xml:lang="es">Que i18n Portlet</display-name>
  <portlet-class>com.examscam.portlet.Multi18nPortlet</portlet-class>
  <expiration-cache>0</expiration-cache>
  <supports>
   <mime-type>text/html</mime-type><portlet-mode>view</portlet-mode>
  </supports>

  <supported-locale>en</supported-locale>
  <supported-locale>fr</supported-locale>
  <supported-locale>es</supported-locale>

  <resource-bundle>
    com.examscam.nl.i18nportlet
    <!-- notice how there is no .properties extension -->
  </resource-bundle>

  <portlet-info>
    <title>IntenationalPortlet</title>
  </portlet-info>
 </portlet>
</portlet-app>
```

Providing the Resource Bundles

The portlet.xml file, through the <resource-bundle> tag, provides the root name of the property files that will perform internationalization. This entry only applies for configurations in the portlet.xml file. JSPs must explicitly reference this file on their own.

```
<resource-bundle>
   com.examscam.nl.i18nportlet
</resource-bundle>
```

Now, with this example, there will not be a file named i18nportlet – there will be a file named i18nportlet.**properties**. The resource bundle entry does not specify the extension of the property being used, nor does the JSTL custom tag. It is assumed that the property file will have a .properties extension.

Furthermore, there should be more than one property file. A property file named i18nportlet.properties should exist, with all text string defined in the default language of the portlet. From there, a properties file should exist for each of the various languages your portlet text strings are translated into. So, if you are supporting French, Spanish and English, the following property files should exist:

- i18nportlet.properties (default)
- i18nportlet_es.properties (Spanish)
- i18nportlet_fr.properties (French)
- i18nportlet_en.properties (English)

Furthermore, these files must be places in a folder appropriate subdirectory of the WEB-INF\classes folder of the war file. So, our properties files should be placed in a folder named:

`WEB-INF\classes\`**`com\examscam\nl\`**

This folder will be directly off the root of the war. All compiled class files are also found under the WEB-INF\classes folder, which includes any of your portlet classes, and utility classes that are defined in your portlet project.

Internationalizing JSP Content

The property files referenced in the portlet.xml file must contain entries for the title, short description, and keywords used to describe your portlet. Those entries are defined with the keys:

- javax.portlet.title
- javax.portlet.short-title
- javax.portlet.keywords

Internationalizing JSP Content

Internationalizing entries in the portlet.xml file, such as the display name of the portlet, and the description of the portlet, is one thing, but internationalizing your JSP files is another. If you want to do a proper job internationalizing your portlet, every piece of text to be displayed to the user must be read from a resource bundle. This requires a JSTL custom tag to reference the resource bundle, and special JSTL custom tags to pull the appropriate strings from the corresponding properties file.

To create a JSP that can use JSTL tags, along with resource bundles, to provide internationalization, you must follow the following step:

- Make sure your portlet application has access to the classes that support JSTL custom tags
- Add a taglib directive to the JSP, indicating that you are using the **fmt** custom tag library
- Use the fmt:setBundle tag to point to your internationalized resource bundles (property files)
- Use the fmt: message tag to pull internationalized strings from your resource bundle, based on access keys
- Make sure your resource bundles contain string mappings for **all** access keys used in your application

Resource Bundle Files

```
# default resource bundle
# i18nPortlet.properties

javax.portlet.title=Default International Portlet
javax.portlet.short-title= Default i18n Portlet
javax.portlet.keywords= i18n Default

view.poemtitle = They Killed Che
```

```
# english resource bundle
# i18nPortlet_en.properties

javax.portlet.title=The International Portlet
javax.portlet.short-title= The i18n Portlet
javax.portlet.keywords= i18n English

view.poemtitle = They Killed Che
```

```
# french resource bundle
# i18nPortlet_fr.properties
javax.portlet.title=The International Portlet
javax.portlet.short-title= The i18n Portlet
javax.portlet.keywords= i18n English

view.poemtitle = Ils Ont tué Che
```

```
# spanish resource bundle
# i18nPortlet_es.properties
javax.portlet.title=Que International Portlet
javax.portlet.short-title= Que i18n Portlet
javax.portlet.keywords= i18n Spanish
view.poemtitle = Mataron A Che
```

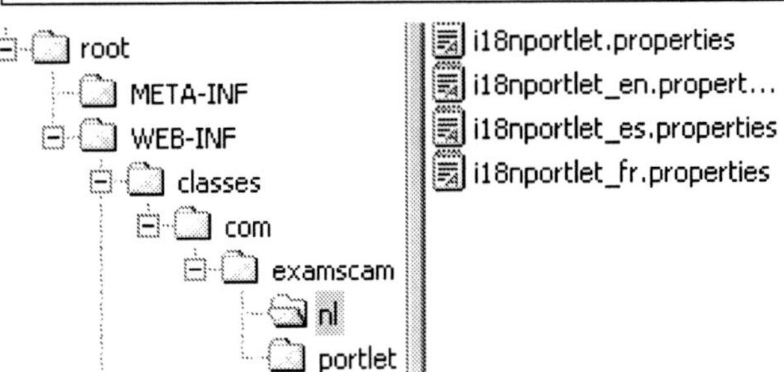

Access to JSTL Tag Libraries

In order to be able to access JSTL tag libraries, you will likely have to import a few jar files into the lib directory of your web module. The required jar files depend upon your environment, but typically, you will need access to:

- jaxen-full.jar
- saxpath.jar
- standard.jar
- jstl.jar

Taglib Directive

To gain access to the fmt custom tag library, you must also add the appropriate taglib directive to any JSP performing internationalization.

```
<%@taglib uri="http://java.sun.com/jstl/fmt" prefix="fmt"%>
```

Pointing to the Resource Bundle

After adding the taglib directive, a JSP must point to the ***base name*** of the resource bundle from which it will pull text strings.

```
<fmt:setBundle basename="com.examscam.nl.i18nportlet"/>
```

Note that we are using the same resource bundle referenced in the portlet.xml tag. Now, part of the magic of the fmt custom tag is the fact that it will figure out the preferred language of the user for us. All we have to do is provide internationalized, and appropriately named, property files, such as i18nportlet_**fr**.properties and i18nportlet_**es**.properties; if we do, the custom tags will take care of the rest.

Using the <fmt:message/> JSTL Tag

To access content that has been internationalized in a properties file, you use the fmt:message custom tag, pointing to the key in your resource bundle that is matched with an internationalized string. Our resource bundles contain a key named ***view.poemtitle***, which is what we will point to with our custom tag:

<fmt:message key="view.poemtitle"/>

The view.poemtitle must map back to a key, and a subsequently internationalized string, in the

Providing i18n Property Files

The whole point of the fmt:message tag is that it pulls data from a resource bundle. Here are two resource bundles, one for French, and one for Spanish:

```
# french resource bundle
# i18nPortlet_fr.properties

javax.portlet.title=The International Portlet
javax.portlet.short-title= The i18n Portlet
javax.portlet.keywords= i18n English

view.poemtitle = Ils Ont tué Che
```

```
# spanish resource bundle
# i18nPortlet_es.properties


javax.portlet.title=Que International Portlet
javax.portlet.short-title= Que i18n Portlet
javax.portlet.keywords= i18n Spanish

view.poemtitle = Mataron A Che
```

The Full JSP, and Resulting Portlet

Here is the completed JSP, with all of the pieces pulled together.

```
<%@taglib uri="http://java.sun.com/jstl/fmt" prefix="fmt"%>

<%@ taglib uri="http://java.sun.com/portlet" prefix="portlet"%>
<%@ page language="java" contentType="text/html; charset=ISO-8859-1"
        pageEncoding="ISO-8859-1" session="false"%>

<fmt:setBundle basename="com.examscam.nl.i18nportlet"/>

<portlet:defineObjects />

<!-- Pull the view.message from the appropriate language bundle -->

<fmt:message key="view.poemtitle"/>
```

When the portlet runs on the server, a Spanish user will see Spanish text, and a French user will see French text.

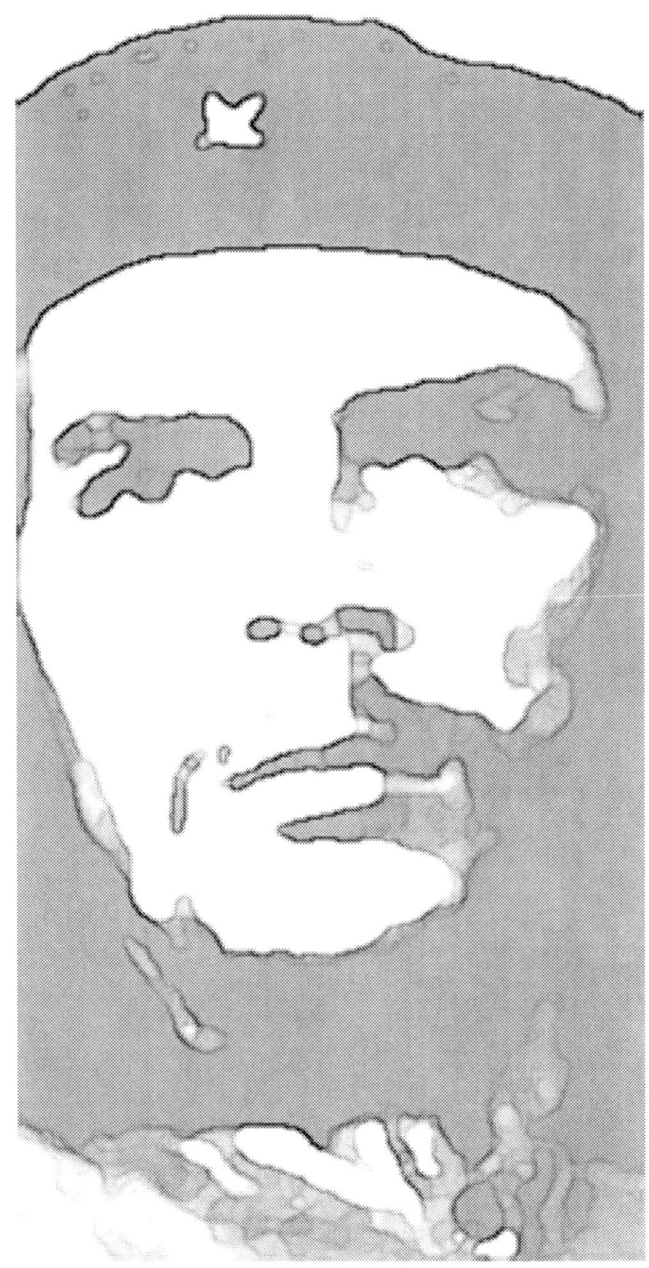

Che Guevara taken by Alberto Korda, March 1960
"The Most Famous Photograph in the World"

Che

They Killed Che.

They cut off his hands,
They put a bullet in his chest,
They let him breathe his own blood.

Because he tried to help them,
We Killed Che.

Question 10-1

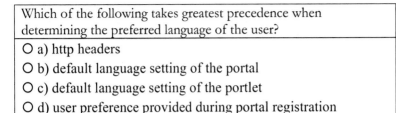

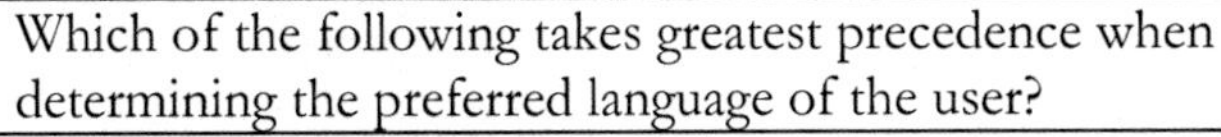
Which of the following takes greatest precedence when determining the preferred language of the user?

- O a) http headers
- O b) default language setting of the portal
- O c) default language setting of the portlet
- O d) user preference provided during portal registration

Question 10-2

A resource bundle named ***quizapp*** has been referenced within the resource-bundle tag in the web.xml file. What will the file containing French language translations be named?

- O a) quizapp_properties.fr
- O b) quizapp.properties_fr
- O c) quizapp.fr_properties
- O d) quizap_fr.properties

Question 10-3

Which tag library contains the fmt tags used for internationalizing a portlet application?

- O a) JetSpeed Standard Tag Library (JSTL)
- O b) JSR-168 Standard Tag Library (JSTL)
- O c) Java Standard Tag Library API (JSTL)
- O d) JetSpeed2 Standard Tag Library API (JSTL2)

Answer 10-1

Which of the following takes greatest precedence when determining the preferred language of the user?
O a) http headers O b) default language setting of the portal O c) default language setting of the portlet O d) user preference provided during portal registration
Option d) is correct. When a user registers with the portal, they are typically asked their preferred language of correspondence. This setting takes precedence over all other language settings used by the portal. Of course, this does assume that the user has logged in. Without logging in, the portal must decipher the user's preferred language through http headers, individual portlet settings, or through an overall language setting of the portal.

Answer 10-2

A resource bundle named ***quizapp*** has been referenced within the resource-bundle tag in the web.xml file. What will the file containing French language translations be named?
O a) quizapp_properties.fr O b) quizapp.properties_fr O c) quizapp.fr_properties O d) quizap_fr.properties
Option d) is correct. A common problem in getting i18n to work, is simply naming your resource bundles properly. Option d) takes the root name of the resource bundle, follows the root name with an underscore and a language code, and then provides the .properties extension. This is the proper way to name an internationalized resource bundle file.

Answer 10-3

Which tag library contains the fmt tags used for internationalizing a portlet application?

- ○ a) JetSpeed Standard Tag Library (JSTL)
- ○ b) JSR-168 Standard Tag Library (JSTL)
- ○ c) Java Standard Tag Library API (JSTL)
- ○ d) JetSpeed2 Standard Tag Library API (JSTL2)

Option d) is correct.

Many custom tag libraries provide i18n support, but the universally accepted mechanism for internationalizing your applications is to use the Java Standard Tag Library, JSTL, for providing the ability to pull language appropriate text strings from property files.

-

Complicating Things With Portlet Frameworks

Portlet Frameworks
A Word from the Author

A Word From The Author:

Now, when I first decided to write this book, I decided that I wanted to write a ***simple***, ***straight forward*** book that deals with the JSR-168 Portlet API, and ***nothing else***.

I decided that I was going to adhere very strictly to documenting and explaining the objects and types defined by the JSR-168 Portlet API, and I wasn't going to diverge from that path. I've seen so many books over the years try to tackle the topic of portlet development, and then get sidetracked by delving into peripheral technologies such as Maven, Velocity, JetSpeed2 administration, and the like. I promised myself, and for that matter, you the reader, that I wasn't going to do that. I wasn't going to confuse the reader by going on wild tangents and covering things that weren't directly related to JSR-168 portlet development. Well, like every other promise I've every made to myself, I'm going to break it by delving into the topics of JSF and struts, portlet framework development.

As I thought about it, I really came to the conclusion that it would be a disservice to the reader *not* to deal with the two most pervasive portlet development frameworks around, so I've thrown in the towel, and very reluctantly, and against my better judgment, added in two very important, and potentially overwhelming chapters, on Struts and JSF portlet development.

I'm going to take on the two most common frameworks, the struts framework, and the JSF portlet framework, and explain how to create a simple, JSR168 compliant portlets, that works properly the JSR168 compliant JetSpeed2 portal server.

It should be noted, no, ***must*** be noted, that there are definite nuances between various portal vendors, and certain parameters need to be tweaked to get the struts and JSF bridges to work properly in different portal environments. The portal bridge page at apache will provide information on any vendor specific configurations or tweaks that need to b made. Furthermore, I know that the IBM struts and JSF portlet frameworks, while similar, use a special set of tested and highly reliable bridges that are provided by IBM. Again, there are nuances between vendors. If you run into problems, and you are not deploying to JetSpeed2, check your portal server's documentation.

Also, it should be noted that this is not a full fledged tutorial on how to develop applications using struts or JSF. Struts and JSF are huge topics in and of themselves, and understanding application development with struts, or JSF, is a book in itself. These tutorials can only demonstrate the most basic aspects of developing a JSR168 compliant, struts or JSF portlet, that will work properly in the JetSpeed2 portal. A full fledged tutorial on JSF or struts will be left to someone much more intelligent and better looking than me.

Chapter 11
The Struts Portlet

Portal Frameworks

So far, the portlets we have looked at have been relatively stateless. Our portlets might take a small piece of data from a user, and display back a response, but none of the portlets we have developed incorporate multiple pages, that must be completed in a step by step manner.

What happens when we need a *wizard-type* of application that requires the user to fill out multiple forms in a specific sequence or order? The portlet API, not to mention the portal as a whole, doesn't really provide any built in facilities for developing a wizard-like, multi-state, multi-page application, yet these types of apps are quite common in a typical enterprise environment.

Creating 'Wizard Type' Portlet Applications

Imagine a web based application such as an online exam, where a user can select a topic on which to be examined, a user can start an exam, can finish an exam, and can even jump between different questions while an exam is in progress. An application like this would incorporate many different presentation pages. An exam application like this would also incorporate several different application states, such as an examinprogressstate, examgradedstate, topicselectedstate and topicnotselectedstate.

Depending upon which state a user is in, only certain page transitions would be legal, and it would be the job of the developer to ensure that any illegal page transition didn't mess up the user's application. How do we perform complex state management such as this in a portlet application?

Form Handling and Error Validation

Furthermore, if we are developing an application that takes a great deal of input from the user, how do we handle input-form validation? And if a user indeed provides bad data, what type of framework are we going to use to provide internationalized error messages back to the user? The portal API doesn't provide any built in facilities for implementing form handling, or for delivering helpful error messages back to the user.

Fortunately though, there are a number of different frameworks on the market with built-in facilities for managing things such as complex application state, multi-page navigation, error handling and input validation. The most pervasive application development frameworks in the Java arena are Struts and Java Server Faces (JSF). For developers who want to create complex portlet applications, not to mention those who want to port existing Struts and JSF applications to the portal, a variety of bridges exist to make it possible to create JSR-168 compliant Struts and JSF portlet applications.

The Rock- Paper-Scissors Struts Portlet

To help demonstrate the struts portlet framework, we'll recreate the old Rock-Paper-Scissors challenge. Of course, we'll always choose rock, because rock *rocks*. When the user chooses rock as well, it's a tie; if the user chooses paper, they win; and if the user chooses scissors, they lose.

Figure 11-1 shows what the landing page of our portlet will look like, and the three potential outcomes of the game.

Figure 11-1

We will use the Rock-Paper-Scissors challenge to guide us through the creation of the struts portlet.

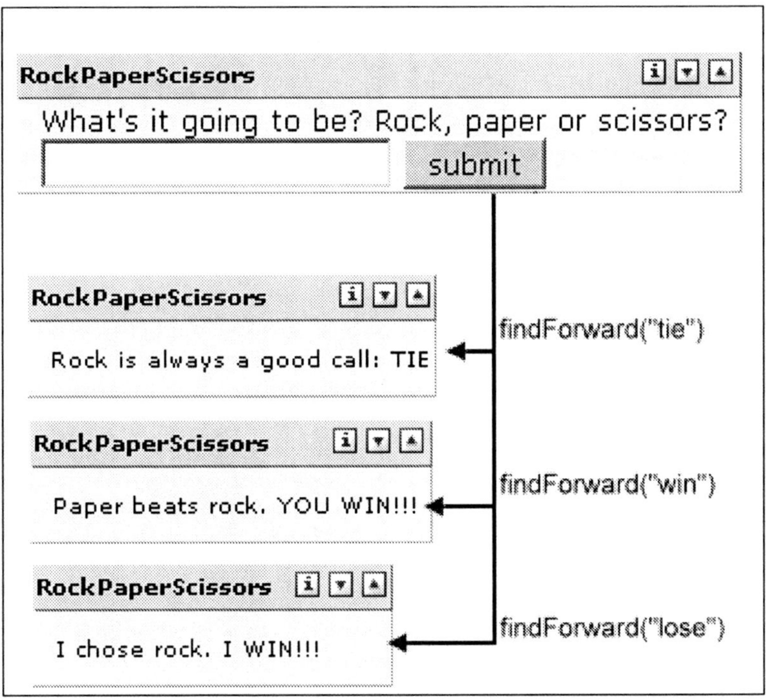

First Step

The first step in developing a struts portlet is to create an empty portlet project, with the proper folder structure needed for a regular JSR168 portlet app. From there, you must download the required JAR files that are needed to get a JSR168 struts portlet to work. The following jar files must be downloaded from apache, and added to the lib directory of the portlet application:

- commons-beanutils-1.7.0.jar
- commons-digester-1.6.jar
- commons-fileupload-1.0.jar
- commons-logging-1.0.4.jar
- commons-validator-1.1.4.jar
- log4j-1.2.8.jar
- **portals-bridges-struts-1.2.7-1.0.jar**
- standard-1.0.6.jar
- struts-1.2.7.jar
- struts-el-1.2.7.jar

Step Two: Edit portlet.xml File

After adding the required JAR files to the lib directory, the portlet.xml file must be edited to define a portlet that uses the struts bridge.

```
<?xml version="1.0" encoding="UTF-8"?>
 <portlet-app
xmlns="http://java.sun.com/xml/ns/portlet/portlet-app_1_0.xsd"
version="1.0" xmlns:xsi="http://www.w3.org/2001/XMLSchema-instance"
xsi:schemaLocation="http://java.sun.com/xml/ns/portlet/portlet-app_1_0.xsd http://java.sun.com/xml/ns/portlet/portlet-app_1_0.xsd"
 id="RockPaperScissorsStrutsPortlet.1c7992b209">

  <portlet id="RockPaperScissorsStrutsPortlet2.id9">
  <description>RockPaperScissors</description>
  <portlet-name>RockPaperScissors</portlet-name>
  <display-name>RockPaperScissors</display-name>
  <portlet-class>
    org.apache.portals.bridges.struts.StrutsPortlet
  </portlet-class>
  <init-param>
    <name>ServletContextProvider</name>
    <value>
     org.apache.jetspeed.portlet.ServletContextProviderImpl
    </value>
  </init-param>
  <init-param>
    <name>ViewPage</name>
    <value>/index.mcnz</value>
  </init-param>
<!-- You can optionally add additional portlet modes
  <init-param>
    <name>HelpPage</name><value>/help.mcnz</value>
  </init-param>  end of commented out help mode -->

  <expiration-cache>-1</expiration-cache>
  <supports>
    <mime-type>text/html</mime-type>
    <portlet-mode>VIEW</portlet-mode>
    <portlet-mode>HELP</portlet-mode>
  </supports>
  <portlet-info>
    <title>RockPaperScissors</title>
    <keywords>Struts</keywords>
  </portlet-info>
 </portlet>
</portlet-app>
```

Step Three: Edit the web.xml File

After editing the portlet.xml file, the web.xml file must be made aware of the PortletServlet, which is essentially the bytecode embodiment of the JSR-168 Struts Portlet bridge.

Typical portlet applications don't edit the web.xml file too often, but this is a total requirement to get the struts framework to run within a JSR-168 compliant portlet.

```
<?xml version="1.0" encoding="UTF-8"?>
<!DOCTYPE web-app PUBLIC "-//Sun Microsystems, Inc.//DTD Web Application 2.3//EN" http://java.sun.com/dtd/web-app_2_3.dtd >
 <web-app id="WebApp_ID_0077">
  <display-name>RockPaperScissors</display-name>
  <description>RockPaperScissors</description>
  <servlet>
    <servlet-name>action</servlet-name>
    <servlet-class>
      org.apache.portals.bridges.struts.PortletServlet
    </servlet-class>
    <init-param>
      <param-name>config</param-name>
      <param-value>/WEB-INF/struts-config.xml</param-value>
    </init-param>
    <init-param>
      <param-name>debug</param-name>
      <param-value>2</param-value>
    </init-param>
    <init-param>
      <param-name>detail</param-name>
      <param-value>2</param-value>
    </init-param>
    <load-on-startup>2</load-on-startup>
  </servlet>
  <servlet-mapping>
    <servlet-name>action</servlet-name>
    <url-pattern>*.mcnz</url-pattern>
  </servlet-mapping>
  <session-config>
    <session-timeout>30</session-timeout>
  </session-config>
  <welcome-file-list>
      <welcome-file>index.html</welcome-file>
  </welcome-file-list>
</web-app>
```

Step Four: Create the Landing Page

Every portlet must support the view mode, and the struts portlet is no exception. The page we create, that is by default, displayed when the portal in view mode, can be referred to as the *landing page*. Since we are modeling the old rock, paper, scissors game, our landing page will contain a form that asks the user to type in one of three words: *rock*, *paper* or *scissors*.

```
<%@ page contentType="text/html"%>
<%@ taglib
  uri="http://portals.apache.org/bridges/struts/tags-portlet-html"
  prefix="html"
%>
<TABLE border=0 cellSpacing=0 width="100%">
  <TR>
    <TD vAlign=top width=100%>

    <html:form action="rpsaction">
     What's it going to be? Rock, paper or scissors?
    <html:text property="rpschoice"></html:text>
    <input type="submit" name="submit" value="submit">
    </html:form>

    </TD>
  </TR>
</TABLE>
```

You should notice two things right away about this example. First, the HTML uses custom tags for defining all of the form elements, including: the form itself, the textfield and the submit button. These custom tags are part of the Struts library, and help with both the implementation of the view layer, and the process of communicating input data back to the control layer of the application. Struts works very tightly with a model-view-controller philosophy.

Secondly, you should notice that the taglib directive references the struts-portal custom tag library. For *struts* programmers, this is unique, as it is not a reference to the standard struts custom tags. For *portlet* developers, this is different, as it is not a reference to the portletAPI custom tag library. This set of custom tags is based primarily on the struts API, and the custom tags traditionally afforded to a regular struts application, although they have been tweaked a little to support the JSR-168 portlet specification.

Creating the struts-config.xml File

You will notice that while the web.xml and portlet.xml file had a number of entries that references resources packaged in the various JAR files downloaded from apache.org, there was no reference to any resources that the developer will *code* to implement their custom application. This is because, in a struts application, all of the information about how the developer's application works is configured in the appropriately named, struts-config.xml file.

The struts-config.xml file resides in the same folder as the portlet.xml and web.xml files, which is the \WEB-INF folder, off the root of the war file.

```
<?xml version="1.0" encoding="ISO-8859-1" ?>
<!DOCTYPE struts-config PUBLIC
"-//Apache Software Foundation//DTD Struts Configuration 1.1//EN"
http://jakarta.apache.org/struts/dtds/struts-config_1_1.dtd >

 <struts-config>

 <action-mappings>
  <action path="/index" include="/index.jsp" />
 </action-mappings>

 <controller
   pagePattern="$M$P" inputForward="false"
   processorClass=
   "org.apache.portals.bridges.struts.PortletRequestProcessor"
 />

</struts-config>
```

There are two important things to note about the content of the struts-config.xml file. First, is the action mapping from /index to /index.jsp. The /index action mapping is used by the view mode of a struts portlet to display content when the portlet is first rendered. We have this action mapped to our landing page, index.jsp.

```
<action path="/index" include="/index.jsp" />
```

Furthermore, the second, more innocuous entry in the struts-config.xml file, is the reference to the PortletRequestProcessor as the *controller* for the application. This entry can usually be left alone, although it should be noted that different vendors may provide their own controller. Furthermore, in the past, when struts portlet applications misbehaved, such as having the action processing phase being invoked twice or something, sometimes this particular class has to be upgraded or changed. For the most part though, this entry can be left alone.

Adding the DynaActionForm Entry

One of the compelling features of struts, is the built-in ability of the framework to both validate client input, and pass that input to the controller part of the application. The component used to pass form input data from the client view to the server side struts controller, is known as an ActionForm object. Complex input validation can be coded into a class that inherits from ActionForm, and subsequently gets called when client input is submitted to the server.

```
<form-beans>
<form-bean name="rpsform"
 type="org.apache.struts.action.DynaActionForm">
 <form-property name="rpschoice" type="java.lang.String" />
</form-bean>
</form-beans>
```

Alternatively, rather than sub-classing ActionForm, an entry can be made in the struts-config.xml file that defines a dynamic form. This dynamic form object, or DynaActionForm, as it is officially called, is created on the fly by the struts framework, and will be used to magically pass the data entered by the user on the client side, to the struts action components running on the serverside. For our application, we will map the textfield on our landing page, which is named **rpschoice**, to a dynaform entry named **rpsform**, which encapsulates the data entered into the rpschoice textfield.

Here is how our struts-config.xml file is progressing:

```
<?xml version="1.0" encoding="ISO-8859-1" ?>
<!DOCTYPE struts-config PUBLIC
"-//Apache Software Foundation//DTD Struts Configuration 1.1//EN"
http://jakarta.apache.org/struts/dtds/struts-config_1_1.dtd >
<struts-config>
  <form-beans>
    <form-bean name="rpsform"
     type="org.apache.struts.action.DynaActionForm">
        <form-property name="rpschoice"
         type="java.lang.String" />
    </form-bean>
  </form-beans>
  <action-mappings>
    <action path="/index" include="/index.jsp" />
  </action-mappings>
  <controller
    pagePattern="$M$P" inputForward="false"
    processorClass=
     "org.apache.portals.bridges.struts.PortletRequestProcessor"
  />
</struts-config>
```

Create the Results Pages

Since this is the rock, paper, scissors game we are emulating, there will be three potential outcomes: win, lose or tie. While it might not be the most efficient application design, in an attempt to emphasize the ability struts provides for managing multi-page applications, we will create three separate JSP pages, one for each of the potential outcomes: win.jsp, lose.jsp, and tie.jsp. These will be simple pages that simply say ***You win!***, ***You lose!***, or ***We tied!***

win.jsp

```
<%@ taglib
uri="http://portals.apache.org/bridges/struts/tags-portlet-html"
prefix="html" %>

<%@ page  contentType="text/html"%>


<P>Paper beats rock. YOU WIN!!!</P>
```

lose.jsp

```
<%@ taglib
uri="http://portals.apache.org/bridges/struts/tags-portlet-html"
prefix="html" %>

<%@ page  contentType="text/html"%>

<P>I chose rock. I WIN!!!</P>
```

tie.jsp

```
<%@ taglib
uri="http://portals.apache.org/bridges/struts/tags-portlet-html"
prefix="html" %>
<%@ page  contentType="text/html"%>


<P>Rock is always a good call: TIE</P>
```

Debriefing the Results Pages

The win.jsp, lose.jsp and tie.jsp pages are all relatively straight forward. They include a reference to the struts-portlet custom tag library, although none of them actually use the struts-portlet tags.

Defining the Action Class in struts-config.xml

As you have probably gathered, the struts-config.xml file is pretty pivotal when it comes to developing a struts application. Within the struts-config.xml file, we have already defined the controlling request processor, an /index path, which represents the landing page of our portlet, and a form-bean object, which will be used to marshal input data back and forth between the client and our server side application. The only thing we are missing is an entry for the action class we are about to code, which will implement the control and flow logic for our application.

We are going to code logic into a custom struts action class called RockPaperScissorsAction, which will be found in the package com.examscam.portlet.action. This action will be invoked by the index.jsp file, and when it is invoked, it will be passed an instance of our form bean, the rpsform, which encapsulates the client input in a field named rpschoice. Furthermore, there will be three possible outcomes from invoking this action, namely win, lose, or tie, which map to the correspondingly named JSP pages win.jsp, lose.jsp and tie.jsp. All of this information must be captured in the struts-config.xml file, as so:

```
<action path="/rpsaction"
  type="com.examscam.portlet.action.RockPaperScissorsAction"
  name="rpsform" scope="request" validate="false"
  input="index.jsp">

  <forward name="win" path="/win.jsp" redirect="true" />
  <forward name="lose" path="/lose.jsp" redirect="true" />
  <forward name="tie" path="/tie.jsp" redirect="true" />

</action>
```

The Completed struts-config.xml File

```
<?xml version="1.0" encoding="ISO-8859-1" ?>
<!DOCTYPE struts-config PUBLIC
"-//Apache Software Foundation//DTD Struts Configuration 1.1//EN"
http://jakarta.apache.org/struts/dtds/struts-config_1_1.dtd >
<struts-config>

  <form-beans>
    <form-bean name="rpsform"
     type="org.apache.struts.action.DynaActionForm">
        <form-property name="rpschoice"
         type="java.lang.String" />
    </form-bean>
  </form-beans>

  <action-mappings>

  <action path="/rpsaction"
   type="com.examscam.portlet.action.RockPaperScissorsAction"
   name="rpsform" scope="request" validate="false"
   input="index.jsp">

   <forward name="win" path="/win.jsp" redirect="true" />
   <forward name="lose" path="/lose.jsp" redirect="true" />
   <forward name="tie" path="/tie.jsp" redirect="true" />

  </action>

  <action path="/index" include="/index.jsp" />

  </action-mappings>

  <controller
   pagePattern="$M$P" inputForward="false"
   processorClass=
    "org.apache.portals.bridges.struts.PortletRequestProcessor"
  />

</struts-config>
```

Creating the Struts Action Class

All of the required entries have been made to the struts-config.xml file, and all of our JSP pages have been created. Now it's time to code the struts Action class.

In struts, the control logic goes into action classes, which inherit from the special struts class, appropriately named, Action. In this action class, we code a very special method called execute, which not only gets passed the standard request and response objects, but more interestingly, it gets passed the ActionForm that encapsulates any data that has been sent to the server by the client, along with another special object called the *ActionMapping* object, which can read the various forward entries in the struts-config.xml file, and subsequently generate an ActionForward object. The job of the execute method is to figure out where to send the client next; correspondingly, the return type of the execute method is a special struts class called an *ActionForward.*

Please, Cut Me Some Slack!!!

If you're new to struts, this is all probably pretty overwhelming. I want to emphasize that ***struts is an entire book on its own***, and I'm trying to fit the pertinent parts into a small chapter. If you are doing struts development, you really owe it to yourself to pick up a book that explains the technology in greater detail. Better yet, find someone on your team that might be able to walk you through this tutorial and point out some of the finer points of struts development. Please don't judge this book on this short chapter on the struts framework. ☺

```
package com.examscam.portlet.action;
import javax.servlet.http.*;
import org.apache.struts.action.*;
public class RockPaperScissorsAction extends Action
{
 public ActionForward execute(ActionMapping mapping,
                        ActionForm form,
                          HttpServletRequest request,
                             HttpServletResponse response)
                                        throws Exception {

    ActionForward forward = new ActionForward();
    DynaActionForm choiceForm = (DynaActionForm)form;

    try {
    /* Use the DynaActionForm to find get the form input*/
      String choice = (String)choiceForm.get("rpschoice");
    /* Given the users choice,forward to the appropriate view page*/
      if (choice.equalsIgnoreCase("rock")){
        forward = mapping.findForward("tie");
      }
      if (choice.equalsIgnoreCase ("paper")){
        forward = mapping.findForward("lose");
      }
      if (choice.equalsIgnoreCase ("scissors")){
        forward = mapping.findForward("win");
      }

    /* Be lazy, and just send to win if there is a problem. */
     } catch (Exception e) {
      System.out.println(e.getMessage()+e.getClass());
      forward = mapping.findForward("win");
    }

  /* the end of a struts action forwards to a view page*/
  return (forward);
 }

}
```

Adding the struts-portlet-config.xml File

One place a struts portlet differs from a regular struts application is with the requirement for a special configuration file named struts-portlet-config.xml. This file goes along side the struts-config.xml file and the portlet.xml and web.xml deployment descriptors in the WEB-INF folder. Essentially, every custom action mapping that appears in the struts-config.xml file should have a corresponding entry in the struts-portlet-config.xml file.

```
<?xml version="1.0" encoding="UTF-8"?>
<config>
  <portlet-url-type>
    <action path="/rpsaction" />
  </portlet-url-type>
</config>
```

Package and Deploy!

Once the struts-portlet-config.xml file is successfully added, you are now ready to package your portlet application in a war file, and deploy the war to the portal server.

Again, this particular tutorial demonstrates how to build a struts portlet that can be deployed to a JetSpeed2 portal server. Each platform has its own nuances, and this particular portlet may not run on every portal platform. If you're not developing on JetSpeed2, this tutorial will help to point you in the right direction, but you should definitely check your vendor's documentation with regards to how to tweak the apache bridge, or the struts framework as a whole, to get the struts framework to run in your environment.

Question 11-1

Which of the following files require a reference to the StrutsPortlet, from the apache-bridges project?
O a) web.xml
O b) portlet.xml
O c) struts-config.xml
O d) index.jsp

Question 11-2

Which of the following files would you not find in a typical struts or portlet application?
O a) web.xml
O b) portlet.xml
O c) struts-config.xml
O d) struts-portlet-config.xml

Question 11-3

What is the extension of a packaged struts portlet?
O a) .war
O b) .do
O c) .mcnz
O d) .jar

Answer 11-1

Which of the following files require a reference to the StrutsPortlet, from the apache-bridges project?
O a) web.xml O b) portlet.xml O c) struts-config.xml O d) index.jsp
Option b) is correct. The StrutsPortlet replaces the reference to the custom coded class that the developer typically creates. This class is provided through the apache portals bridges project. For a struts portlet to behave properly, there must also be a reference to the PortletServlet in the web.xml file.

Answer 11-2

Which of the following files would you not find in a typical struts or portlet application?
O a) web.xml O b) portlet.xml O c) struts-config.xml O d) struts-portlet-config.xml
Option d) is correct. The web.xml file is common to all Servlet and JSP based applications, while the portlet.xml file is common to all portlet based applications. The struts-config.xml file is the standard configuration file used in all struts applications. Of the four files provided, only the struts-portlet-config.xml file is unique to a struts portlet.

Answer 11-3

What is the extension of a packaged struts portlet?
O a) .war O b) .do O c) .mcnz O d) .jar
Option a) is correct. While there may be quite a bit going on in a struts portlet, at the most fundamental level, a struts portlet is just another portlet that gets deployed to a portal server as a web application archive, or WAR file.

Chapter 12
JSF Portlet Development

A discussion of JSR-168 portlet development wouldn't be complete without a discussion of how to leverage the Java Server Faces (JSF) development framework within the confines of a JSR-168 portlet.

Like struts, JSF is a highly pervasive, model-view-controller (MVC) framework for developing web based applications. JSF not only incorporates a number of important design patterns and development best practices, but it also provides facilities for managing many of those difficult challenges that typically stare down web based developers, such as managing application state, providing input validation, and providing feedback to a user when an error has occurred.

A JSF portlet application begins with the same basic structure as any other portlet application, with a WEB-INF folder that contains both a web.xml and portlet.xml file, and a \WEB-INF\lib folder containing all of the required JAR files.

Acquiring the Required JAR Files

A JSF portlet application requires a number of supporting JAR files to work. Some of these JAR files are required for developing against the basic JSF framework, whereas others provide common JSF extensions. Furthermore, the portals-bridges-jsf-1.0.jar actually contains the JSF-portal bridge that allows a JSF application to be ported to a portlet environment.

The following JAR files should be added to the lib directory of the JSF portlet application:

- commons-beanutils-1.6.1.jar
- commons-codec-1.2.jar
- commons-collections-2.1.jar
- commons-digester-1.5.jar
- commons-el-1.0.jar
- commons-logging-1.0.4.jar
- log4j-1.2.8.jar
- myfaces-api-1.1.0.jar
- myfaces-impl-1.1.0.jar
- **portals-bridges-jsf-1.0.jar**
- tomahawk-1.1.0.jar

Updating the web.xml File

A standard JSF application requires a number of entries to be made to the web.xml file, including a number of context parameters, the definition of the JSF FacesServlet, and the mapping of the FacesServlet to *.faces.

One of the things you should notice about the web.xml file of a JSF-Portlet application is the fact that there aren't any references to portlet packages, not even for the definition of the FacesServlet, **javax.faces.webapp.FacesServlet.** One of the compelling reasons for using JSF, especially in a portlet environment, is the fact that JSF is extremely portlet friendly, much more so than struts, and for the most part, relatively few changes need to be made to get an existing portlet application to run inside of the portal.

```
<?xml version="1.0" encoding="UTF-8"?>
<web-app id="WebApp_ID" version="2.4"
xmlns="http://java.sun.com/xml/ns/j2ee"
xmlns:xsi="http://www.w3.org/2001/XMLSchema-instance"
xsi:schemaLocation="http://java.sun.com/xml/ns/j2ee
http://java.sun.com/xml/ns/j2ee/web-app_2_4.xsd">
<servlet>
  <servlet-name>Faces Servlet</servlet-name>
  <servlet-class>
   javax.faces.webapp.FacesServlet
  </servlet-class>
  <load-on-startup>1</load-on-startup>
  </servlet>
  <servlet-mapping>
    <servlet-name>Faces Servlet</servlet-name>
    <url-pattern>*.faces</url-pattern>
  </servlet-mapping>
  <context-param>
    <param-name>javax.faces.CONFIG_FILES</param-name>
    <param-value>/WEB-INF/faces-config.xml</param-value>
  </context-param>
  <context-param>
    <param-name>javax.faces.STATE_SAVING_METHOD</param-name>
    <param-value>client</param-value>
  </context-param>
  <context-param>
    <param-name>
    org.apache.myfaces.ALLOW_JAVASCRIPT
    </param-name>
    <param-value>true</param-value>
  </context-param>
  <context-param>
    <param-name>org.apache.myfaces.PRETTY_HTML</param-name>
    <param-value>true</param-value>
  </context-param>
  <context-param>
    <param-name>
    org.apache.myfaces.DETECT_JAVASCRIPT</param-name>
    <param-value>false</param-value>
  </context-param>
  <context-param>
    <param-name>org.apache.myfaces.AUTO_SCROLL</param-name>
    <param-value>true</param-value>
  </context-param>
<!--continued on next page -->
```

```
<!--continued from previous page -->
  <listener>
    <listener-class>
    org.apache.myfaces.webapp.StartupServletContextListener
    </listener-class>
  </listener>
  <welcome-file-list>
    <welcome-file>index.jsp</welcome-file>
</welcome-file-list>
</web-app>
```

The JSF Configuration File

In my opinion, the most elegant aspect of JSF development is the manner in which the crucial elements of page navigation are tied together in the JSF configuration file, faces-config.xml

For example, in our Rock-Paper-Scissors example, we will have a landing page, named ***index.jsp***, that contains an input form that is used to take data from the user. User input will be delivered to a Java class that acts as a controller, and the controller will decide which one of three jsp files, ***win.jsp***, ***lose.jsp*** or ***tie.jsp***, will be displayed back to the user. This is all elegantly detailed in the faces-config.xml file as follows:

```
<navigation-rule>

  <from-view-id>/index.jsp</from-view-id>

  <navigation-case>
    <from-outcome>win</from-outcome>
    <to-view-id>/win.jsp</to-view-id>
  </navigation-case>

  <navigation-case>
    <from-outcome>lose</from-outcome>
    <to-view-id>/lose.jsp</to-view-id>
  </navigation-case>

  <navigation-case>
    <from-outcome>tie</from-outcome>
    <to-view-id>/tie.jsp</to-view-id>
  </navigation-case>

</navigation-rule>
```

Managed Beans

The custom-coded, logic controller, that handles the client request and figures out which of the possible outcomes to which a client should be routed, also gets referenced in the faces-config.xml file.

We are going to code a Java controller, named **RockPaperScissorsController**, which we'll throw in the package com.examscam.rps.jsf. Here is how the faces-config.xml file entry for the RockPaperScissorsConroller will look:

```
<managed-bean>
  <managed-bean-name>rpscontroller</managed-bean-name>
  <managed-bean-class>
  com.examscam.rps.jsf.RockPaperScissorsController
  </managed-bean-class>
  <managed-bean-scope>request</managed-bean-scope>
</managed-bean>
```

The name, **rpscontroller**, is the name we will use when invoking this component from the HTML page. The JSF framework will then map the managed-bean-name back to the implementation class, RockPaperScissorsController.

The Full faces-config.xml File

There is undoubtedly a great deal of information that can be entered in the faces-config.xml file. However, we're going to keep this example as succinct and simple as possible. The following is the full faces-confg.xml file for this example. Remember, the faces-config.xml file must be placed in the \WEB-INF folder of the portlet application.

```
<?xml version="1.0"?><!DOCTYPE faces-config PUBLIC
  "-//Sun Microsystems, Inc.//DTD JavaServer Faces Config 1.0//EN"
  "http://java.sun.com/dtd/web-facesconfig_1_0.dtd">
<faces-config>

  <navigation-rule>
    <from-view-id>/index.jsp</from-view-id>
    <navigation-case>
      <from-outcome>win</from-outcome>
      <to-view-id>/win.jsp</to-view-id>
    </navigation-case>
    <navigation-case>
      <from-outcome>lose</from-outcome>
      <to-view-id>/lose.jsp</to-view-id>
    </navigation-case>
    <navigation-case>
      <from-outcome>tie</from-outcome>
      <to-view-id>/tie.jsp</to-view-id>
    </navigation-case>
  </navigation-rule>

  <managed-bean>
    <managed-bean-name>
      rpscontroller
    </managed-bean-name>
    <managed-bean-class>
    com.examscam.rps.jsf.RockPaperScissorsController
    </managed-bean-class>
    <managed-bean-scope>request</managed-bean-scope>
  </managed-bean>

</faces-config>
```

The Landing Page: index.jsp

The page that is first displayed by the JSF portlet, also known as the landing page, will be named index.jsp. This page uses the ***core*** and ***html*** JSF custom tag libraries to create a form that will take input from the user, and subsequently be submitted to the server.

```
<%@taglib uri="http://java.sun.com/jsf/core" prefix="f"%>
<%@taglib uri="http://java.sun.com/jsf/html" prefix="h"%>

<f:view>
<h:form id="rpsform">
Rock Paper or Scissors? <h:inputText id="rpschoice"/><BR>
<h:commandButton value="What will it be???"
action="#{rpscontroller.play}"/><BR>
</h:form>
</f:view>
```

Notice the id attribute of the form and the inputText field, ***rpsform*** and ***rpschoice***. To extract what the user has typed into the textfield associated with this form, we will use the call:

```
request.getParameter("rpsform:rpschoice");
```

Also noteworthy is the value of the action attribute, #{rpscontroller.play}. This is part of the JSF expression language, and in plain terms, it reads: when the submit button of the form is clicked, invoke the managed bean named rpscontroller, and call the play method of that bean. The name rpscontroller is mapped to the RockPaperScissorsController class in the faces-config.xml file. The RockPaperScissorsController is the Java class we will code that contains all of the control logic for the Rock-Paper-Scissors application.

```
<managed-bean>
  <managed-bean-name>rpscontroller</managed-bean-name>
  <managed-bean-class>
  com.examscam.rps.jsf.RockPaperScissorsController
  </managed-bean-class>
  <managed-bean-scope>request</managed-bean-scope>
</managed-bean>
```

The Managed Bean: RockPaperScissorsController

The faces-config.xml file refers to a *managed-bean* named RockPaperScissorsController. This is a custom coded class that implements the core logic of our application, or at least, the core logic associated with page navigation. A JSF application can have any number of managed beans associated with it. The more complicated the site, and the more numerous the number of page changes and state transitions, more managed beans will be required. Our simple application will use one, but this is more the exception, not the rule.

Unlike struts, where controllers must subclass the struts Action class, JSF controllers can be simple classes that inherit directly from java.lang.Object. Furthermore, the developer has the freedom to call their action, or control logic method, anything they want. In our case, we will create a class that extends java.lang.Object, with a simple controlling method called play().

```
package com.examscam.rps.jsf;
import javax.faces.context.*;
import javax.servlet.http.*;

public class RockPaperScissorsController {

  public String play() {
/*Implement logic here, and return a String, corresponding
to one of the from-outcome entries in the faces-config.xml
file, such as win,lose or tie.*/
  }
}
```

RockPaperScissors

Rock is always a good call: TIE

The key to coding your controller methods is the fact that they must return a String, and that String must map to a from-outcome entry in the faces-config.xml file. The three from-outcome entries available to our controller, according to the faces-config.xml file, are: win, lose and tie.

Request-Response Programming

Unlike the execute method of a struts action class, the ***doPost*** of a Servlet, or the ***doView*** method of a portlet, methods of a JSF managed-bean are not explicitly passed a request and response object. Instead, to access the request and response objects, a static call needs to be made to the FacesContext, which returns an ExternalContext. From the ExternalContext, you can access the important objects of the Servlet and JSP API, namely the HttpServletRequest, and the HttpServlerResponse.

```
✂✂✂
ExternalContext context =
    FacesContext.getCurrentInstance().getExternalContext();
HttpServletRequest request =
     (HttpServletRequest) context.getRequest();✂✂✂
```

Once we have the request object, we can figure out what the user typed into the form they just submitted, and send the user to the appropriate page:

```
✂✂✂
String result = null;
String choice = request.getParameter("rpsform:rpschoice");
/*we always chose ROCK*/
if (choice.equalsIgnoreCase("PAPER")){ result = "win";}
if (choice.equalsIgnoreCase("SCISSORS")){result = "lose";}
if (choice.equalsIgnoreCase("ROCK")){result = "tie";}
return result; ✂✂✂
```

Notice how the result maps to one of the three navigation-case elements in the faces-config.xml file.

```
<navigation-case>
  <from-outcome>win</from-outcome><to-view-id>/win.jsp</to-view-id>
</navigation-case>
<navigation-case>
  <from-outcome>lose</from-outcome><to-view-id>/lose.jsp</to-view-id>
</navigation-case>
<navigation-case>
  <from-outcome>tie</from-outcome><to-view-id>/tie.jsp</to-view-id>
</navigation-case>
```

It should be noted that if a null String is returned, the JSF framework simply redisplays the originating page to the user.

The Full RockPaperScissorsController

```
package com.examscam.rps.jsf;

import javax.faces.context.ExternalContext;
import javax.faces.context.FacesContext;
import javax.servlet.http.HttpServletRequest;

public class RockPaperScissorsController {

  public String play() {
  /*Gain access to the request object*/

  ExternalContext context =
       FacesContext.getCurrentInstance()
                       .getExternalContext();
  HttpServletRequest request =
     (HttpServletRequest)context.getRequest();

  String result = null;
  /*Grab the user's input from the form*/
  String choice =
     request.getParameter("rpsform:rpschoice");

  /* we always chose ROCK */
  if (choice.equalsIgnoreCase("PAPER")){
    result = "win";
  }
  if (choice.equalsIgnoreCase("SCISSORS")){
    result = "lose";
  }
  if (choice.equalsIgnoreCase("ROCK")){
    result = "tie";
  }
  /*return the navigation string to the JSF framework*/
  return result;
  }
}
```

The JSP Files

The *navigation-case* in the faces-config.xml file lists three JSP files, win.jsp, lose.jsp and tie.jsp, as possible outcomes. These three, simple JSP files, will be placed in the root of the portlet application, in the same directory as the WEB-INF folder.

```
<!-- win.jsp -->
<%@taglib uri="http://java.sun.com/jsf/core" prefix="f"%>
<%@taglib uri="http://java.sun.com/jsf/html" prefix="h"%>

<H1>You WIN!</H1>
<H2>Paper beats rock. You win! </H2>
```

```
<!-- lose.jsp -->
<%@taglib uri="http://java.sun.com/jsf/core" prefix="f"%>
<%@taglib uri="http://java.sun.com/jsf/html" prefix="h"%>

<H2>Rock beats scissors. You lose!!!</H2>
```

```
<!-- tie.jsp -->
<%@taglib uri="http://java.sun.com/jsf/core" prefix="f"%>
<%@taglib uri="http://java.sun.com/jsf/html" prefix="h"%>

<H2>Rock is always a good call: TIE</H2>
```

Each of the JSP files reference the html and core JSF tag libraries. Since no tags are actually being used in the JSP files, the declarations are not needed, but I threw them in to emphasize the fact that they are often used in a JSF application.

Moving to the Portlet World

Believe it or not, but so far, we've developed a completely valid, JSF application, that could run quite ruggedly in any standard Servlet and JSP container. We really haven't done anything portlet specific. This is actually the great thing about porting JSF applications to the portal world – there is very little configuration that needs to be done once the JSF application is working properly. To *portalize* a JSF application, the toughest part is creating the portlet.xml file.

```
<?xml version="1.0" encoding="UTF-8"?>
<portlet-app id="jsf-demo" version="1.0">
 <portlet>
  <description>JSF RPS Portlet</description>
  <portlet-name>JSF RPS Portlet</portlet-name>
  <display-name>JSF RPS Portlet</display-name>
  <portlet-class>
  org.apache.portals.bridges.jsf.FacesPortlet
  </portlet-class>
  <init-param>
    <name>ViewPage</name><value>/index.jsp</value>
  </init-param>
  <init-param>
    <name>HelpPage</name><value>/help.jsp</value>
  </init-param>
  <init-param>
    <name>EditPage</name><value>/edit.jsp</value>
  </init-param>
  <expiration-cache>-1</expiration-cache>
  <supports>
    <mime-type>text/html</mime-type>
    <portlet-mode>VIEW</portlet-mode>
    <portlet-mode>EDIT</portlet-mode>
    <portlet-mode>HELP</portlet-mode>
  </supports>
  <portlet-info>
    <title>JSF RPS Portlet</title>
  </portlet-info>
 </portlet>
</portlet-app>
```

Examining the JSF portlet.xml File

For the most part, the portlet.xml file associated with a JSF portlet is made up of all of the usual suspects, such as the name, description, title, etc. The key to the JSF portlet is the fact that the portlet-class entry maps to the JSF bridge from apache, or more specifically: **org.apache.portals.bridges.jsf.FacesPortlet**

```
<portlet-class>
org.apache.portals.bridges.jsf.FacesPortlet
</portlet-class>
```

The other unique part of the JSF portlet.xml file is the *init-param* elements. For each of the various portlet modes you want your JSF portlet to support, you define an init-param element, with the mode as the name element, and the page to be rendered by default when that mode is invoked, as the associated value. Since we want our landing page, index.jsp, to display when the portlet is initially displayed in the view mode, we specify /index.jsp as the value for the named parameter ViewPage.

```
<init-param>
  <name>ViewPage</name>
  <value>/index.jsp</value>
</init-param>
```

Multiple Modes with the JSF Portlet

The portlet.xml file allows you to specify any number of supported modes for the JSF portlet. To support multiple modes, simply make the required entries under the *support* tag, as you would with any portlet, and then add init-param entries for each of the supported modes, using HelpPage and EditPage as the named value for the name-value pair. The value in the pair should point to the landing page for the given mode.

```
<init-param>
  <name>HelpPage</name><value>/help.jsp</value>
</init-param>
<init-param>
  <name>EditPage</name><value>/edit.jsp</value>
</init-param>
```

The last thing our JSF portlet application needs is the JSF files that will act as landing pages for the help and edit modes:

```
<!-- The edit.jsp file -->
<%@taglib uri="http://java.sun.com/jsf/core" prefix="f"%>
<%@taglib uri="http://java.sun.com/jsf/html" prefix="h"%>

<P>This is the edit mode.
```

```
<!-- The help.jsp file -->
<%@taglib uri="http://java.sun.com/jsf/core" prefix="f"%>
<%@taglib uri="http://java.sun.com/jsf/html" prefix="h"%>

<P>This is the help mode.
```

Admittedly, the edit and help mode JSP files are pretty lame, but they do the job. Potentially, these pages could also take advantage of navigation and state management configured through a faces-config.xml file.

Question 12-1

Java Server Faces (JSF) is an API managed primarily by:
O a) apache
O b) struts
O c) Sun
O d) IBM

Question 12-2

Navigation rules are defined in which of the following files?
O a) web.xml
O b) portlet.xml
O c) faces-config.xml
O d) struts-config.xml

Question 12-3

Given a form named goodform, and an input field named badchoice, how would this field be retrieved through the getParameter method of the request object?
O a) goodform::badchoice
O b) badchoice::goodform
O c) goodform:badchoice
O d) badchoice:goodform

Answer 12-1

Java Server Faces (JSF) is an API managed primarily by:
O a) apache O b) struts O c) Sun O d) IBM
Option c) is correct. While the open source community delivers some fantastic solutions, many people find great relief in the fact that JSF is supported and backed by the inventors of Java, Sun Microsystems.

Answer 12-2

Navigation rules are defined in which of the following files?
O a) web.xml O b) portlet.xml O c) faces-config.xml O d) struts-config.xml
Option c) is the correct answer. The key file for configuring and managing a JSF application, which includes many, potentially complex, navigation rules, is the faces-config.xml file.

Answer 12-3

Given a form named ***goodform***, and an input field named ***badchoice***, how would this field be retrieved through the getParameter method of the request object?
○ a) goodform::badchoice ○ b) badchoice::goodform ○ c) goodform:badchoice ○ d) badchoice:goodform
Option c) is correct. While there are several ways to obtain data from a JSF form, the most basic way is to reference the form, and then the name of the input field, with the two names separated by a colon.

Chapter 13
The Ajax Portlet

Portal page aggregation is a fairly resource intensive process. Just think about what goes on when the portal server has to render a page containing half a dozen portlets appearing on it. The portal not only has to invoke the doView method of every portlet on the page, but it must also validate the user's credentials and access rights, render a theme, invoke the action processing phase if an event has indeed been triggered, and then, just generally provide all of the services that the various portlets on the page need in order to be rendered propertly.

So, how can we deliver content to a user, through a portlet, or any web based, content delivery vehicle for that matter, without triggering the overhead of having to regenerate, and deliver, and entire web page back to the user? Short of going back to applet technology, small snippets of dynamic content can be easily delivered back to a web based clients by taking advantage of something called *Ajax* technology.

What is Ajax?

So, what is Ajax, or AJAX, as it should more accurately be called? I'm going to leave it to the Wiki to explain it:

*"**Ajax** (also known as **AJAX**), shorthand for "Asynchronous JavaScript and XML", is a development technique used for creating interactive web applications. The intent is to make web pages feel more responsive by exchanging small amounts of data with the server behind the scenes, so that the entire web page does not have to be reloaded each time the user requests a change. This is intended to increase the web page's interactivity, speed, functionality, and usability. Ajax is also usable on many operating systems and architectures as it's based on JavaScript and XML."*

The Magic Ajax Ball

So, Ajax is a neat technology that allows updates to go out to web based clients, without requiring an entire page to be delivered to, and re-rendered by, the client. If you appreciate the overhead in putting togther a portal page, having a technology that allows individual portlets to interact with a client, without having to rerender the entire page is a fabulous idea.

As a little example, I'm going to create a Magic Ajax Ball portlet. Essentially, the user will think up a question, like, *will I find love*, or *will my charges be dropped*, and the portlet will generate a response, such as *Without a doubt*, *It is decidedly so*, *or Better Not Tell You Now*. Basically, the user will click on a link that says ***seek guidance***, and a response will come back to the client, from the server, and be displayed in the portlet. Of course, this will all be accomplished using AJAX, so rather than the entire portal page being aggregated, and sent back to the client, only a small part of the page, the part where the response needs to be displayed, will be regenerated. You'll like AJAX; it's a really kewl, and really slick, technology.

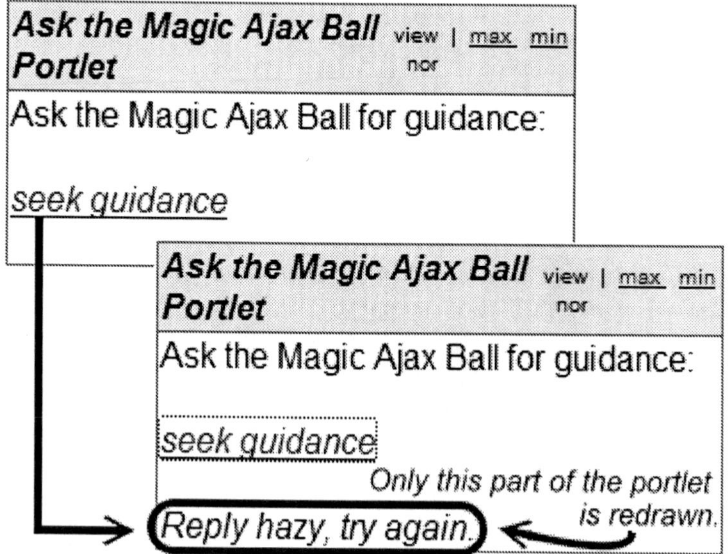

The guidance.jsp

The web based component that will be asynchronously invoked by the client will be a very simple JSP, that simply spits out one of ten response. The JSP will simply be called guidance.jsp, will be placed in the root of the war file, and will be coded like this:

```
<%!
/* Create an array of responses */

static String[] fortunes =
 {"<B>Better not tell you now.</B>",
  "<I>You may rely on it.</I>","<B><I>Yes.</I></B>",
  "<B>It is decidedly so.<B>","Concentrate and ask again.",
  "<U>My reply is no.</U>","Yes - definitely.",
  "Without a doubt.","<I>Reply hazy, try again.</I>"};

%>

<!--  display a response to the client  -->

<%=fortunes[(int)(System.currentTimeMillis()%fortunes.length)] %>
```

As you can see, the guidance.jsp simply defines an array of Strings, and randomly spits one of the Strings in the array back to the user. This will essentially make up the content displayed between the <SPAN> tags, named suggested_guidance, on the landing page of the portlet, index.jsp.

The MagicAjaxBallPortlet.java File

The code for the MagicAjaxBallPortlet class really isn't overly interesting. Basically, it just points to the landing page of the view mode of the portlet, which is quite uncreatively named index.jsp. It's in the index.jsp file where all of the really interesting stuff happens.

```
package com.examscam.portlet;

import java.io.*;
import javax.portlet.*;

public class MagicAjaxBallPortlet extends GenericPortlet {

  protected void doView
    (RenderRequest request, RenderResponse response)
                    throws PortletException, IOException {

    response.setContentType("text/html");
    String url = "/index.jsp";
    getPortletContext().getRequestDispatcher(url)
                              .include(request,response);

  }
}
```

The Landing Page: index.jsp

As far as Ajax and JavaScripting goes, all of the really interesting stuff happens inside of the landing page of the view mode, index.jsp.

When the index.jsp page initially appears, it simply displays a link to the user that says ***seek guidance,*** along with a little message prompting the user to think up a question to ask the Magic Ajax Ball.

```
<%@ page session="false" contentType="text/html" %>
<%@taglib uri="http://java.sun.com/portlet" prefix="portlet"%>
<portlet:defineObjects/>

Ask the Magic Ajax Ball for guidance: <BR/><BR>

<!-- clicking this link triggers the AJAX request -->

<A href="javascript:seekGuidance();">
<i>seek guidance</i>
</A>

<!-- where the AJAX response goes -->

<span id="suggested_guidance">
<!--  AJAX CONTENT GOES IN HERE!!!  -->
</span>

✂✂✂✂✂✂ <!-- more jsp content to follow --> ✂✂✂✂✂✂
```

Ask the Magic Ajax Ball Portlet view | max min nor

Ask the Magic Ajax Ball for guidance:

seek guidance

Portlets and JavaScript

Notice how the *seek guidance* link triggers a JavaScript method named seekGuidance(). It is this seekGuidance() method that sends a request to the server, for the content delivered through the guidance.jsp file. The returned data is then displayed between the open and closed span tags. The <SPAN> tags really are a key part to the whole delivery of content to the end user with Ajax.

✂✂✂

```
<span id="suggested_guidance">
<!—AJAX CONTENT GOES IN HERE!!!-->
</span>
```

✂✂✂

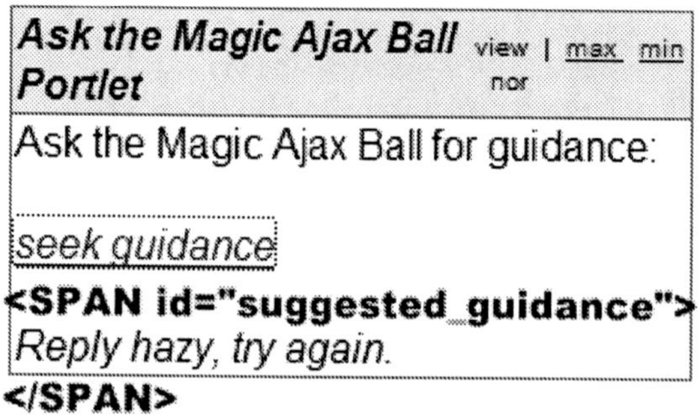

Ask the Magic Ajax Ball Portlet view | max min nor

Ask the Magic Ajax Ball for guidance:

seek guidance

<SPAN id="suggested_guidance">
Reply hazy, try again.
</SPAN>

Invoking the AJAX_RESOURCE

The key to invoking the guidance.jsp file from the the landing page is the funky JavaScript in the seekGuidance() method of the index.jsp file. Basically, in the seekGuidance() method, the XMLHttpRequest object, called receiveReq, opens a call to the AJAX_RESOURCE, which is really the encoded guidance.jsp file, which was defined as a global variable for the page.

```
var AJAX_RESOURCE =
 "<%=renderResponse.
       encodeURL(renderRequest.getContextPath())%>"
            + "/guidance.jsp";
```

Notice how the path to the guidance.jsp file must be encoded. This is one of those extra complexities we see with portlet applications that we don't have to deal with in typical Servlet and JSP applications. Still, a little extra code won't hurt us. We just code a reference to the encodedURL of the guidance.jsp file once, and then we can simply use the variable name AJAX_RESOURCE from there on in.

```
<!-- triggers the AJAX request -->
function seekGuidance() {
<!-- use a GET to call the guidance.jsp file on the server -->
  receiveReq.open("GET", AJAX_RESOURCE, true);
<!-- tell the XMLHttpRequest what to do when a response comes in -->
  receiveReq.onreadystatechange = handleSeekGuidance;
<!-- Request the resource from the server.  -->
  receiveReq.send(null);
}
```

So, if the seekGuidance() method makes a request to the guidance.jsp file, the handleSeekGuidance() method handles the response that is returned. Basically, when a response is sent back to the XMLHttpRequest object, the handleSeekGuidance() method is invoked, which takes the textual content deliverd back to the XMLHttpRequest object from the server,

<SPAN id=”suggested_guidance>

and displays it within the open and closed span tags.

</SPAN>

```
<%@ page session="false" contentType="text/html" %>
<%@taglib uri="http://java.sun.com/portlet" prefix="portlet"%>
<portlet:defineObjects/>

Ask the Magic Ajax Ball for guidance:<BR/><BR/>
<!-- clicking this link triggers the AJAX request -->
<a href="javascript:seekGuidance();">
<i>seek guidance</i>  </a>  <BR/>  <BR/>
<!-- the AJAX response returned from the server, guidance.jsp-->

<span id="suggested_guidance"></span>

<SCRIPT language="JavaScript">

<!-- AJAX_RESOURCE points to the server side rendering component -->
var AJAX_RESOURCE =
 "<%=renderResponse.encodeURL(renderRequest.getContextPath())%>"
     + "/guidance.jsp";
var receiveReq = getXmlHttpRequestObject();

<!-- triggers the AJAX request -->
function seekGuidance() {
<!-- use a GET to call the guidance.jsp file on the server -->
  receiveReq.open("GET", AJAX_RESOURCE, true);
<!-- tell the XMLHttpRequest what to do when a response comes in -->
  receiveReq.onreadystatechange = handleSeekGuidance;
<!-- Request the resource from the server.  -->
  receiveReq.send(null);
}
<!-- This method is invoked when the XMLHttpRequest is updated -->
function handleSeekGuidance() {
  <!-- make sure the XMLHttpRequest is ready -->
  if (receiveReq.readyState == 4) {
<!--    change    the    contents    within    the    <span
id="suggested_guidance"></span> tags -->

  document.getElementById('suggested_guidance').innerHTML =
    receiveReq.responseText;
 }
}
<!-- Take into account the various browsers -->
function getXmlHttpRequestObject() {
  if (window.XMLHttpRequest) { <!--not IE -->
    return new XMLHttpRequest();
  } else if(window.ActiveXObject) { <!-- IE -->
    return new ActiveXObject("Microsoft.XMLHTTP");
  } else {
    alert("Your browser doesn't support Ajax!");
  }
}
</SCRIPT>
```

Broswer Checks and the XMLHttpRequest

Finally, the last method to mention is the getXmlHttpRequestObject() method. There's nothing overly tricky about this method – all it really does is initialize the receiveReq variable to a real, instantiated, XMLHttpRequest object. Different browsers initialize this object in differet ways, so this method makes sure the XMLHttpRequest object is appropriately initialized, regardless of whether the client is using Microsoft's Internet Explorer, or Mozilla's Firefox.

```
<!-- Take into account the various browsers -->
function getXmlHttpRequestObject() {
  if (window.XMLHttpRequest) { <!--not IE -->
    return new XMLHttpRequest();
  } else if(window.ActiveXObject) { <!-- IE -->
    return new ActiveXObject("Microsoft.XMLHTTP");
  } else {
    alert("Your browser doesn't support Ajax!");
  }
}
```

Working with Ajax

So, when you put it all together, Ajax is a pretty powerful technology for delivering dynamic content quickly to the client, without burdening the server with the task of aggregating and delivering an entire web page to the client.

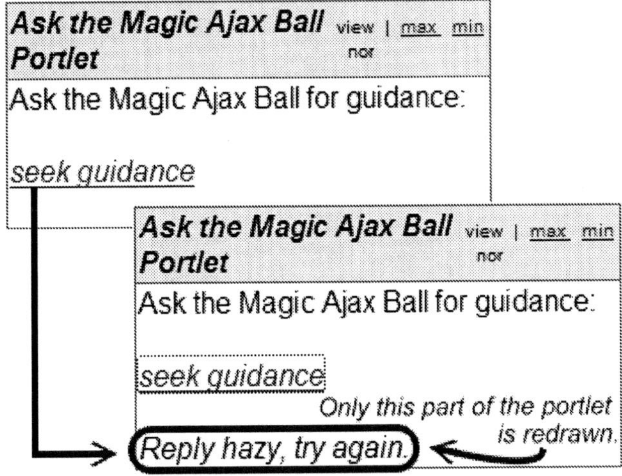

Chapter 14
Portlet Development Best Practices

So far, we've concentrated quite heavily on the JSR168 API, and how to create portlet applications that can be deployed to a JSR168 compliant portlet container. However, there's a big difference between ***how***, and ***how best,*** to develop a portlet application. As with any application, there are no right ways to develop, there are only ***wrong ways,*** and the best we can do is not come up with a ***wrong way***. This section will simply discuss a few best practices for coding, developing, and getting the most out of a JSR168 portal framework, and hopefully, help you avoid a wrong answer.

Don't Use PortletPreferences

Okay, telling you never to use PortletPreferences is a pretty over the top statement. There are actually good uses for PortletPreferences. My problem with PortletPreferences is the fact that the object is so overly used and abused in a typical development environment.

The PortletPreferences object provides the ability to store information persistently about how a client wants to use a particular portlet, on a particular page. For example, with the weather portlet, a user can provide postal code information to the portlet, and the portlet will store that information persistently using the PortletPreferences object. The next time the user visits the view mode of the portlet, the weather for that user's postal code will be displayed. Persistently storing this information, and tying the corresponding data to the user and the portlet, is all done behind the scenes for you by the portal framework. This all sounds good, right?

Well, let me ask you: *how does the portal server save PortletPreferences information?* Does it write it to the hard drive? Does it write it to a small, lightweight database like

Derby? Does it store it in 16 kilobyte blocks in a DB2 database? Well, the answer is, I don't know. How data is stored is completely up to the portal vendor, and the portlet developer, and for that matter, the database or portal administrator, has very little control over it. Go ask your database administrators what they think about having very little control over data. I have a feeling they won't like it; and neither should you.

Imagine you stored a true/false flag in PortletPreferences. I can guarantee you that PortletPreferences isn't storing that as a boolean value in a database. The information is probably being turned into character data, or a CLOB, or something very inefficient. If you wrote a little program to store that true/false flag in your own database, you could use a boolean datatype, and consume only one tiny bit of drive space, as opposed to the overhead of using some large and unwieldy character type.

Furthermore, how do you mine information stored to PortletPreferences? Imagine you had a little tax portlet, that estimated a user's tax burden, based on their income. Imagine you stored the user's income as a PortletPreference. How would you go back and mine that income data? If your boss comes to you and says "*You know how we keep track of a user's income in that tax portlet you created? Well, I'd like a list of all the users with income greater than $100,000 a year. Get it to me this afternoon.*" How are you going to do that?

If you don't know how the portal stores your PortletPreferences data, and you don't know how the portal ties a particular preference to a particular user, you're going to have a pretty hard time mining your own data. And in a world where information is power, you are giving up a lot of power when you hand your data over to the PortletPreferences object.

Now I'm not saying you should ***never***, ***ever*** use PortletPreferences. PortletPreferences are great when used for what they are intended – a simple, configurable, portlet ***preference***. If a user wants their portlet to have a pink background colour, then store that information in PortletPreferences. If a user wants a 14 point font, store that information in the PortletPreferences object. If the user wants to tell you where they live, or how much money they make, well, that's something I would really hesitate about storing as a PortletPreference.

When you store information in the PortletPreferences object, you are giving up control over where the data is stored, how the data is stored, and how easy it is to potentially mine that data in the future. That's a whole lot of control to be giving up.

Get Service Oriented

Don't try to do too much in your portlets. Behavior coded into one portlet is very difficult to reuse in another portlet. Instead, factor our useful and potentially common behavior into a service layer.

Portlets themselves should be fairly thin, and really focused on client side presentation. Making a portlet too complex can slow down the portal, and create a frustrating experience for the user.

When common and useful behavior is factored out into a service tier, the service layer can be accessed by many different portlets, workload managed, and updated in a much more controlled fashion.

Servlet and JSP Rules Apply

The Portlet API draws heavily from the Servlet and JSP API, so many of the rules pertaining to JSP and Servlet development apply equally to Portlet Development.

Three rules of Servlet and JSP development that rarely get violated are 1. don't spawn new threads in a Servlet, 2. don't declare instance variables in a Servlet and 3, don't synchronize Servlet methods. These rules apply equally well to portlets.

The portal server is already threading client invocations. Spawning new threads will only wreak havoc on the portal server.

As far as instance variables go, there *are* times when they are appropriate, but those times usually involve extending the Servlet or Portal framework, as opposed to creating a portlet or servlet that corresponds to a business case. When you are tempted to place an instance variable in a portlet, think instead about how the various scopes, such as the PortletSession or the PortletContext, might be a more appropriate place to maintain the data.

Synchronizing methods is also a bad idea in a portlet. This can create a bottleneck in your applications. Move complex logic as far away from the portlet tier as possible, and if you really need to synchronize a method, synchronize it in that far away place, not in the portlet itself.

Use Good Variable Names

It annoys the life out of me when I go into a development shop, and see thousands of KLOCs hacked out, without a single variable name being more than four letters long. It also annoys the life out of me when people have abbreviated common words by removing the vowels, as if typing out an 'e' or an 'o' is going to be the difference between making a deadline, or being out of a job. Application development is not an episode of Wheel of Fortune. You do not have to spin for a letter, and you do not have to pay $500 for a vowel.

And reading code shouldn't be a fun game of trying to figure out the meaning of an obscure, personalized license plate. The variable name ***h8s10s*** shouldn't indicate that the user hates tennis.

Minimize Session Bloat

For managing state information about a user, the PortletSession is great. But remember, managing the PortletSession requires a great deal of effort from the Portal Server. When the vendor that provided you your portal server implemented the PortletSession, they did it in such a way that the data stored in the PortletSession could be clustered, and managed across many servers, in a horizontally and vertically scaled, workload managed, environment. Implementing this type of solution takes a lot of thought, and a lot of effort, not to mention a lot of overhead at runtime.

Furthermore, most application servers serialize the information stuffed into the PortletSession, and save all of that information as a character string, or potentially, a CLOB, in a centralized database. That will probably imply a somewhat inefficient storage of your data, not to mention the overhead of reading and writing data to a database when session data is accessed or updated. With large object graphs, it's sometimes more efficient to create your own temporary database table to store the information, as opposed to using the PortletSession.

Poor session management, and database connection management, are the two most common performance bottlenecks I encounter when troubleshooting performance issues. Minimize the potential of a session bottleneck by not throwing too much into the PortletSession, keeping the data you put into the PortletSession fairly small, and remove items from the PortletSession when you're done with them.

Comment Your Friggin' Code

I do believe that good code comments itself. Good variable names, and a proper use of the API, should make it fairly easy for a new developer to figure out what your code is doing. But I also, strongly believe, that good code is commented.

Commenting your code makes it extremely clear to other developers what your code was trying to accomplish. It also makes it easier for you to clear your thoughts and think about what you are trying to achieve as you write your code. Commented code is also a great reminder about what you were trying to accomplish when you first wrote the code. You'd be surprised how many times you come back to a piece of code and think "what the heck was I trying to do there???"

I will admit that many of the examples in this book do not contain comments. ***But that's because this entire book is a comment.*** Yes, I have left out a few, one line comments in my code, only because the code is then followed by three pages of text trying to explain it. ☺ I also think that when learning how to use an API, it makes it a bit easier to learn when you're just looking at the code, and not a mass of comments. But code in a tutorial is different from code written in the development phase of an application. Comment your code. It's important.

Handle IO Exceptions

When the portal invokes your portlet, but decides that it's not going to wait for your portlet to finish processing, your portlet will encounter an IOException. You should handle the IOException in your code, to ensure that when there is a problem, your clients get a message that's a little more informative than simply "Portlet Unavailable."

If a portlet consumes a massing amount of processing time, and the portal server doesn't want to wait for your portlet to finish processing, your portlet will encounter an IOException. In fact, if you're doing a lot of heavy lifting in a portlet, you should occasionally check the flush method of the PrintWriter and handle a potential IOException. If you call the flush method of a PrintWriter or OutputStream in a portlet, and you get an exception, the portal server has put the kibosh on your portlet, and your portlet will not be rendered. At that point, you can end all of your complex computations, because nobody is ever going to see the results of them.

Look out for the IOException in your portlet code. It will make your portlet applications all the more robust.

Encode Your NameSpaces

Many portlets, from potentially many different portlet providers, can appear on a portal page. Each of those vendors can potentially throw a textfield on the page named ***password***, or a JavaScript method called ***validate***. These types of name collisions can result in portlets reacting to the wrong input data, or even worse, scripting errors when the web page is delivered to the user.

To avoid name collisions on the portal server, all scripts, URLs, HTML form attributes, and the like, should be namespace encoded. Without encoding a namespace, your portlets will likely work properly in a sequestered, local test environment, but may encounter some very obscure and difficult to reproduce errors when your portlets go into production.

Use the expiration-cache Tag

Each portlet can have an expiration-cache entry in its deployment descriptor. This entry allows a portlet to cache content for a specified period of time. Caching of content can significantly improve the response-time of a portlet, and subsequently relieve the portal server from doing unneeded processing.

Furthermore, the RenderRepsonse object can be used to override the time specified in the deployment descriptor by using the EXPIRATION_CACHE property:

```
renderResponse.setProperty(EXPIRATION_CACHE, time);
```

Note, that the time is entered in seconds, and setting the time to –1 means the cache will never expire, and setting the cache to zero, 0, means the caching mechanism for the portlet is completely disabled.

Think about the life expectancy of your portlet content, and set an expiration-cache tag appropriately.

Not Every Portlet is a Framework Portlet

I always hate jumping onto a project with a bunch of developers who just took a design-patterns class, because everything they see is either a friggin' factory, or a friggin' singleton. Similarly, when portlet developers are introduced to the JSF portlet framework, or the struts portlet framework, everything they see is either a JSF or a struts portlet.

JSF and struts portlets certainly serve a purpose, but not every portlet needs to be a framework portlet. Sometimes, having a subclass of GenericPortlet acting as a controller, and then calling on a JSP or two, is all you really need. Don't go seeing framework portlets where you don't need them.

And framework portlets aren't an all or nothing thing. You don't have to decide on whether to use JSF in your portal or not. Some portlets can be JSF portlets, some can be PERL or struts portlets, and some portlets can be just regular, vanilla ice, portlets. All of the various portlet types can co-exist in the portal server.

Appendices

Appendix A
Creating and Deploying a Simple Portlet

Developing, packaging, deploying, and testing a simple portlet can be a fairly involved endeavor.

Choosing a Development Environment

First of all, you need to set up a development environment, and that in itself is not a simple and easy decision. Will you use a Sun development tool like NetBeans? Will you use an open source tool like Eclipse, or something a little more refined, like Lomboz? Will you be deploying to WebSphere, because if you are, you'll probably be using IBM's Rational Application Developer (IRAD). And hey, maybe you're just hacking around, and want to use the simplest tools available – Windows Notepad and the good old javac compiler.

Choosing the Deployment Environment

And once you've decided upon a development environment, you have to decide upon a deployment, or testing, environment. You could choose one of the many versions of Pluto, which is the reference implementation of the Portlet API. Or, you could choose the open source, JetSpeed2 portal, which is the highly refined, open source portal, designed for production use.

Of course, if you're learning portal for work, you probably work for a big company. Portal server environments tend to make the most sense for large and intimidating organizations such as banks, insurance companies and governments. If that's the case, you'll probably be deploying to a vendor portal, such as BEA's WebLogic, or IBM's WebSphere Portal Server. You may even be testing and staging an a crazy, hybrid portal environment. I've even seen some really messed up environments in my time, where local testing happens against Pluto, dev testing happens with JetSpeed2, and regression, preprod and performance testing, not to mention production, all happens against IBM's WebSphere Portal Server.

Anyways, the point is, there are a myriad of development and production servers out there, and when you mix in the various platforms and operating systems on which they run, there are just too many combinations to cover.

In the first printing of this book, I didn't even broach the topic of how to set up an environment for deploying a simple, HelloWorldPortlet. Inevitably, if I do, a reader gets insulted that their particular Portal server wasn't discussed, or the latest, greatest version of Pluto or JetSpeed wasn't covered, and they end up writing nasty reviews on Amazon. I've seen some great books on Java and J2EE get completely slammed on Amazon because a reader couldn't get their development environment up and running; it's a real shame.

So, as you can see, I'm quite trepid about describing how to install and configure the various tools needed to develop, deploy and test a basic portlet, but I'm going to do it anyways. In this section, I'm going to describe how to install the resources needed to develop a basic portlet application using the JDK, and subsequently deploy that portlet application to the open source, Pluto portal server.

Don't Be Afraid to Ask For Help

One thing I do want to stress is that it is incredibly important to get some form of a portlet development and testing environment up and running. If you run into a problem getting things configured, don't waste any time reaching out to a friend, co-worker, manager, teacher, professor, or even an Internet message board. There's alot to learn with the Portal API, but you won't learn anything if you spend all day trying to figure out how to correctly configure the JAVA_PATH variable. If you run into problems, swallow your pride, and reach out for some help.

Setting the Expectation

The goal here is to develop, and deploy, from scratch, a simple portlet application. The Operating System will be a basic, Windows 2000, Intel machine. A simple text editor, in this case, Windows Notepad, will be used to write the Portlet and the required XML files, compilation will be done using the javac utility of the JDK, and deployment and testing will be done using Pluto as the Portal server.

```
THE BASIC CONFIGURATION

Windows 2000 Operating System
Text Editor, such as Notepad
JDK 5.0 (aka 1.5)
Pluto Portal Server 1.0.1
```

Downloading and Installing the JDK 1.5

The very first step towards getting a portlet development environment up and running is installing the Java Standard Edition (SE) Development Kit, also known as the JDK. The implementation of Pluto, version 1.0.1, which was the first full version to provide JSR168 Portlet support, will be the taget portal server. Sure, there's an updated version, but for the sake of simplicity, and ease of installation, I'm going to use Pluto 1.0.1. Version 1.0.1 of Pluto requires version 1.5 of the JDK, or as it's colloquially known, Java 5, in order to run properly.

Now, as I said, Pluto 1.0.1 requires version 1.5 of the JDK. You can use version 1.6 if you want, but the documentation says to use 1.5, so that's what I recommend using. If you're configuring a development environment for the first time, don't go around second guessing the recommended components. Get things working with Java 1.5, and then, if you really want access to all of the new and kewl features of Java 1.6 that you're never going to use, then upgrade your JDK. But initially, I recommend sticking with what is proven to work.

Finding the JDK on Sun's Site

In order to get your fingers on the JDK, you have to go to Sun Microsystems's website, at http://java.sun.com, or http://www.javasoft.com. Both urls pretty much take you to the same place. There's usually a link on the landing page called 'Popular Downloads,' which will probably change as soon as I finish writing this, but nevertheless, there should be a link that allows you to download Java SE. Java SE is what you want.

Now, when you go to the downloads page, you'll see all sorts of links to download JDK 6, or JDK 6u1, or something like that. You don't want Java 6. You want Java 5, so you'll have to find a link on the page that says "Previous Releases" or something like that. Dig around until you find a link for J2SE 5.0 Downloads.

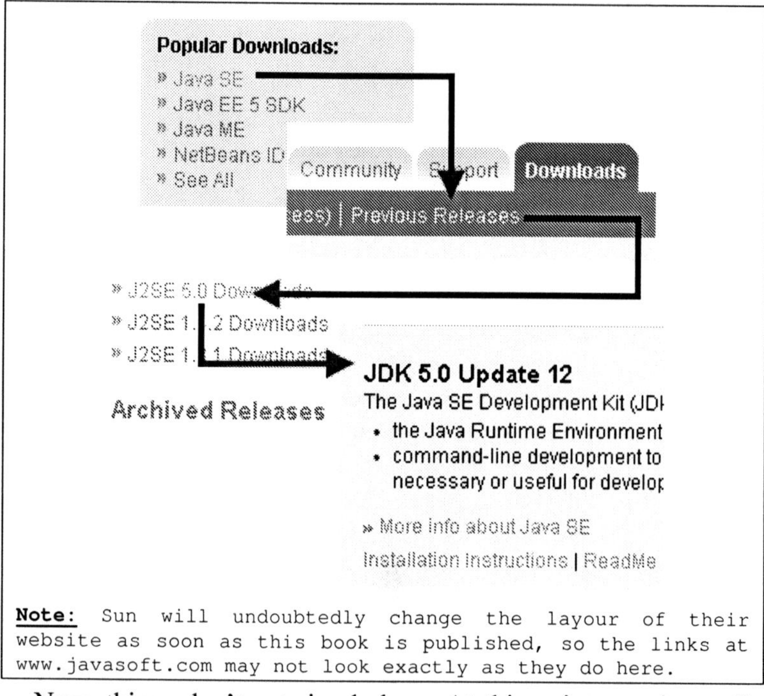

Note: Sun will undoubtedly change the layour of their website as soon as this book is published, so the links at www.javasoft.com may not look exactly as they do here.

Now, things don't get simple here. At this point, you have all sorts of Java 5.0 download options. There's options with NetBeans IDE. There's download options with Java EE. There's probably options for the JRE, and there's probably options for J2SE Documentation. All of these are really great links, but they're not what you want. There should be a link to simply download **JDK 5.0 Update 12**. Now personally, that sounds like the link just allows you to download update 12 for an already installed JDK, but that's not the case. This link will allow you to download and install the full blown **J**ava SE **D**evelopment **K**it (JDK) with update 12 already applied. This is the download that you want. Just for the record, the installation file I downloaded was 52,560 kilobytes in size.

Installing the JDK 1.5

Now, when you install the JDK, the tool will ask for an installation directory. On Windows, this usually defaults to C:\Program Files\jdk1.5.0.12 or something crazy like that. Personally, I recommend you install it into a folder right off the root of C:\, preferably **C:_jdk1.5.0** I like to have the underscore in there, because it puts the JDK right at the top of the list when you open up the file system explorer.

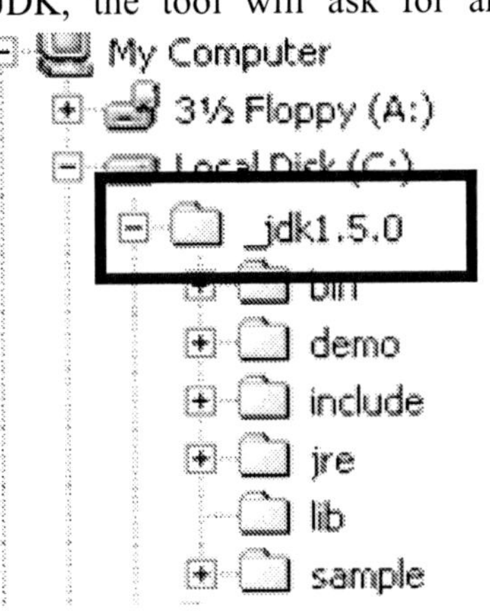

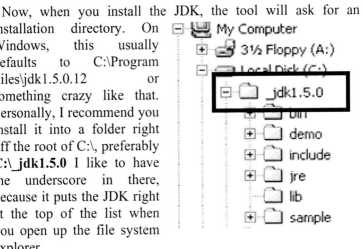

Configuring JAVA_HOME

Once the JDK has been successfully installed, you need to configure the JAVA_HOME environment variable, and point this variable to your installation directory of the JDK, which for me, would be C:_jdk1.5.0

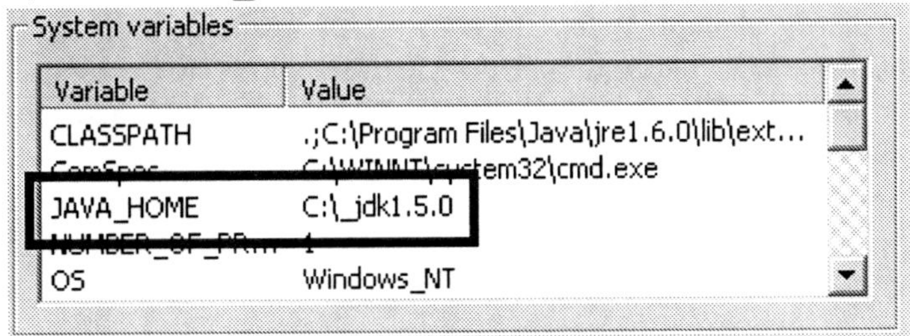

Environment and system variables are set up in the **Advanced** tab of the **System** applet, which can be accessed through the Windows **Control Panel.**

Start → Settings → Control Panel → System → ***Advanced Tab***

Configuring JAVA_HOME is one of those steps people tend to screw up. If you mess up this step, your portal server won't run properly, so it is important to be careful here. The JAVA_HOME variable must point directly to the installation directory of the JDK. It's not good enough to have a *close* spelling, and it's not good enough to change the caSinG of the letters. Be very careful and deliberate when configuring the JAVA_HOME variable.

Downloading Pluto

With the JAVA_HOME variable configured, it is time to download and install Pluto.

Pluto is an open source portlet *container*, that runs on Tomcat, and is designed to run and test JSR168 compliant portlets. In and of itself, Pluto is not a full scale portal server. For a full scale, open-source portal server, with all the bells and whisltles, you need to look at Apache's JetSpeed. But for testing portlets, Pluto is a perfect choice.

Pluto is open source, and maintained by the apache foundation. So, to download Pluto, you have to point your browser to www.apache.org, find the link for portals (http://portals.apache.org) and then find the Pluto sub-project. (http://portals.apache.org/pluto).

Now I really hate having a URL in a book, because sometimes, apache.org changes their URLs without consulting me, and my book becomes inaccurate. If the URLs result in 404 errors, use your brain and dig around the Apache website to find the correct download link.

Once you've found the Pluto page, you need to head over to a download distributions link, look for downloadable BINARIES, and from there, download pluto-1.0.1.zip For the record, the edition I downloaded had a datestamp of 18-May-2006, and was 9.9M in size.

You will notice that there are a few Pluto downloads that end with an rc1 or rc2 extension, such as pluto-1.0.1-rc2.zip. Do not download these files as your portal server. These downloads lack the admin link that allows you to upload portlet applications and configure page layouts. Make sure the file you download from apache.org is named pluto-1.0.1.zip.

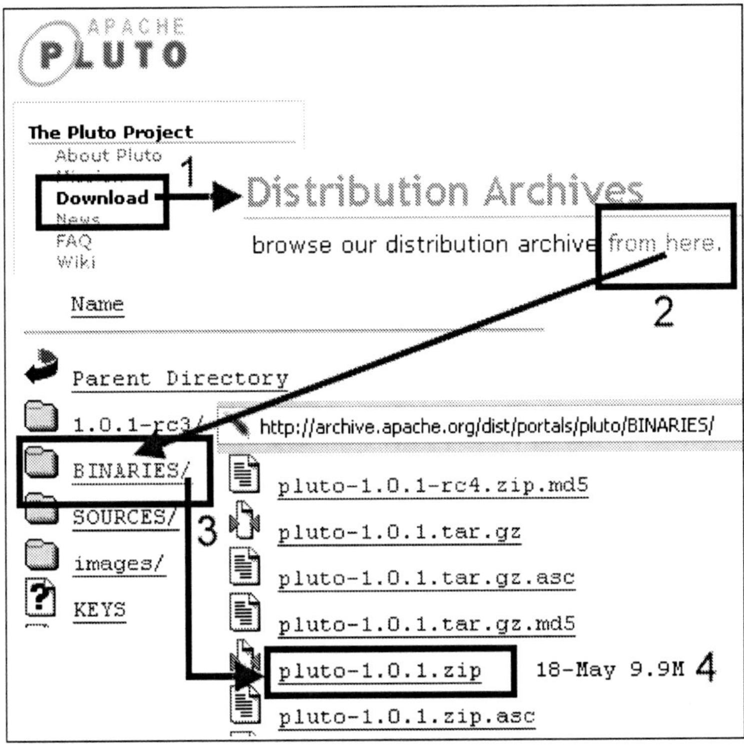

Installation (Extraction) of Pluto

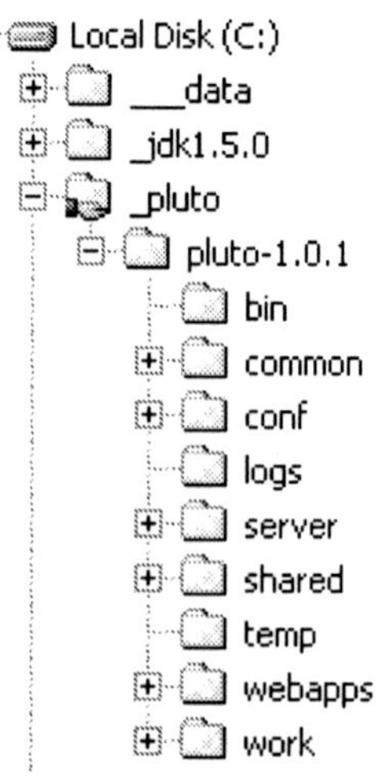

Once downloaded, you can extract the contents of the zip file, which essentially represents the installation of Pluto. I personally created a subfolder off the root of C:\ named _pluto, so after extraction, I ended up with a folder structure that looked like this: C:_pluto\pluto-1.0.1

tomcat-users.xml

A quick edit must be made to the tomcat-users.xml file, which resides in the conf sub-directory of the Pluto installation folder (C:_Pluto\Pluto-1.0.1\conf\tomcat-users.xml). A ***pluto*** rolename must be added as a new role, and the Pluto rolename must be added as a role of the tomcat/tomcat user. After a quick edit, your tomcat-users.xml file should look like this:

```
<?xml version='1.0' encoding='utf-8'?>
<tomcat-users>
  <role rolename="pluto"/>
  <role rolename="tomcat"/>
  <role rolename="role1"/>
  <role rolename="manager"/>
  <user username="tomcat" password="tomcat"
                      roles="tomcat,pluto"/>
  <user username="both" password="tomcat"
                           roles="tomcat,role1"/>
  <user username="role1" password="tomcat" roles="role1"/>
  <user username="manager" password="manager"
roles="manager"/>
</tomcat-users>
```

Starting Tomcat and its Pluto Portlet Container

In the subdirectory of Pluto-1.0.1, there should be a folder named bin, which will contain a file named ***startup.bat***. Double-clicking on this file will launch the Pluto portlet environment, along with the tomcat servlet engine on which the portlet environment is deployed. If the JAVA_HOME variable has been properly configured, the server should start without any major errors. Once the portal has started, you should be able to access the Pluto portal environment through the following URL:

http://localhost:8080/pluto/portal/

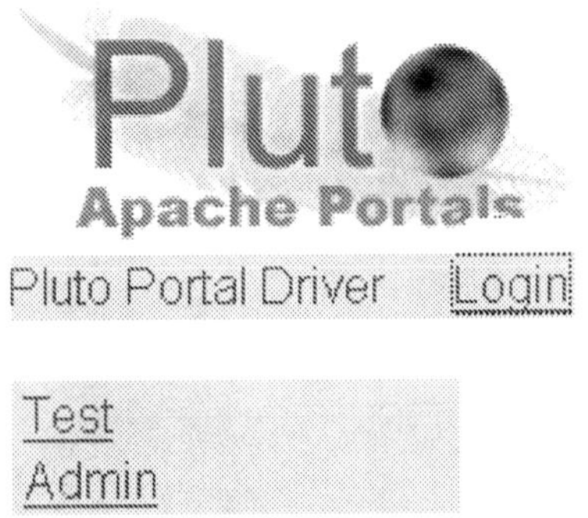

You should be able to log in to Pluto with the username of tomcat, and the password of tomcat.

Two links should appear on the left hand side of the landing page: one for Test, and one for Admin. If the Admin link does not appear, you have downloaded an incorrect binary file from apache. Go back to the downloads page, and look for the pluto-1.0.1.zip file, Make sure the letters rc do not appear towards the end of the name of the file, otherwise you won't have any admin links in your Pluto portlet engine.

The Poor Mans Portlet Application

Once you have the JDK installed, and the Pluto portlet engine running properly on Tomcat, it's time to create a simple portlet application.

Now, in creating the following portlet application, I'm going to take every shortcut possible. I'm not going to create any packages, and I'm going to place my Java source code smack dab in the middle of the bin directory of the JDK. These are by no means recommended practices, but they will make it easier to get a basic portlet application built and packaged, which is the goal.

Coding a Portlet

Using Microsoft's Notepad application, I code a simple HelloWorldPortlet. Here's the code:

```
import java.io.*;

import javax.portlet.*;

public class HelloWorldPortlet extends GenericPortlet {

  public void doView
    (RenderRequest request, RenderResponse response)
                       throws PortletException, IOException {

    response.setContentType("text/html");
    response.getWriter().println("Hello World!");

  }
}
```

Once this has been coded, I save this with the filename HelloWorldPortlet.java, in the bin directory of the JDK (***not*** the Pluto bin directory, but the ***JDK*** bin directory!), which for me, is C:_jdk1.5.0\bin. Be careful, as Notepad has this insidious habit of adding a **.txt** extension to the end of files. Make sure your portlet file ends with a .java extension, and not a .txt extension.

With the HelloWorldPortlet.java file saved in the bin directory of the JDK, it's now time to compile your portlet. Open a command prompt, aka DOS prompt, and navigate to the bin directory of the JDK, which for me, is C:_jdk1.5.0\bin.

When in the bin directory, execute the command >**dir *.java** This command will list all the files in the bin folder that end with a .java extension. Make sure the HelloWorldPortlet.java file is identified by this dir *.java command.

Linking to the Portlet API

Now, if we were dealing with a typical, standard Java source file that didn't use any classes or APIs outside of the standard, J2SE environment, we could compile our portlet using the following command:

>javac HelloWorldPortlet.java

However, any attempt to do this right now would generate the following compile error: **package javax.portlet does not exist.**

You see, when you create a Portlet, you are leveraging the Portlet APIs, which exist outside of the standard J2SE environment. In order to compile a portlet using the JDK, you must link to a special JAR file that contains the various classes and interfaces that make up the JSR168 API. And where do we find this magical JAR file? Well, this magical JAR file is found in the **\shared\lib** subdirectory of the Pluto portal, which in my environment, is **C:_pluto\pluto-1.0.1\shared\lib**, and this magical JAR file bares the name **portlet-api-1.0.jar.**

So, to compile a the HelloWorldPortlet, you need to reference this jar file when invoking the javac utility. The command to compile the HelloWorldPortlet.java file, while referencing the portlet-api-1.0.jar file, would look something like this, although the entire command should be on a single line, and not broken up across three:

```
C:\_jdk1.5.0\bin>javac
     –classpath C:\_pluto\pluto-1.0.1\shared\lib\portlet-api-1.0.jar
                                          HelloWorldPortlet.java
```

Personally, I hate having to deal with a huge classpath like that. What I usually do is just copy the portlet-api-1.0.jar file to the root of C:\, which makes the command much simpler:

```
C:\_jdk1.5.0\bin> javac –classpath C:\portlet-api-1.0.jar HelloWorldPortlet.java
```

Anyways, the point is, if you want to create a portlet application, you must compile some source code, and to do this with the javac compiler of the JDK, you must include the Portlet API libraries on the classpath, which can be done by simply referencing the portlet-api-1.0.jar file that is packaged with the Pluto portal.

Once compilation of the Java source file is complete, a file named **HelloWorldPortlet.class** should appear alongside the HelloWorldPortlet.java file, in the bin directory of the JDK.

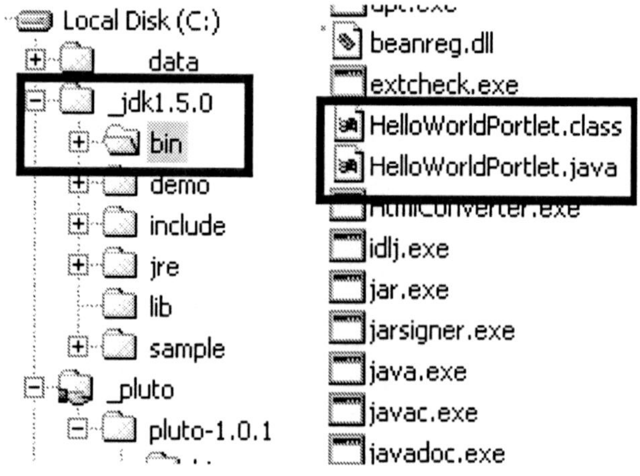

Setting up the Portlet Applications

Coding and compiling a portlet is only a small part of the much larger process of getting a portlet application ready for deployment. Portlet applications themselves must be deployed as Web Application aRchives, or WAR files, and those war files must maintain a structure that is consistent with the JSR168 specification.

The first step in preparing our portlet application for packaging is to create a directory folder off the root of C:\, under which all of our components will reside. I'm going to suggest creating a folder name _portletapp01, which will be directly off the root of C:\. This folder will represent the root of the portlet application.

C:_portletapp01

The WEB-INF Directory

According to the JSR168 specification, every portlet application must contain a WEB-INF folder directly off the root of the war. So, you need to create a WEB-INF folder under the C:_portletapp01 directory.

In the WEB-INF folder, each portlet application must contain a **web.xml** file. These files are fairly simply, usually just indicating a welcome file.

```
<?xml version="1.0" encoding="UTF-8"?>
<!DOCTYPE web-app PUBLIC
   "-//Sun Microsystems, Inc.//DTD Web Application 2.3//EN"
     "http://java.sun.com/dtd/web-app_2_3.dtd">
<web-app id="WebApp_ID">
  <display-name>BasicPortlets</display-name>
  <welcome-file-list>
    <welcome-file>index.jsp</welcome-file>
  </welcome-file-list>
</web-app>
```

The Portlet Deployment Descriptor: portlet.xml

Along with the web.xml file, every portlet application needs a **portlet.xml** file that describes all of the portlets contained in the portlet application. Here is the contents of our portlet.xml file, which like the web.xml file, must be saved in the WEB-INF folder

```
<?xml version="1.0" encoding="UTF-8"?>
<portlet-app
xmlns="http://java.sun.com/xml/ns/portlet/portlet-app_1_0.xsd"
version="1.0" xmlns:xsi="http://www.w3.org/2001/XMLSchema-instance"
xsi:schemaLocation="http://java.sun.com/xml/ns/portlet/portlet-app_1_0.xsd
http://java.sun.com/xml/ns/portlet/portlet-app_1_0.xsd"
id="BasicPortlets.413e4e0df0">
<portlet>
  <portlet-name>HelloWorld</portlet-name>
  <display-name>HelloWorld Test</display-name>
  <display-name xml:lang="en">
   HelloWorld Test
  </display-name>
  <portlet-class>
  HelloWorldPortlet
  </portlet-class>
  <expiration-cache>0</expiration-cache>
  <supports>
    <mime-type>text/html</mime-type>
    <portlet-mode>view</portlet-mode>
  </supports>
  <supported-locale>en</supported-locale>
  <portlet-info>
    <title>Testing HelloWorld</title>
  </portlet-info>
</portlet>
</portlet-app>
```

Moving the Compiled Class File

Finally, once your portlet.xml and web.xml files have been created, you need to add your HelloWorldPortlet.**class** file to a **classes** subdirectory under the WEB-INF folder. So, create a classes subdirectory under WEB-INF, and copy in the HelloWorldPortlet.class file from the bin directory of the JDK.

```
C:\_portletapp01
      \WEB-INF
         -web.xml
         -portlet.xml
         \classes
            -HelloWorldPortlet.class
```

Packaging the Portlet Application in a WAR File

Once the C:_portletapp01 directory has all of the required contents, including the portlet.xml and web.xml files under the WEB-INF directory, and the HelloWorldPortlet.class file under the WEB-INF\classes directory, it is time to package the portlet application up in a WAR file.

WAR files can be created using the JAR utility that comes with the JDK. Simply open a Command Prompt and navigate to the C:_portletapp01 directory. From there, invoke the JAR utility and ask it to compress the contents of the C:_portletapp01 directory, and all subdirectories, into a single file, with a .war extension. We'll create a file named testportlet.war. The command to do this is as follows:

C:_portletapp01> **C:_jdk1.5.0\bin\jar -cvf testportlet.war *.***

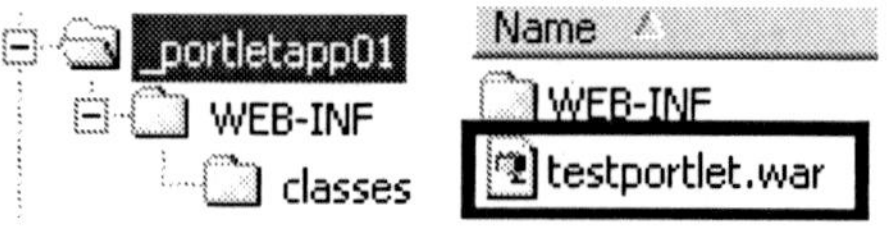

Portlet Deployment to Pluto

With the war file created, it is time to deploy the portlet application to Pluto. Make sure Pluto is started, by running the startup.bat command in Pluto's bin directory. From there, bring up the Pluto home page by navigating to: http://localhost:8080/pluto/portal/

Login to Pluto using tomcat as both the username and password. This assumes that you appropriately edited the tomcat-users.xml file, as outlined in a previous step.

Once logged in, click on the admin link, and where it says Deploy War, click on the upload button, and search for the testportlet.was file, which should be in the C:_portletapp01 directory. Upload the file by then clicking Submit.

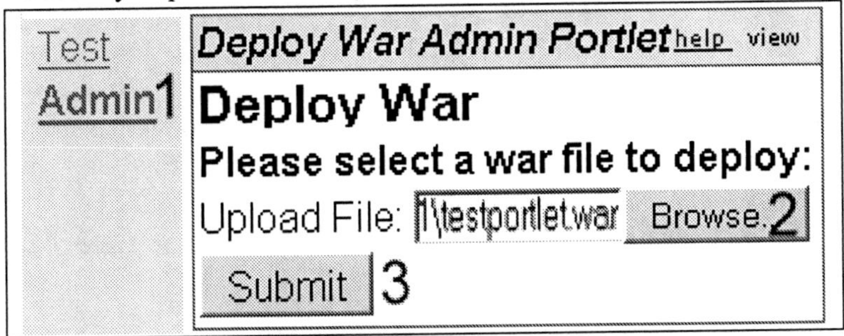

After clicking the Submit button, you will be prompted for layout information. For the Title, type in ***Test Portlet***, for the Description, type in ***Test Description***, keep the number of rows and columns at 1, and then click Submit.

Deploy War Admin Portlet help view
Enter layout information
Title: Test Title
Description: Test Description
Layout for the 1 portlet :
Number of columns: 1
Number of rows: 1
Submit

On the following screen, click submit, allowing for our portlet to appear in the space defined in the previous step.

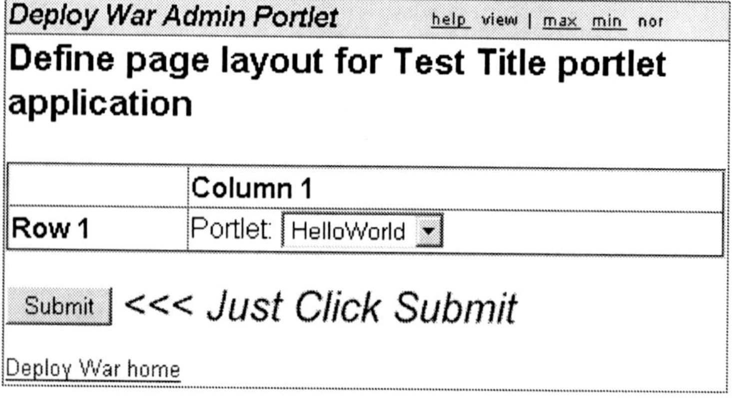

On the following window, it will look like you have been taken back to the original deployment screen, but there is a difference. There is now a link at the bottom of the portlet window that says: ***Hot deploy 'testportlet' portlet application.*** Click this link to immediately deploy the test portlet.

After choosing to *hot deploy* your portlet, you will be taken to a new portal page, with a new link named ***Test Title*** appearing at the left hand side, and the test portlet, shouting out Hello World, displaying in the content rendering pane of the portal page.

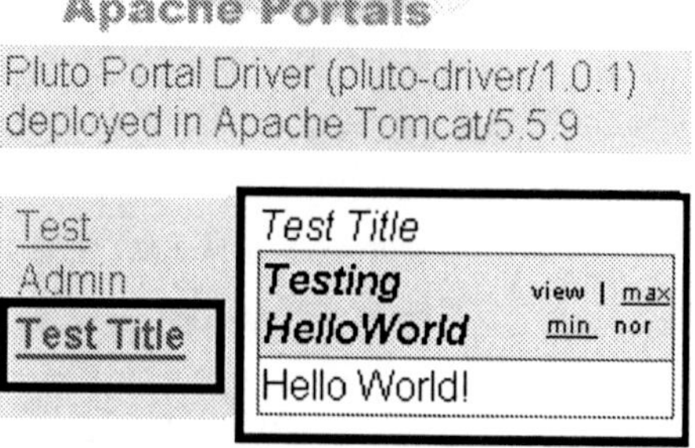

Congratulations! You just created and deployed a portlet application!

Appendix B
Manual Deployment to JetSpeed2

Pluto is a basic portlet container, that allows you to test your JSR-168 portlets against a standard implmentation of the specification. However, Pluto is not intended to work as a full scale, portal server. For an open source, full scale portal server implementation, you will want to install the JetSpeed portal server from Apache, or, as release two-point-one is called, JetSpeed-2.1

JetSpeed-2.1 can be downloaded from the portals section of www.apache.org, and the installation of JetSpeed2 follows very much in line with the installation of Pluto, in so much as you need to download and install the approprate version of the JDK and you need to configure your JAVA_HOME variable appropriately. Furthermore, a very nice and slick wizard now takes you through the various installation steps for JetSpeed2.1. If you are interested in working with, and installing JetSpeed2.1, consult the installation documents at www.apache.org.

Deployment to JetSpeed2

Given a JSR-168 compliant portlet that has been packaged as a war file, deployment to JetSpeed2 is fairly straight forward. All you have to do is drop your war file in the following directory:

```
<JetSpeed_ROOT>\webapps\jetspeed\WEB-INF\deploy
```

I installed JetSpeed2.1 in a directory named C:_Jetspeed-2.1, so the actual location of the folder that I need to place portlet war files is:

```
C:\_Jetspeed-2.1\webapps\jetspeed\WEB-INF\deploy
```

Processing of the Portlet Application

Assuming the JetSpeed portal server has been started, JetSpeed will recognize that a war file has been placed in the deploy directory, and JetSpeed will subsequently process the portlet application. After placing the testportlet.war file created in Appendix A into the deploy directory of the JetSpeed portal, the command window used to start JetSpeed displayed the following output:

```
Found WEB-INF/portlet.xml
Found web.xml
Attempting to add portlet.tld to war...
Adding portlet.tld to war...
Creating war C:\_Jetspeed-
2.1\webapps\testportlet.war ...
War C:\_Jetspeed-2.1\webapps\testportlet.war
created
June 14, 1928 3:57:49 PM
org.apache.catalina.startup.HostConfig
deployWAR
INFO: Deploying web application archive
testportlet.war
JetspeedContainerServlet: starting
initialization of Portlet Application at:
testportlet
JetspeedContainerServlet: initialization done
for Portlet Application at: testportlet
```

Adding a Portlet to a Portal Page

With a portlet deployed to JetSpeed2, the next step is to actually add the deployed portlet to a portal page, and test the portlet's runtime behavior. To do this, you need to log into the JetSpeed portal. The default username and password for the JetSpeed2.1 portal is: admin admin. The URL to access the JetSpeed2.1 portal is:

```
http://localhost:8080/jetspeed/portal/
```

Manually Editing the Portal Page

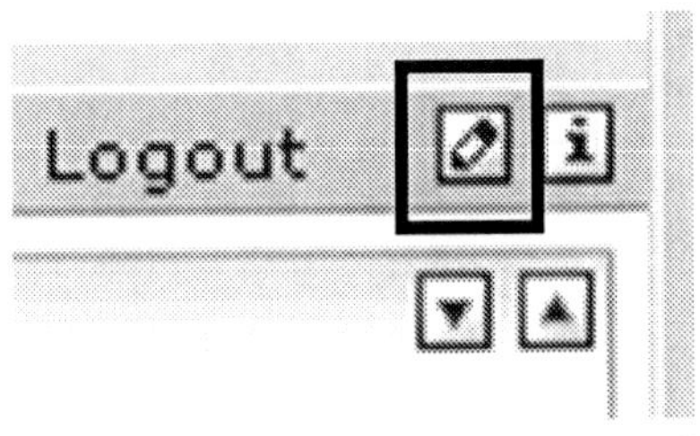

After logging into the portal, you need to click on the pencil icon in the top right-hand corner of the portal page, next to the **Logout** link.This pencil icon takes you to the ***page edit mode,*** where you can add new portlets, and change the layout of the portal page. All we want to do is add our test portlet to the page.

Adding a Portlet to the Page

In the ***page edit mode***, click the link towards the top right-hand corner that says Add Portlets +. Clicking on this link will take you to a new page that will allow you to add portlets to the page.

The JetSpeed2.1 Portlet Selector

On the Portlet Selector page that appears, you can either search for the HelloWorld test portlet, or simply click the add link for the HelloWorld test portlet, which should appear on the initial screen.

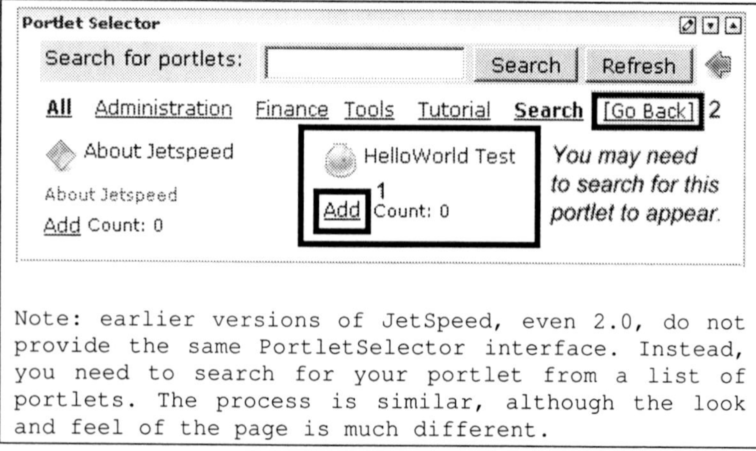


```
Note: earlier versions of JetSpeed, even 2.0, do not
provide the same PortletSelector interface. Instead,
you need to search for your portlet from a list of
portlets. The process is similar, although the look
and feel of the page is much different.
```

Clicking the add link will increase the count to 1. After the count has increased to one, simply click the **Go Back** link towards the top of the page to take you back to the page editing mode. In the page editing mode, click the restore icon, , in the top right-hand corner of the page to restore the original landing page of the portal. When the landing page is restored, your portlet will appear at the top of the page.

Admiring Your Completed Work

And that's it! That's how easy it is to deploy a JSR-168 portlet to JetSpeed2.1

This novella is dedicated to the memory of my father, Cecil McKenzie, who left us on June 21st, 2007.

In a time when so many kids grow up without fathers, and so many men just walk out on their responsibilities, I was blessed with a father that loved being just that, a father, despite the fact that he never had a father of his own.

Discerning Bombs

The following work is novella, pulled from Cameron McKenzie's collection of writings, poems, digital photography and short stories.

For obvious reasons, this novella has been pulled out for individual distribution. However, it represents just one in a collection of many interesting, and at times disturbing, stories about the people that live their lives in the 905.

If you enjoy this novella, do yourself a favor, and pick up a copy of Cameron McKenzie's *Discerning Bombs on Oshawa*. You won't regret it.

Available no on Amazon.com

The City

Pickering is Springfield

Do you know the difference between a *good* story and a *great* story? I didn't for the longest time.

Good stories are the ones you love to tell your friends. *Great* stories are the ones your friends beg you to retell to *their* friends. If I went over my entire inventory, I'd have to say that this is the only great story I've got. It's the only story that people beg me to tell over and over again.

This whole thing started out a few years back when I accepted a job doing entity analytics with a tiny little high-tech company based out of Las Vegas, Nevada. I was to be in *Lost Wages* for the week, as the local talent worked to get me up to speed on their nifty little piece of software.

When I travel, I'm fairly particular about the hotels in which I stay. In Vegas, I always stay away from the strip. It's overpriced, and filled with tourists. It's a great place to vacation, but the strip isn't the place to be when you need to get some business done.

Personally, I always like to find a hotel that has a bit of a gathering spot; something friendly, informal and inviting; nothing too overly ostentatious. I much prefer a sweet, honest hotel with a relaxing little bar close to the lobby where I can sit down, have a drink, and eat a few pretzels as the evening slips away. Sometimes, if it's quiet, I can usually convince the keeper of the bar to switch off the baseball game, and switch on the hockey game; at least, that's what they did the last time I stayed here.

On this particular evening, I headed down at around seven in the evening, which is kinda early to be hitting the hotel bar, but I was still on eastern time, so it felt more like nine o'clock to me. Early as it was, I wasn't going to be the first at the bar. Exiting the elevators, I could see the side profile of a pretty brunette sitting alone at the bar, munching on some pretzels, and sipping away at a mixed drink. Sometimes you just get a feeling, and I had a feeling that this was going to be a good night; although, at that point, I had absolutely no idea just how memorable an evening this would turn out to be.

Seeing a woman sitting by herself at the hotel bar this early in the evening is a pretty unusual sight. Normally, when people congregate at the hotel bar, they congregate in groups of five or six, all of them usually being from the same company, all in town for the same conference or training seminar. They sit together and chat cordially, working to maintain a fun and casual atmosphere, trying hard not to do or say anything that might raise an eyebrow or two. If you're trying to be social, that's always a tough crowd to crack into, because they don't really want outsiders in their little clique. If I'm going to chat up a woman in an entourage like that, I've got to wait for the majority of the group to disappear, and then, if one or two ladies are left behind, I can gregariously introduce myself. A giggle of three ladies, although preferably a sniggle of two, is much easier to break into that a full guffaw of business types.

But to see an attractive young lady, sitting all by herself, well, that's a rarity. The only time that usually happens is if the woman is dating the bartender, but this time, the guy behind the bar was a girl, and the two of them weren't carrying on like they knew each other.

With half a dozen empty chairs at the bar, I confidently and presumptuously took the open stool next to the empty one next to her. She gave me a bit of a look that said '*who the hell are you?*' to which I just kinda smiled and said "So, tell me a story."

I always ask people to 'tell me a story.' It's a line from the movie Reservoir Dogs, used when one thief is chatting with another. But it's a good line, and now I've stolen it for myself.

I say it to all my friends. '*Tell me a story.*' I say it to my acquaintances. I say it to the people I work with. And most of all, I use it as an opening line, especially when I haven't got anything better to say, which quite frankly, is most of the time.

It's actually a great opening line. It's pretty innocuous and unassuming. *'Tell me a story.'* It's an opening line that feigns interest in someone you may or may not be interested in at all, and even more importantly, it opens up a bevy of responses.

Most women, especially if I'm approaching them without any context or reason, will just look a little surprised, and tell me they don't have a story to tell. Then they usually ask *me* to tell *them* a story, which opens up a great big door, because I've got a bunch of stories. They're not necessarily great stories, but they're *my* stories, and I love to tell them.

Alternatively, a woman *will* have a story. If that's the case, I'll just sit there and listen, asking the questions that dig deeper and deeper. It's amazing how good you can make other people feel when you take an interest in their stories. And I do take an interest in people's stories. As they say, everyone's got a story to tell; I just happen to like listening to them.

Susan didn't respond well to my *'tell me a story'* line. Actually, I can't definitively remember if Susan was really her name. Over the years, as I have related this tale, I have always referred to her as Susan. Somehow, I think I've convinced myself that her name *was* Susan, but I really don't think it was. That's the problem with trying to track her down, three years later. I don't even have a name with which to start. But for the sake of argument, let's just say her name was Susan.

Susan neither provided a story, nor did she ask for one of mine. Susan's reply was curt, and Susan's reply was terse, if not somewhat aggressive and possibly, slightly rude.

"I get paid to tell stories, so if you want to hear a story from me, you better cough up some dough. And I don't work for scale. If you want to hear my story, you'll be lightening a very, very heavy wallet."

So, right away, Susan put me in my place. With one smart-ass comment, she not only cut me down to size, but she defeated both of the gambits that my patented *'tell me a story'* line usually opens up. I liked this girl already; either that, or I hated her. I really couldn't make up my mind, not that it really mattered.

And the thing is, not only did she completely shut down my opening gambit, but she simultaneously rooked me on some of my most trusted, first date, first contact, material. You see, whenever you meet someone, the conversation usually veers into a conversation about what you do; like, do you drive a truck for a garbage company, or do you day trade on the stock exchange. When the conversation comes to what I do, I always tell women that I'm a writer.

Now telling a woman that I'm a writer isn't entirely untrue. I've actually written a couple of half-decent computer books. Of course, when you tell people that you're a technical writer, you can actually see the look of excitement instantaneously zap from their face.

GIRL: What do you do for a living?

ME: I'm a writer.

GIRL: (enthusiastically) Really, what do you write?

ME: Computer books.

GIRL: Oh. (Which is said with such a look of disappointment, I may as well have told her that I just killer her cat.)

The other great thing about saying that you're a writer is that it gives you the ability to ask the question *"if you were to write a book, what would it be about."* This is another great line to get someone talking. Still, I figured that if she *was* a real writer, or storyteller as she put it, getting her to talk about her work was probably the best way to get the conversation moving.

"So, what do you write? Anything I'd be familiar with?"

"No, not unless you're into kids cartoons."

"Are we talking anime?"

"Why? Are you telling me that the thirty year old man sitting across from me spends time at home watching Japanese animation films?"

"I was just asking a question. To be honest, I don't really spend too much time watching TV. And very little of that is spent watching kids cartoons."

"Well, then you wouldn't be familiar with any of my work then, would you? Besides, I don't really want to talk about work. I came here to get away from all of that bullshit for a while."

She was here to get away from all of that *bullshit* for a while. Something was definitely eating at her, and I was hoping she might open up to me about it.

"So, do you fly to Vegas and gamble your worries away every single time you get tired of dealing with life's bullshit?"

"Well, first of all, I drive, I don't fly. And secondly, I don't gamble."

"You drive?"

"Yeah, I've got a little place, in a little town, just outside of L.A. With a good tailwind, I can make it out here in less than four hours. And besides, I'd never actually fly into Vegas. I'd prefer to crash land in Barstow, and drive a rental the rest of the way. I *hate* flying into Vegas"

"Wow. Aren't we just full of venom tonight?"

"It's not venom. I just hate being on a plane with a bunch of tourists bound for Vegas. How often do you fly?" she asked

"ALOT"

"Well, then you should be able to appreciate how annoying it is being on a passenger jet bound for Vegas. A plane bound for Vegas is different, and more annoying, than a plane bound for any other destination on the planet."

"And why is that?"

"Because, everyone on that damn plane is a tourist. Flights bound for just about any city, other than Las Vegas, are predominantly filled with business people, with the occasional tourist mixed in for good measure. But a plane bound for Vegas is the inverse: mostly tourists, with the occasional, unfortunate, businessperson.

"Tourists have no idea how to behave on a plane. They have no appreciation for etiquette or customs. Everyone gets up and stands in the aisle when the plane lands. Everyone rushes to use the washroom as soon as the fasten seatbelt sign goes off. Nobody knows to stand to the right, and walk to the left on an escalator. It's purely amateur hour when you're walking around Carson International. People who are walking will just all of a sudden stop and stand, with no regards for anyone walking behind them. You've heard of *road rage*? When I'm in Carson, I get *walk rage*. I'd be more than happy to die without seeing that airport again."

"You know, I hadn't even noticed. The only thing that really stands out to me when I head to Vegas is how different the crowd is. It's a much older crowd than I'd expected, with the occasional, young, newlywed couple. But the percentage of people fifty and older is definitely much higher on a flight to Vegas than a flight to anywhere else."

"Yes, newlyweds and shiny-bottoms. That's what Vegas is all about."

"Shiny-bottoms?"

"Yeah, shiny-bottoms. That's a select group of Vegas elite, that fly in from all around the country, are approximately fifty years of age, and have worn the same pair of polyester pants for so long, that the material has actually become part of their skin, giving the polyester a glossy, reflective, shine. They can sit all week long in front of a slot machine, and quite often, do."

That made me laugh, if only because I knew exactly the type of people she was talking about. Back home in Ontario, they'd opened up a bunch of casinos, and the stories about gambling addicts were always enough to make you shake your head. Some would wear diapers so they could relive themselves without moving away from their slots. Others had configured pee jugs, or alternatively would urinate into those plastic cups that are supposed to hold all of your coins. Imagining one of those gambling addicts wearing the same pair of polyester pants, day after day, until the fabric actually became part of their skin, wasn't really all that much of a stretch.

"That's the thing about Vegas" she said. "It's a total smoke and mirrors job; a real Potemkin facade. I mean, when they advertise Vegas, it's always show girls and square jawed men throwing sevens at the craps table. But when you walk the strip, it's just a bunch of late to middle-aged morons, who have made that once in a lifetime trip to Vegas, as though they were Muslims making a pilgrimage to Mecca."

The thing was, I actually knew exactly what she meant. A few years ago, I met this fantastic girl at a bar in Buffalo, New York. Her name was Angela, and she was far and away the prettiest girl I had ever met. After two dates, I told her I wanted to take her to Vegas. Angela was completely into the rave and techno scene, and she was anxious to get to the mighty Las Vegas strip and see some of the biggest names spin. On the Saturday night, Angela and I got all dolled up, and headed out to some big name clubs.

The thing was, the crowd was a far cry from what you would have seen in a hip club in Toronto or New York or Chicago. Instead of the club being filled with the usual suspects of college kids and young adults in their early to maybe, mid twenties, the clubs, with names like Studio 54 and Coyote Ugly, were filled with middle-aged men and middle-aged women whom hadn't been to a club in maybe ten years. They were in Vegas with their friends, or with their husband of fifteen years, or their coworkers at the place they've worked at for the past decade, and everyone has decided to go out and 'party.' They end up doing things they did twenty years ago, and they'll have a great time doing it. They'll go home and tell their kids that they partied at Studio 54, or Coyote Ugly, and their kids will think their parents actually went out to a hip club in a happening city. But it's all smoke and mirrors. It's all make-believe, like a children's game of pretend.

But in Vegas, everyone else is in the same, make-believe world; and people actually believe that what they are experiencing is real. As we stood on the second floor balcony of Studio 54, across from the hot, young, go-go dancers hired to dance above the floor in a cage, I remember Angela turning to me, as we were looking down on the crowd of thirty and forty somethings dancing and having fun, and she said, disappointedly "this really isn't what I expected." I just kinda gave her a nod, as though to say "I know, but don't ruin the fun for everyone else in here. Just keep your thoughts to yourself, and let them all think they were dancing in a club that a young and beautiful girl like yourself might actually frequent on a weekend."

The Girl

"But you don't come here to gamble? You know, gambling is pretty big thing in this town. I think there are a few one arm bandits in those big hotels downtown. You should try it." My sarcasm is neither clever, nor necessary, but it is perpetual. She just kinda rolled her eyes.

I continued. "You know, for someone with such a sandpaper like personality, I actually feel pretty comfortable around you."

Now that actually sounds like a line, and I am probably guilty of saying something lame like that to another woman in the past, but as much as it may have been a line, it was also true. There was something very comfortable and familiar about her.

"Of course you're comfortable around me. I'm the first person you've talked to since you got off your flight that talks like you."

"Come again?"

"Well, I should say, I'm the first person you've talked to that talks *somewhat* like you. I've lost my soft vowels. They've hardened over the years. But we're close."

"Er...What are you talking about?"

"You're Canadian. I can tell by your accent."

"I don't have an accent." I said, a little insulted. She just laughed.

"You don't think you have an accent? Your vowels are softer than my.." she hesitated "well, I shouldn't say that. That's rude." She flashed me a devious little smile. "You have an accent. Trust me. You're from Toronto, right?"

I was now becoming a little disconcerted, wondering how a woman I just met knew things about me. "Yeah, pretty much. How'd you know?"

"I was at the vending machine when you checked in. I saw the Toronto Maple Leafs pendant on your suitcase. It always catches my eye when I see something that reminds me of home. It's ballsy sporting a pendant for the most miserable hockey team in Canada. I will say though, I'm impressed by anyone who is proud to be a perpetual loser."

"You're not a big Leafs fan?"

"Actually, I don't watch alot of hockey, but I do like watching the people that watch hockey, especially Torontonians. Now that Boston's won a world series, Torontonians are truly the most pathetic fans in the sporting world. They've got the best center in team history, but they long for the glass defenseman that struggled to put in twenty games a season."

"So, you're from Toronto, *eh*?" I asked, emphasizing the *eh*, to help further that Canadian bond.

"Well, not really Toronto. I grew up in the 'burbs, mostly the east end. I got bounced between parents quite a bit, and ended up living all over. Went to school in Whitby and Oshawa, and spent most of my summers with my Dad in Pickering."

Now the funny thing is, these types of coincidences are surprisingly common in my life. I guess, when you meet enough people, or visit enough places, coincidences tend to become statistical probabilities. Still, it's funny when they happen.

I was in San Francisco doing some work for The GAP a few years back. One of the web architects had just moved to San Bernardino from a suburb of Chicago. It was actually the same suburb that I was currently living in. In fact, not only was it the same suburb, but I was living in the same apartment building he had just left a few months earlier.

Even more peculiar was when I was teaching a seminar for a bunch of bankers in Dublin, Ireland. Part of my seminar included the filling out of a form, and I quickly typed in my hometown address in Ajax, which was displayed for all to see on the overhead projector.

"Er, is that your real address?" one of the bankers politely queried as I was pecking at the keyboard.

"Yeah, why do you ask?"

"I lived on that same street when I lived in Canada." In fact, when we chatted further, it appeared that she had lived just four houses down from me, five years prior. Curiously enough, it took a six hour flight to Dublin to finally make her acquaintance; funny.

"You're kidding" I said to Susan. "I was born and raised in Ajax. We're pretty much neighbors."

"Ah, *Ajax*. How's that shopping mall of yours coming? Have they built a movie theatre there, yet?" That was a jab. There was always a bit of a rivalry between the people of Shmickering and the residents of Ajax. "What a sweet little lemon town. We may have been neighbors once, but I haven't lived in Canada for quite a while."

"When did you leave?"

"I headed to Los Angeles about fifteen years ago. I finished High School and I was gone. But that little town where I spent most of my summers growing up has never been far from my heart. I head back practically every summer."

"You live in LA, but you miss Pickering? How does that make any sense?"

"Well, I don't know if I'd say that I *missed* it. Being a teenager in a middle-class Toronto suburb isn't exactly exciting. But I've always thought the town of Pickering was interesting. I've always thought of it as Toronto's wanting little sibling. Anything Toronto didn't want, they could always pawn off on Pickering – a sewage treatment plant, an incinerator, a landfill site, an airport, *a nuclear power plant...* It's actually pretty comical."

"Well, you'll have to excuse me for not being a historian on the topic of Pickering, Ontario. Maybe you can enlighten me?"

"And why should I just enlighten just you?" She asked. "I've taken it upon myself to enlighten *everyone*."

And it was here that the encounter really started to get interesting.

The Show

"You know that little children's show I told you I contribute to?"

"Kids cartoon, I think you said."

"Yeah. Well, it takes place in Pickering."

"Really?"

"Okay, it doesn't exactly take place in a town *named* Pickering, but if you watch the show, you'd be able to catch enough details to realize that it's all actually taking place in Pickering, Ontario."

"Is that so?"

"Yeah, it's my own little secret. It's not really public knowledge. A few hints. A few obvious references. A few events that are a little too coincidental, if you catch my drift?"

"Well, I've never been too good at catching drifts. The only things I tend to catch are colds. Maybe you could give me an example."

She sorta laughed. "I could probably give you one for every episode if you wanted me to. But there are some hints that are bigger than others. You see, if you watched the show, you'd think it was a typical American town, and an American family at that, but there's hints that it's not."

"Such as?"

"Well, there's the state motto in the show. It's *'Not Just Another State.'* Which is true, because it's not a state at all, it's a *province.*" She smiled. "I thought that was clever. Most Yankees would never get it."

"That's cute." I said, not being overly impressed. "Anything else?"

"And the town's crest is based on Pickering's"

"Pickering has a crest?"

"Yeah, I guess not too many people have ever seen it. But it was draped over my left boob for two consecutive years when I played soccer for the Pickering Atoms. It was part of the uniform. Pickering's coat of arms has a sheaf of wheat, a spinning atom, and the sun on it."

"Well, in the show, the town's crest has a star for the sun, an ear of corn for the sheaf of wheat, and the same spinning atom. Plus, I threw in a beaver to emphasize that it was Canadian."

"If you really wanted it to shout out Canada, you should've had the beaver drinking a beer and eating a donut." She actually laughed a little too hard at that remark. I mean, it really didn't seem all that witty.

"Well, the main character in the show does consume alot of Canadian bacon and maple syrup. Plus, you get to see his drivers license in one episode, and the *state* abbreviation is NT"

"Okay. I don't get it, but it sounds good."

"NT? You don't get it? First of all, there's no state with the abbreviation NT. But beyond that, the Americans used to refer to Canada as the Northern Territories before Canada was even called Canada. *NT* is the *Northern Territories*, or Canada"

The girl actually seemed rather tickled by herself. Personally, I wasn't all that impressed that she'd somehow hijacked a frame or two in a local children's cartoon, but she seemed rather tickled by it, and her enthusiasm was more infectious than annoying, so I probed a little more.

"The letters NT hardly bind a place to Pickering, Ontario. And the pure existence of a state motto still implies the fact that a state is involved. Surely you can do better than that?"

"Well, there are some hints that are bigger than others. You said you were from Ajax, right?"

"Born in Ajax Pickering hospital. Raised on Clover Ridge." I said smugly.

"Well, there's one episode where the kids all go to the Ajax Steel Mill."

"Ajax has a textile plant, not a steel mill."

"True, but a 'textile plant' wouldn't exactly resonate with the children who watch the show. Besides, the episode was a tip of the hat to a couple of guys I dated from Ajax when I was a teenager. A steel mill is a great way to show how rugged and manly the men of Ajax are."

"Was that a compliment?"

"An indirect one, I guess." It wasn't really a compliment though. I actually fumbled over the episode she was talking about. When the five o'clock whistle blew, the steel mill turns into a gay bar.

"There's one episode where the characters in the show jump on the highway, and head to the capital to watch their major league baseball team play. We did that episode back when the Toronto Blue Jays were still a big deal. I always loved going to see the Jays play when I was a kid. Dad used to take us there whenever he could scrape up enough to buy a couple of cheap bleacher seats. I even made *Jay* the middle name of one of the characters in the show.

"Anyways, the capital is just a short drive away, and there's a great shot where the characters jump on the highway to get there. Do you want to guess which highway they jump on?"

"It's an easy guess, right?

"Well, if you're from Pickering it is."

"What is the 401?" I said, in my very best Jeopardy voice.

"Yup, they jump on the 401." She had this proud and sinister little smile on her face as she completed the sentence.

"That's cute, but that hardly pinpoints Pickering, Ontario on a map. I mean, lots of cities in the states have highways running through them." Susan looked a bit insulted, but not the slightest bit deflated.

"No they don't." She said defensively, as though I had personally attacked her. "Not four hundred highways, they don't. In Canada, it's all four hundred highways. There's the 401, the 403, the 409, the overpriced 407. But in the states, they have interstates. It's all I-65, and I-69. Heck, even the freak states have interstate highways."

"The freak states?"

"Yeah, the freak states: Alaska and Hawaii. They have interstates as well, although I'm not sure which other states their interstate highways are connected to?"

"I thought I saw a 401 in California."

"We'll there's a 401 connecting North and South Carolina, there's one I know of in Oregon, and there's a bypass called 401 in California, which is why I think it slid it by the writers so easily. People who live in LA don't realize there's a world outside of California. That makes it easy to slip things by them. But I will tell you this – if you want to jump on a 401 highway, take a short drive, and watch a major league baseball game in a Capital City, there's only one place you can do it, and that's in Ontario, by driving down the MacDonald-Cartier freeway to Toronto. Although we called it the Michael Jackson Freeway in the show. I thought it kinda rhymed."

I started sorta laughing to myself. The idea of some Canadian hack putting tidbits of trivia about her hometown into a little Los Angeles children's show was delightfully devious. But still, hijacking the storyline in a show or two wasn't all that impressive, although it was pretty cute. Nevertheless, I wasn't overly convinced that there was anything that would single out Pickering in this little show of hers.

"You know, the 401 runs through alot of cities in Ontario; *Hundreds*, actually."

She looked like she was more than ready to handle my objection.

"Yeah, but of those, how many of them have a garbage dump. I think the answer is none." She smiled that sinister little smile of hers, again.

The Inspiration

"The great thing about Hollywood writers is that they don't have an original thought in their heads. If you want to become a writer for Fox, here's all you have to do: go to Harvard for four years and get great marks, using up every original idea in your head. Once every original and interesting thought in your head has been used up, you'll get your degree, and *then* you'll be ready to write for a network TV show. That's how it works."

"You went to Harvard?" I said.

"Screw that, I'm not a *writer*." she said, with palpable disdain for the word. "I never said I was a *writer*. I'm a contributor, at best. But the thing is, when a bunch of writers are around, all rehashing their completely unoriginal ideas, it's easy to plant a few seeds in their heads. And that's why everyone loves me; because I never went to an Ivey league school, I don't have any letters after my name, and I've still got some original ideas left in my head. Plus, I grew up in Pickering, which is simply a fountain of fresh ideas and storylines.

"As I said, the thing I love about Pickering is the fact that it's like Toronto's wanting younger brother. The town's so seeking of Toronto's attention and approval, Toronto can get Pickering to do just about anything a rationally run city would never even contemplate. Deciding to take on the role of Toronto's trash can is just one of them."

"But they closed the dump a few years ago."

"Yeah, I know. I always got a kick out of reading the newspapers when Toronto had to figure out what to do with all their trash once Pickering began to burst at the seams. Do you know what they actually decided?"

"No. Enlighten me."

"They decided to ship it all to Michigan! Can you believe that? Like, thirty or forty trucks a day take Toronto's trash, and it gets shipped to some place outside of Detroit. That's just *precious*.

"Have you ever been to Detroit? I used to always say that if crap rained down on Detroit, it could only be considered an improvement. But now, Toronto's actually doing it. It's the largest cross-border beautification project in the history of the world, as Toronto ships all of its trash to Michigan."

"Ha. Ha. Cute. But what does this have to do with your show? Do they ship their trash to Michigan?"

"Well, not quite. In one episode, we put the main character in charge of the landfill site. Toronto kept talking about shipping their trash to an abandoned mine up by Kirkland lake, so that's exactly what we did in the show; of course, things then went awry, and the town ended up bursting at the seams with garbage."

"So, *then* they ended up shipping everything to Michigan?"

"Heh. No. Not quite.

"They actually moved the entire town, which I thought was kinda symbolic of what Toronto did. I mean, it's the same thing, right? Whether you ship your garbage away, or leave the garbage there and just move the entire city, it's the same thing. It doesn't deal with the problem. It just leaves it for someone else, at some other time, to deal with."

"This show of yours. It sounds pretty deep."

"Well, it is and it isn't. The whole idea is to keep people interested. That's what Hollywood does – it *entertains* people. So you have to have bright colors, simple storylines, sight gags, and lots of physical comedy to keep people from flicking around the dial. But if you do all that other stuff right, and you end up having people's attention for twenty minutes or so, you may as well try to deliver a bit of a message as well."

"Still, it sounds pretty deep for a children's show. What did you say it was called?"

"I didn't tell you. In fact, I think I've told you enough already. Why, do you find children's television particularly stimulating?"

"If the show's about my hometown, well, I might tune in. Besides, you said you were trying to educate everyone about Pickering, Ontario. How can I get educated if I don't watch the show. Is it aired in Canada?"

"It might be. I'd have to check the broadcast listings." She said, with another coy little smile."

"Well, if you tell me, I'll buy you another drink. How's that?" Her glass was nearly empty, so I though it was a decent proposition.

"Sorry, mate; no deal." And as the bartender, at that very moment, brought her a brand new glass of clear, yellow liquid, she rhymed, as though she was quoting from a song: "I get my Long Island Ice Teas, *for free*."

The Simpsons

She took a sip of her drink and asked: "If I told you the name of the show, would you promise not to tell anyone?"

"I promise. I won't tell a soul. This will be our little secret."

"Somehow I don't believe you."

"Honest Engine" I said, as I crossed my heart in a gesture of trust.

"Well, I still don't believe you. But I don't really care anymore. I'm not going to be working with those fucks again." And just to note, she pronounced it more like *Fox*, than like *Fucks*.

"Do you ever watch *The Simpsons*." She said, with that coy little smile of hers making another appearance.

"Yeah." I just kinda paused after my response, waiting for her to tell me how her show was related. Like, was it produced by the same producer, or drawn at the same studio, or did it pilfer from the same set of writers. I just kinda paused, waiting for her to fill in the blanks. A few empty seconds passed.

"The show I'm talking about is called ***The Simpsons***"

Now I'd love to be able to describe the look on my face at the moment where I finally clued in to what she was saying, but I can't. I simply can't.

I'd like to say that I didn't initially believe her. All of my better judgment told me that this woman must be completely full of it, just like I am when I tell women in the club that I'm a *NASA astronaut*, or the *author* of *Catcher in the Rye*. But when I toss around crap in the clubs, I do it to get a laugh, to capture a young woman's attention, or to keep her interested in me for just a little bit. But this woman really didn't seem the slightest bit interested in 'keeping my attention.' I mean, I was clearly the one casually pursuing her. There was no discernable impetus for her to tell me any tales, and bullshitting just for the sake of bullshitting just didn't seem like her modus operandi. Plus, in a very discomforting way, things just kinda made plausible sense. I mean, here we were, in a nice hotel in Vegas, only a four or five hour drive from LA. If I met someone in Antigonish, Nova Scotia, who told me they wrote scripts for Hollywood, well, I'd have a hard time believing them. But it wasn't that improbable in Vegas.

"*Fuck off.*" That was the most intellectually honest response I could give. I'm not sure if it captured my combined disbelief and incredulousity, but it was all that I could muster.

"You don't have to believe me if you don't want to. *You* asked *me*. I didn't ask to tell you. If you want to change the subject, we can. When did you start shaving your head?"

"Seriously, you write for The Simpsons?"

"I told you. I'm *not* a *writer*." It's funny, I always boast about being a writer, but she considered it to be an insult of the highest order. She didn't like being referred to as a writer, that was clear. "You can call me a *contributor*. I don't write, but I am around when things get written. Let's just say, *I have influence*. Or at least, I *had* influence before I came out here." She looked into her drink as she said it. It was the first time she spoke without having the confidence to look me in the eye. But her lack of temerity was short lived, as she raised her head back up to chat with me.

"And you plant little tidbits of information about Pickering in ***The Simpsons.*** C'mon? You expect me to believe that?"

She smiled again. This was totally her little secret, and you could tell that she enjoyed the chance to share it with someone. I doubt there were too many people in California or Nevada that cared too much about a little suburb outside of Toronto.

"Oh, I've been doing that for a long, long time, I assure you."

"Since when?"

"Well, when did the first show air? That was pretty much the start" She smiled again. "I used to watch as Matt put together a bunch of skits for the Tracey Ullman show..."

"Matt?" I interrupted.

"Yeah, Matt Groening." She seemed to over-emphasize the *groan* in Groening. "He's the one that's credited with creating The Simpsons."

"You said *credited*, as opposed to *responsible for*. Are you trying to telling me something else?" Now *I* smiled.

"No. Don't read anything into that. When it comes to creating poorly drawn stick figures, and coming up with dry, two minute story lines, Matt's very talented. He's definitely the originator. That's a good word – originator. But things changed for Matt when Fox turned the whole thing into a Television show. They brought in writers and producers and all these people that were supposed to know what they were doing. You know, the brainless Harvard types that networks love so much.

"It was when they were putting together the first episode that I realized how easy it'd be to influence the direction of the show.

"The first episode was really weird. I mean, it was to air in December, so it had to be a Christmas show. If you're not a writer, you probably don't understand how difficult it is to write a Christmas episode. Most shows don't even attempt a holiday episode until their second or third season, after the characters are developed, but we were asked to write a holiday episode as the *first* prime-time show. That's a pretty tall drink to order.

"All the Harvard types wanted to do the same old, unoriginal, sugary, Frosty the Snowman type crap. Every character was going to be all lovey-dovey, and life was going to be happy, and it was a totally crap idea. I mean, that's not the way any of us wanted the show to go. I think the writers even knew that it wasn't the right direction, but they had no idea how to combine edginess with Christmas. It's hard to believe that a room full of Jews would be so sensitive about the birth of Christ, but they were.

"For us, the idea of The Simpsons was that it had the *look* of a Children's TV show, which was then contrasted against a very sad and dark storyline. We didn't want The Simpsons to be another Cosby Show."

"Sad and dark?" I asked.

"Yeah. Of course. The Simpsons is totally sad and dark, right to the core; or at least, it was supposed to be. I mean, the father is an alcoholic, the mother is ineffectual, the son is uncontrollable, the daughter's genius is suppressed, and the baby is pretty much ignored. It's not a *Father Knows Best* type of storyline. But it's real, and it's how real families are. And it was important for us to keep it that way.

"Anyways, it was when they were trying to figure out how to combine initial character development with a Christmas theme, when I related a personal story about one Christmas I had when I was a kid."

"My Mom and Dad were separated when I was pretty young. My Dad had some problems, and my Mom didn't want her kids exposed to his instability. We spent most of the year living with Mom, while Dad drifted all over Durham.

"When I was about eleven, my Dad made all of these promises about the things he was going to get us for Christmas. He made promises every year, and by time I was eleven, I learned not to expect anything from him anymore. Not presents anyways.

"But that year, he actually decided to make good on his promise. He'd been working for a few months, and getting back on his feet. He even took a job as a Santa at the Pickering Town Center. I actually went in and saw him one time. I don't know why, but that was probably the proudest day of my life. I mean, you'd think I'd be embarrassed, being eleven years old and seeing your Dad play Santa at the mall, but I wasn't. I was so proud of him. He was working, and he was working hard, and I guess I knew that he was doing it for me." She looked back at her Long Island Ice Tea again, exposing for a second time that slight hint of humility that she had shown a few minutes before.

"So, what did you get for Christmas?"

"Nothing. I got nothing. Nothing from Dad, anyways. Lots of stuff from Mom, but nothing from Dad."

"What happened?"

"Well, he just disappeared. I mean, he always had an excuse as to why he couldn't get us anything, and every year we were disappointed, but he was our Dad and he could never do anything wrong, even though he never seemed to do anything right. We just liked spending time with Dad at Christmas, even if he didn't get us anything. But that Christmas he just disappeared. We didn't even hear from him again until the summer." Her eyes looked towards her drink again.

"What happened?"

"You know, it wasn't until a few years ago, well, maybe more now, that I actually found out the whole story. I was talking about it with my Mom, and she laid it all out for me.

"Apparently he hadn't come up with enough money to buy us the things we wanted. Or he blew too much on booze and drugs, which is probably closer to the truth, but that's not what my Mom told me. I don't know what the exact truth was; it doesn't really matter. But what money he did have, he took to the track. He headed over to Picov Downs or something and bet it all on a horse, all on the eve of Christmas Eve.

"I'm guessing the horse didn't come in."

"The horse didn't come in, and he didn't show up for work the next morning. The mall actually called my Mom, wondering where their Santa was on the day before Christmas. But Dad had just picked up and left. He was so ashamed, he couldn't even face us."

"Wow, that's quite a story."

"Well, it's not all that strange. Actually, it's probably more common that you think. Worse things happen to better people than me, I can promise you that. But it was a good story, and I gave it to the writers.

"And?"

"Well, have you ever seen the first episode? Homer gets fired from the Nuclear Power Plant, just before Christmas, and can't tell Marge. So, he goes out and gets a job as a Santa Claus at the Pickering Town Center."

I started to laugh, which was good, because the conversation was getting a little heavy. "Um. I think Homer got a job at the *Springfield Mall*, not the *Pickering Town Center*."

She blushed a little bit, and giggled. "Sorry. It's just such a personal story. That's not Homer and the Springfield Mall in that episode. It's my Dad and the PTC. And when Homer goes to the track in that episode to bet on the greyhounds, well, that's my Dad putting all his money on that horse. And when Patty and Selma, Homer's sister in laws, shame him about not being a good man or a father, well, that's my Dad being too ashamed to see his own kids on Christmas."

"That's a pretty dark story."

"Well, life is dark, isn't it. It's real. Shit like that happens everyday. And that's what we wanted The Simpsons to be about, real life, and the real things that happen everyday. But we also wanted it to be done in a way that allowed you to laugh about it. I mean, that's the whole point; to take the things that hurt you to your core, and laugh about them. That's why The Simpsons resonates so deeply with so many people."

"But that episode did have a happy ending, if I recall correctly. Doesn't sound like your story did."

"Well, mine has a pretty happy ending; I think, anyways. But in L.A., the happy endings come at the end of a thirty minute episode. In life, that happy ending takes a little bit longer to come about."

The Facts

"Okay, so Springfield is actually based on Pickering, Ontario. If that's so, then where is the Moe's tavern in Pickering?"

That question pissed her off.

"Oh my God. I can't believe you just asked me that. I friggin' hate it when people say that. I've only confided this truth to a couple of friends, and that's the exact same, stupid, idiotic question I get.

"The Simpsons is a television program. It's not a show about Pickering, Ontario. Homer and Marge are not *real* people, raising three kids in a *real* city named Springfield. It's not a reality show, it's a television program.

"No, you're right. There's no *Moe's Tavern* in Pickering. Sorry. So, I guess that means you're right – Springfield can't possibly be based on Pickering because Pickering and Springfield aren't *exactly* the same."

"*Sorry*" I said. "I thought it was a valid question. I take it back." I'd clearly pissed her off.

"But it's not a valid question. It's myopic and short sighted, and whenever a pea-brain asks a question like that, it makes me just want to terminate the conversation."

"Are you calling me short-sighted and myopic?"

"I think I just did. And I'd probably end this conversation as well, if you weren't the only person at the bar to talk to." She gave me a slight smile to let me know that my comparative faux pas had been forgiven, while indicating at the same time, more stupid questions wouldn't be tolerated.

"I mean, did you ever see Citizen Kane?" she asked.

"I think I was forced to see it once in film class."

"You were *forced* to watch Kane? That's like being forced to eat candy, or drink a cold beer on a sweltering hot day."

"It was black and white, and filmed in the fifties."

"And The Simpsons is a two-dimensional cartoon that looks like it was drawn for kids. What's your point?"

"Okay. I saw it. I saw Kane. What about it?"

"Well, what was the main character's name in the movie?"

"I have no idea."

"Charles Foster Kane. That was the name of the protagonist. And what was the name of his mistress?"

"Rosebud?"

"It was Susan Alexander. And what was the name of the Newspaper Kane ran?"

"I think you're going to tell me."

"I am. It was The Chronicle. And what was the name of Kane's palatial home in Florida?"

"I'm not sure."

"It was Xanadu. And what was Kane's nick-name for his wife's private parts?"

I decided to interject and put an end to the Orson Wells movie trivia moment. "Look, I think we've established the fact that I don't know anything about antiquated, 1950's movies. What's your point?"

"Citizen Kane was based on the life of newspaper mogul William Randolph Hearst. In fact, Hearst was so insulted, he had it banned from all of the movie theatres he owned, which was practically all of them. The characters names in the movie were different. The name of the mistresses in the movie, and in real life, were different. Hearst lived in a palace called *The Ranch* in San Simian, California, while Kane lived in a palace named *Xanadu* in Florida. Kane ran a newspaper called *The Inquirer*, while Hearst ran a newspaper called *The Examiner*. Kane bought his mistress an *opera theatre*, Hearst bought his mistress a *film studio....*" I cut her off again.

"Okay, I get it. The character Kane was based on Hearst."

"No, but from what you just told me, you don't fucking get it. That's the problem. Nobody does. Everyone wants the most obvious of clues, which they're *not* going to get.

"I mean, I've lurked around in a bunch of Internet chat rooms that prognosticate about which town Springfield is based on, and what they do is look at each state that has a city called Springfield, and start there. That's as stupid as going to a telephone book and looking up people named *Charles Foster* to figure out who the movie Citizen Kane was based upon. Americans always want easy answers, but thinking the real Springfield will share everything, including the name, with the fictional one, is just plain *dumb* and *foolish*.

"I mean, the idea behind The Simpsons is that it could take place just about anywhere, and The Simpsons could be anyone, or everyone's, next door neighbor. We picked the name Springfield because it was such an ubiquitous name. I think of the 52 states, 34 of them have a Springfield, and some of them have two or three."

"There's only 50 states." I said.

"I was including Canada and Mexico." she quipped, happy that I'd walked right into her setup.

"If you're looking for a town named Springfield, that has a family with the last name Simpson, living at 742 Evergreen Terrace, you're not going to find it. But if you pick up on the more subtle hints, you'll find out where the real Springfield is. And a subtle hint isn't a tavern named Moe's."

"Take this for an example. I remember one time I came home for the summer, and they had introduced a new area code. My phone number never needed an area code; I just dialed the seven digits. But all of a sudden, I had to dial a 905 before the seven digit number, and 905 wasn't even my original area code. Then every time I started dialing friends, I always dialed 905, but half the time their numbers were 416 numbers. And then there was this whole set of numbers in the 905 area code where I actually had to dial a one before the number because they were long distance, even though they were in the same area code."

"Okay. Calm down." I said jokingly. "It'll be okay. It's just a telephone network you know."

"Well, that frustrated the hell out of me. It still does.

"So that whole 4-1-6 and 9-0-5 silliness inspired an episode where Homer marches right down to city hall to denounce the introduction of a second area code. I think the numbers we used in the show were 6-3-6 and 9-3-9, which are area codes in Missouri. So everyone started saying that this was proof that Springfield was in Missouri, even though the story made absolutely no sense in that context. If anyone paid attention, they'd totally realize that the episode was about the area code change for Toronto and the golden horseshoe, not Springfield, Missouri."

"Okay, I get it." I said, trying to calm her down a bit. She was starting to take this personally.

"Don't get mad. I get it. There are enough similarities between the two to demonstrate that Pickering and Springfield are one in the same. But they're not identical. There's no tavern named Moe's, the mayor isn't named Quimby, Pickering doesn't have a Krusty the Clown, and the nuclear power plant isn't run by a guy named Mr. Burns."

She smiled that devious little smile again. "Well, you're half right. There's no tavern named Moe's, and the mayor isn't named Quimby."

"But?"

"Well, child entertainer Mr. Dressup was from Pickering. I'd say Ernie Coombs is the Canadian equivalent of Krusty the Clown, although in a much more Christian and Canadian sense. I don't think Mr. Dressup ever had a gambling problem, and I don't think his sidekicks *Casey and Finnegan* every tried to murder anyone."

"But Mr. Burns doesn't run the power plant, right?"

"Well, he doesn't exactly *run* it.

"You know, there's alot of debate on the Internet about where Springfield really is. The hammer you can drop on any argument is whether the city has a nuclear power plant or not. People argue for and against a bunch of cities, but if the city doesn't have a nuclear facility, it's just out of the running. And not only does Pickering have a nuclear power plant, but it's got the second largest nuclear power plant in the world?"

"What's first?" I asked.

"Darlington, just 100 kilometers down the road. You're from Ajax, right? You live smack-dab between the two largest nuclear power plants in the world. How does it feel?"

"Hasn't effected me a bit." I said, as I erratically flinched my left shoulder, making it look like I suffered from some type of strange, radiation induced, birth defect.

"So, was it your idea to have Homer work at a nuclear power plant?"

"No, not at all. A fortuitous occurrence for sure. I think Matt just liked the idea of an nincompoop like Homer working for a nuclear facility. But that was indeed partially responsible for motivating me to make Springfield as much like Pickering as I could. I mean, having a power plant is a pretty good start. Everything after that is just gravy.

"But about Burns running the power pant; here's a tidbit you'll like. Do you know Mr. Burns' full name?"

"Monty or something?"

"Close. Charles *Montgomery* Burns. That's the full name. It was originally going to be Charles Foster Burns, as a tip of the hat to Orson Wells' classic movie. I mean, Burns was supposed to be a very Kane like figure. In fact, there's a bunch of episodes where we've totally stolen scenes from the movie Citizen Kane, but put Burns in Kane's place. But I hated the overt symbolism of using the same first *and* second name. I mean, if you want overt symbolism that any idiot can understand, listen to a Rush song. But we're beyond that. So, I pushed to drop the Charles or the Foster bit, and replace it with something a little bit more majestic."

"So they dropped the Foster, and replaced it with Monty?" I wanted to show her that I was still paying attention.

"*Montgomery.* They replaced it with *Montgomery.*" The word was clearly important to her.

"Did you ever play baseball or soccer by the power plant?"

"They have soccer fields by the power plant?"

"Yeah, I always thought it was a bit odd to have a kids park right next to a nuclear generator, but they do. My Mom used to take us down there all the time when we were kids. It was like the place to go on Sundays when she wasn't working; an easy bike ride from home."

"Sounds like a nice story. What's your point?"

"Well, do you know what the name of the park is?"

"I've never been there, so obviously I don't."

"Well, if you'd ever been there, you'd know that it was called *Montgomery Park.*" She smiled a big smile. "And no, the person that runs the Pickering Nuclear Power Plant isn't named Montgomery Burns, but the nuclear power plant *is* located on *Montgomery Park Road.* In fact, it borders the power plant to the east and the north. To the south and the west, it's just water."

"I don't believe you." I started feeling a little sheepish over my apparent lack of familiarity with the suburbs in which I grew up.

"Fine. You don't have to believe me. But if you MapQuest it, you'll see that I'm telling the truth. The power plant owner in The Simpsons is named after the very street the Nuclear Power Plant is located on in Pickering. MapQuest it if you don't believe me."

To be honest, I really didn't believe her. I wanted to head up to my hotel room and do a quick search to prove her wrong, but I was afraid she'd be gone by the time I got back. I did look it up a little later, and while I have to admit that it scared me in an inexplicable way, she was dead on in what she told me. She wasn't making anything up.

The Hint

"Okay, lets just say I believe you. What can you tell me that will prove it, beyond a shadow of a doubt, to my friends back home?"

"I thought you promised you weren't going to tell anyone?"

"And I thought you said you didn't care anymore?"

"Well, that's true. What do you want? Storylines? Landmarks? Distances? It's all in there, over and over again."

"I don't know? *Landmarks*. I mean, does Pickering have an elevator to nowhere? Or a tire fire? Or anything like that?"

She smiled. "There's no elevator to nowhere. But there was a tire fire. Okay, that wasn't actually in Pickering, but it *was* in Ontario. I think it was in Hagersville, Neil Pert's home town. I think it took them a month or something ridiculous like that to actually get the thing under control."

"You're joking, right? There really was a tire fire?"

"Yeah, totally. You didn't hear about it? I wasn't even living in Ontario at the time, and even *I* heard about it. To be honest, I'm not sure which came first there, the episode, or the event. That's the really strange thing. I mean, it started off with me putting little tidbits about Pickering in The Simpsons, but there came a point where the storylines we wrote for The Simpsons actually started coming true for Pickering. It was like we were prognosticating the future. That's why I always shied away from doing any shows where a natural disaster hit Springfield. I was afraid it'd work like a curse.

"I mean, I remember how we did that show about some Europeans coming in to take over the power plant. Some Germans bought it off Monty Burns. Then the next thing I know, then Premier of Ontario, Mike Harris, is talking about deregulation, and the privatization of electricity, and then some European consortium of Brits came in and invested. It was weird."

"Well, maybe if this whole writing thing doesn't pan out, perhaps you can go into Tarot card reading or something?"

"I told you, I am *not* a writer.

"And to answer your other question, no, there is no ***escalator*** to nowhere. But do you recall which episode that came from?"

"No, but I think you're going to tell me."

"That was the monorail episode, where Springfield wastes all this money on a transit system that links Springfield, Shelbyville, and North Haverbrook. But what happens when they actually start the monorail? The brakes fail, and the monorail speeds out of control."

"So?"

"Well, have you ever been to the Toronto Zoo?"

"Yeah?"

"Do you know where the zoo is located?"

"It's in Scarborough, right?"

"Actually, it's on the Scarborough-Pickering border. The monorail at the zoo used to take you down the Rouge River Valley, which represents the western border of Pickering. Actually, when you see the episode with Bart trying to jump over the Springfield Gorge, just think of the Springfield Gorge as the Rouge River Valley."

"*You're too much.*" I said, and we started laughing fabulously. She continued.

"Well, the Toronto Zoo had to shut the monorail down after its brakes failed, twice, during the nineties. The final straw was when the monorail lost it's brakes going up a hill, slid back down, and slammed into another packed monorail sitting at the station below."

"That doesn't exactly sound like a funny story."

"Well, it's not funny. But it *is* interesting, and when you've got writers without anything better to write about, any story is a good story. In real life, I think there were over sixty people with broken bones and other injuries. Apparently, the driver of the monorail that got hit jumped out in just enough time to save her life. It could have been truly tragic."

"So, what else can you give me? Anything a little less gruesome?"

"Look, I'm heading down to the strip to watch some shiny-bottoms play the slots. Why don't you just watch the shows. There's hints in practically every one."

"C'mon, just a few more. I told you, I don't watch all that much TV."

"Well, just remember that The Simpsons isn't about Pickering. And the show changes locations every time it suits the writers, and there's alot of writers, all contributing their own personal experiences to the storylines. I mean, even the address of Homer's house changes from 742 Evergreen Terrace, to 50 Evergreen Terrace, to 42 Evergreen Terrace. Plus, the writers always put things in there to shake thing up.

But if you follow the clues, there's really only one conclusion you can come to."

"Well, what other clues? At least tell me what to look for."

"Distances are good clues. There's one episode where the family has to go to Branson, Missouri, and Lisa complains 'Branson Missouri, that's a thousand miles away.'"

"And I'm guessing Pickering is a thousand miles away from Brandon?"

She smiled. "Actually, I think it's more like nine-hundred and eighty two miles. At least, that's what my odometer read when *I* made the drive. I stayed with a family friend in Branson when I made my way to California. Branson was a bit of a milestone, because it meant I had put a thousand miles under my belt. Everything seemed real after that point."

"Oh, and you know how I told you the 401 takes the family to Capital City? Well, the first time they jump on the highway to get there, it's 30 miles away."

"Which is pretty much the distance from Pickering to Toronto, right?"

"Yeah. It was 48 kilometers from my driveway to my Dad's work, which was just off Richmond Street by the CN Tower. That works out to almost exactly thirty miles. But it gets better.

"There's another episode where The Simpsons go to Capital City, and the indication is that it will be a 220 mile trip on the 401. That really messed everyone up on the message boards."

"Well, which is it? Thirty or two-hundred and twenty?"

"Couldn't it be both?" She said, with that mischievous little smile of hers. "Have you ever driven to Ottawa?"

I started to laugh. "I'm guessing it's about 220 miles away?"

"Well, whenever my Mom drove there, it took about three hours and forty five minutes to get there, and 60 miles per hour is the speed limit in the states, so I guessed the distance at 220 miles. I think it's closer to 250 when you actually map it, but it's the same idea."

"This is good stuff!" I was actually getting excited, trying to memorize as much as possible, while thinking who the first dozen people I'd phone with this news would be. Would it be my brother Marcus? Would it be Chris, or Rob, or Eddy or Greg, the guys who actually spent their first two years of University doing little other than watching The Simpsons? Would it be my buddy Andy or Kev or Boppers?

"There's also a few references to actual streets and landmarks in Pickering. I remember one episode where Patty and Selma are told to redesign the drivers test. When one of them asks 'where will we do the three point turn', the manager responds 'oh, just do it on Bayly Street.' You know, that's just a throw-away line, but if you're from Pickering, and you realize that it'd be impossible to do a three point turn on Pickering's four lane thoroughfare, it actually becomes pretty funny. There's plenty of throw away lines in the show that are only funny to me. Well, maybe they'll be funny to you now, as well.

"Look for the little things. The little things all add up. I mean, find another town that has a 401 highway running through it. Look for another town with a garbage dump, a dysfunctional monorail, a sewage treatment plant, a pioneer village, a lighthouse, and a nuclear power plant that leaks."

"The nuclear power plant leaks? In Pickering, or in Springfield?"

"In both, *you dipstick*. For how long did you live in the 905?"

"Pretty much all my life."

"And you don't know about any of the valve breaks or radioactive water leaks? Like the one in the early eighties? It cost a billion dollars to fix. As a taxpayer, you might be interested in knowing where your tax money is being wasted."

"I didn't pay taxes in '83. I was eleven."

"Doesn't matter. You're paying for it now. A billion dollar sunk cost doesn't just disappear.

"Hmmmm. I never even heard of it. You're making that up. A nuclear power plant doesn't just *leak*."

"I could go on about it. There's been plenty of spills. Trust me. I used to be a real granola girl when I was younger, fighting for human rights, and against nuclear power and global warming. Don't worry though, I'm over that whole delusion now; Hollywood got me through it.

"As I said, I think I'm going to head out to the strip. I didn't plan on staying here at the hotel bar all night.

"Oh, and there's one more, pretty huge giveaway. In one episode, Marge is ordering something over the phone, and she has to give her address. She says "742 Evergreen Terrace, Springfield O---, " Marge is about to say O-ntario, but Ned Flanders walks in, and she changes her pitch from O-ntario, to O-h, hi, Ned." I always smile when I see that clip.

"There's also one huge tip in an early episode, but you'd have to decipher it to get it. Still, if you figured it out, it'd remove any doubt. But it'd ruin the mystery too, so I'm not going hand it over to you. It's in there though, if you want to look for it."

"What, does it spell out the word Pickering?"

"Close to it. Something like that, but not quite. Anyways, nobody'll ever get it, so don't worry about it. And don't look for any more clues after this season. I'm done with those assholes. They can find someone else to steal ideas from. I've let them steal from me for long enough."

"So you're through?"

"Well, the way I feel now, I'm through. But to be honest, this isn't the first time I've come down to Vegas to cool off for a while. Actually, after our little chat, I don't feel quite as pissed off anymore. Tell you what, if I ever go back, you'll know."

"Should I give you my email address or something?"

"No. I mean...watch the show. You'll know."

"Why, you'll put something else about Pickering in there?"

"No. I'm saying *you* will know. Just *you*. Get it?" I didn't get it then, but I do now. She continued. "Anyways, I'm off. I'm heading down to the strip."

"Do you want some company?"

"No, not really. I didn't come down here to make any new friends. I came down to get away from the people that I thought were my friends, and to just be alone for a while."

"And your version of being alone includes being on the strip with a hundred-thousand other people?"

"Every one of those people is just as alone as me. Sometimes, it's only when you're in close proximity to other people, that you realize just how alone you really are."

"That's deep."

"Well, that's me."

And that's when she unaffectionately put her hand on my knee to help push herself off her chair. She walked out the first set of automatic doors, turned around, and gave me a smile and an unaffectionate wave. Then, after the second set of automatic doors closed behind her, she jumped in a cab, and I assume, headed down to the strip.

Anyways, I've now probably told that story a hundred times, if not more. I'm not sure if every detail that I can recall is one-hundred percent accurate. I now get constant updates from the people I know, telling me more little tidbits from the show that point to Pickering as the true foundation of the fictional city of Springfield. I'm starting to lose track of which tidbits she told me about, which ones I figured out on my own, and which ones have come through family and friends. I really wish I'd paid more attention when I met her that evening, but disappointingly true to form, I didn't.

www.pickeringisspringfield.com

Since meeting Susan, I've watched alot of episodes of the Simpsons, and I've never actually figured out what the big hint, was. My guess is it's either totally indecipherable, or it's not really in there at all. Who knows? And for that matter, who really cares?

What I do know is that Susan, or whatever her name was, is back, and up to her old tricks. And Susan, if you ever read this, well, I think I got the little hint you were talking about. It was cute. And thanks.

The End

Media Opportunities

Cameron McKenzie is always pleased to make himself available for media opportunities. From radio talk, to television interviews, from book signings to public speaking engagements, Cameron is a memorable guest. For booking information, contact media relations at:

media@cameronmckenzie.com

Discerning Bombs

For more great writing, pick up a copy of Cameron McKenzie's ***Discerning Bombs on Oshawa***. If you're a 905er, or just someone compelled by the state of the human condition, you'll find it to be a very captivating read. Plus, there are pictures. ☺ **Available now on Amazon.com**

Index

Printed in the United States
107281LV00005B/46-48/A

9 781598 729047